View From The Exterior

Serge Gainsbourg

Alan Clayson

View From The Exterior

Serge Gainsbourg

Design: David Houghton
Printed by: MPG Books, Bodmin

Published by: Sanctuary Publishing Limited, 82 Bishops Bridge
Road, London W2 6BB

Copyright: Alan Clayson, 1998

Photographs: All Action, Redferns Picture Library, Rex Features,
Pictorial Press and Jean Pierre Leloir

ISBN: 1-86074-222-X

About The Author

Born in Dover, England in 1951, the author lives near Henley-on-Thames with his wife Inese and sons, Jack and Harry.

Described by the *Western Morning News* as the "AJP Taylor of the pop world", Alan Clayson has written many books on music – including the best-selling *Backbeat*, subject of a major film – as well as for journals as disparate as *The Independent, Record Collector, Medieval World, Folk Roots, The Times, Discoveries, The Beat Goes On* and, as a teenager, the notorious *Schoolkids Oz*. He has been engaged to broadcast on national TV and radio, and lecture on both sides of the Atlantic.

Before he become better known as a pop historian, he led the legendary Clayson And The Argonauts in the late 1970s, and was thrust to "a premier position on rock's Lunatic Fringe" (*Melody Maker*). The 1985 album, *What A Difference A Decade Made*, is the most representative example of the group's recorded work.

As shown by the formation of a US fan club in 1992, Alan Clayson's following has continued to grow, along with demand for his production talents in the studio, and the number of his compositions performed by such diverse acts as Dave Berry – in whose Cruisers he played keyboards in the mid-1980s – and (via a collaboration with ex-Yardbird Jim McCarty) New Age outfit, Stairway. He has worked with the Portsmouth Sinfonia, Wreckless Eric, Twinkle and Screaming Lord Sutch among others.

Alan Clayson is presently spearheading a trend towards an English form of *chanson*, and feedback from both Britain and North America suggests that he is becoming more than a cult celebrity. Moreover, *Soirée*, a new album released in autumn 1997, may stand as Alan Clayson's artistic apotheosis if it were not for the promise of surprises yet to come.

Also available from Sanctuary by Alan Clayson

THE QUIET ONE: A Life Of George Harrison

RINGO STARR: Straight Man Or Joker?

DEATH DISCS: An Account Of Fatality In The Popular Song

JACQUES BREL: The Biography

HAMBURG: The Cradle Of British Rock

ONLY THE LONELY: The Life And Artistic Legacy Of Roy Orbison

"We must embrace the unacceptable in all spheres"

Hangman Communication 0001

To Mike Robinson

Contents

Prologue   **Hier Ou Demain**........................ 13

Chapter One   **Incapable Of Thinking About Tomorrow** 19

Chapter Two   **Du Chant A L'Une!**........................ 37

Chapter Three   **Le Temps Des Yoyos**........................ 55

Chapter Four   **Baby Pop** 73

Chapter Five   **L'Horizon** 83

Chapter Six   **Blow Up** 91

Chapter Seven   **Contact**................................. 99

Chapter Eight   **69 Année Erotique** 109

Chapter Nine   **Gallic Symbol** 119

Chapter Ten   **Love For Sale**........................... 129

Chapter Eleven   **The Oldest Teenager In The Business** 143

Chapter Twelve   **Gainsbourgmania**........................ 157

Chapter Thirteen   **Gain-Gain**.............................. 173

Chapter Fourteen   **Requiem 91** 185

Epilogue   **Versions** 199

Chronology   203

Compositions   205

Index   213

Hier Ou Demain

A couple of years ago, a middle-aged Italian and I were thrown together on a train journey from Bournemouth to Basingstoke. A former pop star on his home turf, my companion – who I shall call "Giuseppe" – had written and directed a multi-media ballet-on-ice that was touring the provinces. As a composer myself, I was hoping to compare notes, but instead I was treated to Giuseppe's unconsciously hilarious monologue – that the whole carriage could hear – about his manifold sexual conquests at this European song festival or that record industry exposition. Giuseppe also imparted graphic pointers for my own use should I find myself in similar locations. Every sentence seemed to end with the phrase, "*ya know whad I mean?*" and the flexing of a phallic forearm.

He was an appalling fellow really – but I liked him. Nevertheless, a few weeks earlier, I had seen his ballet in a theatre in Southend, and I wondered now how one so brutish and foul-mouthed could have been capable of creating a work of such sensitivity.

The purpose of this story – if it has one – is that Giuseppe was much how I imagined Serge Gainsbourg would turn out when my research gave him a sharper definition. It was not an unreasonable supposition, particularly as Gainsbourg in the merciless eye of a TV camera came across as a debauched if intellectual drunk during an infamous chat show incident in 1986 when he was frank and unashamed about what he wanted to do to a female guest, US vocalist Whitney Houston. When the resulting fuss spread like ink on blotting paper across France and then English-speaking territories, such appearances by Gainsbourg in future were restricted to pre-recorded slots.

To the man-in-the-street perusing a newspaper the following day in Basingstoke, Houston or Alice Springs, Serge Gainsbourg was synonymous with 'Je T'Aime...Moi Non Plus', but this most controversial of his many controversial discs was but a single episode in a career in which he bestrode Gallic culture as a showbusiness jack-of-all-trades – and master of some. As well as being a singing hit parade composer, he functioned too as a film director, screenwriter, photographer, novelist, and an actor rated by thespians as discerning as Yul Brynner and Catherine Deneuve.

Yet compared to a "drowsy turtle" in one teenage magazine, his heavy-lidded homeliness did not mark him out as either a darling of the ladies or an obvious focus for popular acclaim. Indeed, he'd started as a painter moonlighting as a pianist in Parisian jazz clubs where, though esteemed by victims of the same passion – such as trumpeter Alain Brunet who was to release a 1994 album consisting entirely of Gainsbourg compositions – no-one was under the impression that he was to become a big name in France, let alone a wider world.

Until a victory in 1965's Eurovision Song Contest, the man born Lucien Ginzburg in 1928 didn't have much going for him, except as a reluctant pop singer, a dependable jobbing tunesmith and a provider of incidental music for so-so movies (in which he was given the odd bit-part). Modest achievements kept his head above water financially, and, now and then, a record he'd issued in his own right would precipitate a brief flurry of media attention and rise in booking fees before a foreseeable slide back to an interminable sense of marking time until another such peak came his way. There was always sufficient incentive to carry on.

However, he'd already thrown in the towel as a stage performer when he got lucky with, first, a televised musical, *Anna*, and, in 1967, a professional (and personal) liaison with Brigitte Bardot – with whom he taped the original version of 'Je T'Aime...Moi Non Plus'. Yet it was with the English actress – and his third wife – Jane Birkin, that this BBC-banned *kitsch* classic swept to Number One all over Europe in 1969, and hovered around the middle of the US *Hot 100*. Even today, it fills dance floors with groping smoochers as surely as 'My True Love' by Jack Scott before, and 10cc's 'I'm Not In Love' after it.

With English the only language for pop contenders with longterm global ambition, later Gainsbourg releases were confined mostly to domestic charts. Though new guidelines from the United States and Britain did not pass him by, there was bitter division about the quality and commercial suitability of his music. "He had a typical French feel for rock," *Guardian* reviewer Caroline Sullivan was to scoff, "he was hopeless at it." Yet Nicolas Godin of Air, a French duo picked to click in 1998, would contend that, "When Serge Gainsbourg used to make very good albums in the 1970s, where were you, in England – eh? You weren't interested, but now it's true that club culture which doesn't rely so much on spoken language has opened a lot of doors."

Before this barricade was broken, Gainsbourg's name had continued to rear up in headline-hogging outrages that were thought newsworthy in those areas that remembered his and Jane's gasps and moans. Attempts to replicate the 'Je T'Aime...' furore on disc included output that touched on masturbation and Nazism; a scandalous arrangement of 'La Marseillaise'; 'Lemon Incest' (a duet with his daughter, Charlotte); a rapping paean to oral sex, and further naughtiness that kept pace with the frittering away of his talent and capital. While many later Gainsbourg offerings were dismissed by even the most snow-blinded fans, his death in 1991 at the age of sixty-three elevated him to cult celebrity in Britain, Australasia and North America – where *Rolling Stone* wrote of his "Sinatra-like magnitude" – and lines were drawn further over whether he was a dirty old lecher who was, so he was reported as saying, "only interested in two things: eroticism and money (in that order)" – or a misunderstood genius whose daring vulgarity, intricate *double entendres* and negative love ballads were rich contributions to France's performing arts. Leaning towards the latter opinion, Laetitia Sadier, French *chanteuse* with London avant-gardeners Stereolab, insisted that "songs like 'Je T'Aime...' and 'Lemon Incest' aren't anti-women. They explore the eroticism of the language and the French themselves."

If affected profoundly by pop's internationalism, Gainsbourg was steeped in the cohesive stylistic precedents of Gallic song. 1959's 'Mambo Miam Miam' was new words to the folk ditty 'Boule De Neige' ("Snowball"), and 'Hier Ou Demain' from *Anna* – about a girl's suicide attempt halted by concern about her pet – could be mistaken for a *chanson* by Jacques Brel. Like the great Belgian too, Serge could be simultaneously personal and universal; subversive but encroaching upon public consciousness through the popular media; romantic but pertinent to real life interactions and outcomes within likely human situations.

Yet he was no *chansonier* in the grand tradition. Though Gainsbourg's 300-odd librettos have been published to be read as poems, they cannot be divorced from musical settings anywhere as comfortably as those of Brel, Georges Brassens or Charles Aznavour. Whereas melodies by these artists were often no more than a repeated series of notes used to carry lyrics, Gainsbourg, if as verbally complex, seemed to regard language as a vast and entertaining game of patterned phonetics and syllables through which he could give vent to a frosty wit, a sense of irony peculiar to himself – and a casually shocking candour, especially in his caustic attitude towards the sexes. Certainly, his approach was more Anglo-Saxon in that meaning was conveyed as much in timbre and metre as in words.

I have, therefore, been inclined not to quote Serge Gainsbourg's lyrics directly, but to paraphrase their substance. *Dernières Nouvelles Des Etoiles* (Librarie Plon, 1994) – an essential compilation that embraces every extant lyric that Gainsbourg committed to paper – and a comprehensive French-English dictionary are recommended for supplementary investigation.

Such is the volume of literary spin-offs (nearly all in French) both before and after his death that someone ought to write a book about books about Serge Gainsbourg. Therefore, rather than attempt a long – and probably incomplete – list of dry titles, it makes more sense to mention two items that are still in print and comparatively easy for readers in English-speaking countries to obtain, namely Yves Salgues' *Gainsbourg Ou La Provocation Permanente* (Jean-Claude

Lattes, 1989) and *Gainsbourg* by Gilles Verlant (Albin Michel, 1985) (containing appendices of detailed discographical and like listings that a certain type of enthusiast would not find too insignificant to be interesting).

Much new and rediscovered evidence was brought to light as I waded through oceans of press and other archives, and screwed myself up to interview complete strangers, often at very short notice, as I accumulated a filing cabinet of Gainsbourgia, exercise books full of scribble to decipher, cassette tapes to transcribe, hour after hour of music to analyse, and a deadline I'd never meet.

Much was learnt from secondary sources, some with inconsistent spellings of proper nouns – especially Russian ones like "Ginzburg", Gainsbourg's preferred rendering of his born surname. In particular these sources provided verbatim accounts that recreated the feeling of being there. Unlike people, they are not influenced by the fact of being observed: *litera scripta manet* (what is written down is permanent).

At other times, I was riven with self-disgust when wheedling an interview from someone who only wanted to crawl away and hide. It may be evident to the reader that I have received help from sources that may prefer not to be mentioned. Nevertheless, I wish to express my appreciation for what they did.

Particular debts of gratitude are owed to Inese Clayson and Frederic Pierre for invaluable assistance with translation.

For their co-operation, trust and supplying of privileged information, I am also beholden to Christine Burridge, Marie-Jo Forsyth, Spencer Leigh, Chris Phipps and, especially, David Scott who, in his capacity as a Gainsbourg consultant and connoisseur, commands the highest respect.

Whether they were aware of providing assistance or not, thanks are also due in varying degrees to Carol Boyer, Bruce Brand, Clem Cattini, Billy Childish, Jack Clayson, Harry Clayson, Don Craine, Margaret Cutts, Tim Day, Kevin Delaney, Jackie Doe, Peter Doggett, the Drummond family, Tim Fagan, Dave Hill, Robb Johnston, Garry Jones, Jon Lewin, Jim McCarty, Giselle Mehenett, Joan Redding, Imogen Setterfield, Bob Stanley, John Tobler and Twinkle Rogers.

Please put your hands together too for the BBC Music Library, the

National Sound Archives, Westminster Music Library, Colindale Newspaper Library and L'Institut Français.

Finally, I'd like you all to put your hands together for Penny Braybrooke, Jeffrey Hudson, Michelle Knight and Eddy Leviten at Sanctuary Publishing for encouragement and patience that went beyond the call of duty.

Alan Clayson, February 1998

chapter one

Incapable Of Thinking About Tomorrow

The twentieth century belongs historically to Adolf Hitler for the difference he made, but strong contenders for its ownership have been the grandees of the Russian Revolution if only for those multitudes who, carrying pathetic bundles, also fled an intolerable native land. An infinitesimal twitch in the death throes of the Czarist regime was the exit in 1919 of twenty-three-year-old Joseph Ginzburg, a Jew from Kharkov in the Ukraine, and his wife Olia, who stumbled via Istanbul towards the safety of Paris. When it became obvious that there would be no welcome back by Mother Russia, Joseph became a naturalised French citizen, a status that the law conferred too upon his spouse – though, like all other French women, she had yet to be granted the vote.

Ostensibly, Olia's place was in the home while her husband, a gifted pianist, made ends meet by providing trickling background music within the walls of a retinue of cellars, music halls and similar venues that orbited round the courtyards and narrow pavements from Montmartre across to Montparnasse, the city's "Artists' Quarters". He would also accompany cabaret singers paid a pittance by hard-nosed managements whose establishments – so they made clear – attracted slumming showbiz moguls among a late night underworld of gamblers, racketeers, prostitutes and practising homosexuals: all those that nice people had been taught to fear and despise.

Frequently, the personality of a given act and the efforts of its backing ensemble, dapper in stiff evening dress, were an underlying noise to boozy chatter until, in the hullabaloo, someone would catch a fragment of melody, and a wine-choked mouth would trigger unison singalongs ranging from the filthiest barrack-room ditties to sentimental ballads about my blue heaven and Ida, sweet as apple cider.

Even after his work spectrum extended beyond Paris to residencies in Deuville and Biarritz, Joseph glowered inwardly from behind owlish spectacles as he vamped triplets into an atmosphere almost liquid with cigarette fumes, and wondered if this was all he'd ever do, drift from pillar to post, from bandstand to unsatisfactory bandstand.

Rather than the mind-numbing requests for some drunken clown's girlfriend, the sounds from the yellowing ivories beneath Joseph's long fingers (if he had the privilege of choice) tended towards jazz. In its infancy then, this embraced both semi-classical items like *An American In Paris* from Gershwin (another of many jazzers from Russo-Jewish stock) or a form derived as much from the Yiddish *klezmer* style – improvisations round European and Middle Eastern dance tunes, marches and folk melodies from time immemorial – as any toot-tooting from black America.

Commanding respect from other city musicians for his exacting standards, Joseph Ginzburg led his own jazz combos in the late 1920s, among them *The* Tortorella's (*sic*), a septet featuring trombone, trumpet, banjo and piano and deviations from prescribed Dixieland precedent in its use of saxophone – and button-accordion, the only visual indication of the outfit's origin in Montmartre which, within the shadow of the Basilica De Sacré Coeur, had an ambience of bistros where you could sit for hours; overhanging windows; street-sweepers with twig brooms, and, lacing the air, the purr of accordions and an aroma of coffee and Gauloise.

The haunt of Modigliani and Sartre, Montmartre was also the traditional home of existentialism with its "nothing matters" engrossment with death and impoverished romantic squalor – well, squalor anyway as exemplified by Modigliani, starving in a garret, burning his furniture against the cold of winter, and going to an early grave for his art.

This, however, was not the way of refugees like Joseph and Olia Ginzburg who, having settled into exile in the free West, established a pattern whereby they moved onwards and upwards to homes that were always improvements on the ones before, and instilled into their growing family the value of money and what they considered ought to be admired about material gain through effort.

No child of parents more steeped in the detours of culture than most could have avoided an early understanding of what music, literature and art was worth experiencing and what was not. Evidence of hard listening to every root and branch of classical music, and more than cursory poring over the deeper fathoms of Baudelaire, Rimbaud, Sartre and Nabokov was to inform the output of Joseph and Olia's only surviving son, Lucien.

Prints of Cézanne, Renoir, Matisse and Vlaminck hung in the small flat in forlorn Rue de la Chine where Lucien – commensurate with a boy being called something like "Lindsey" or "Hilary" in Britain – and his twin sister Liliane were prised into the world after a traumatic pregnancy on a showery Monday, 2 April 1928. Though his parents, Liliane and big sister Jacqueline would come to know him as "Lulu", he was named, for the sake of morbid tradition, after an elder brother who had died of bronchitis in infancy.

A wider world's preoccupation with the impending Great Depression did not trouble the Ginzburg offspring as they caught and held a Parisian rather than Russian accent and began thinking, speaking and dreaming in French. Of the three, gawky Lucien most resembled his rather unprepossessing father. Yet the angularity of the jug-handle ears, hooded eyes and Roman nose was offset by a more intangible delicacy of the cheeks and jawline. From Olia too came a full, almost fleshy, mouth.

A fascinated listener when Papa was seated at the household's upright piano, Lucien's inherited musical strengths were formalised shortly after his investigative pounding with plump fists on the keys. He endured rather than enjoyed lessons from a carping father who'd reduce him to tears as he sweated over Scarlatti and Chopin, and drum in music theory as a kind of mathematics that proved the conjecture that a tone-deaf person could compose a symphony.

Nonetheless, as well as being endowed with a handsome capacity to try-try again, Lucien was sufficiently self-contained to disassociate the music from the drudgery of daily practice. If no young Mozart playing blindfold, he was to become as well-known for his keyboard skills as the class bully and lacrosse captain were in their chosen spheres when, in short trousers and gabardine raincoat, he commenced a formal education which was disrupted by changing schools when, for instance, Joseph's work took the family to Algeria for much of 1934 before a return to France when he landed a job at Maxim's – arguably, the most prestigious Parisian club – and the wherewithal to move everyone to a bigger apartment.

The third floor of 11b Rue Chaptal was closer to both the capital's bustling consumers' paradise and the heart of its music industry. Indeed, one afternoon, Lucien, full of himself after gaining a *croix d'honneur* for attainment at school, ran into Frehel, a sort of precursor of Edith Piaf, whose inbred professionalism smothered any annoyance as she asked the tongue-tied youth to join her in a café for a soft drink and strawberry tart.

Within ten equidistant minutes dawdle of 11b too were both the SACEM (Société Des Auteurs-Compositeurs) offices – the French equivalent of the Performing Rights Society – and bastions of Gallic jazz – also on the itinerary of visiting Americans – like the Hot Club of Paris where a teenage Ginzburg was to appreciate the mainstream fiddling of Stefan Grappelli and the "gypsy jazz" of guitarist Django Reinhardt. He was also to be a denizen of the Blue Note where he heard Billie Holliday (with whom he'd come to share similar self-immolatory inclinations). Two numbers she sang that night, 'Gloomy Sunday' and 'Stormy Weather', were to remain eternal favourites with Lucien.

These pivotal events lay, however, in an unimaginable future to a schoolboy languishing under the unimaginative and often frightening policy exemplified by multiplication tables chanted mechanically *en masse* to the rap of a bamboo cane on an inkwelled desk. Some teachers had to struggle to write anything remotely extraordinary on termly reports about the academic progress of one who meant little more than a name – sometimes rendered in error as "Gainsbourg" – on a register. He was solid enough in most subjects. As well as a sound conceptual grasp of mathematics, there were hints of a flair for drawing and creative writing, but there was always the feeling that he was afraid of articulating his dark humour and further areas within the inner space of a private cosmos. Likewise, shy Lucien was loathe to take part in formal discussions or bring his exercise book to a master's desk for fear of getting into trouble.

He did just that outside school hours on the solitary occasion when he was caught shoplifting. Other routine episodes included truancy – for which he was given a ritual hiding by Joseph – and rare playtime disputes in which he preferred to be placatory before putting up his fists and trying hard not to look the sissy that his forename implied he might be.

Yet Lucien's phase of disregarding the opposite sex was far briefer than that of other pre-adolescent lads. Later, he'd confess to being only eight when he first became lost in the beauty of a female classmate, gazing at her with blatant, slack-jawed wonder. He'd be in raptures if she cast an eye in his direction, and bitterly jealous if she spoke to any other boy. His infatuation was soundtracked by 'J'Ai Ta Main Dans Ma Main', a Charles Trenet record forever on the radio.

It is likely that Lucien's exultations and melancholies were not noticed by the girl or anyone else. To outward appearances, he was just an expressionless nondescript, mooching around the playground, a detached observer of the capers, smiling placidly while the others guffawed.

Reserved at home too, he was never particularly close to even his twin. A fancy that he'd like to make his way in the world as a painter was yet unspoken to parents who were floating an idea of the children entering medicine, law and similarly lettered professions, jobs with suits and half a century of security before retirement and the presentation of a gold watch to tick away the seconds before they went underground.

The Second World War put paid to long-term notions like that – particularly after Hitler's rape of France in 1940, and the creation of the collaborationist Vichy government that assisted the Nazi annihilation of over 70,000 Gallic Jews via the Drancy concentration camp near Paris, and on to the gas chambers of Auschwitz. Indeed, the *nacht und nebel* raid that began this process was as likely to be by the local *gendarmerie* as the Gestapo.

While the country quailed before the long shadow of the modern-day Attila, Joseph Ginzburg had seized the opportunity in 1939 to evacuate the family to the comparative safety of Dinard, a small market town on the coast of Normandy. If rural tranquillity was novel at first,

Lucien came to find it suffocating – and the least opaque memory of his year there would be of watching from across the estuary the burning of petrol tanks by retreating British forces in St Malo.

Now that Dinard had as much potential for persecution as anywhere else in occupied France, the Ginzburgs returned to the devil they knew. In the capital, many buildings and streets were now *verboten* to even non-Jewish dwellers in a realm of queues for essential commodities so scarce that you could only buy them with weeks of saved-up ration coupons. When groceries couldn't be acquired by this means, all that was left was either the black market or cheap return railway tickets into the countryside with the determination that if there were butter, eggs, potatoes and like prized foodstuffs to be had there, they were going to be had.

Of course, Jews – identifiable by the ordained wearing of a demeaning yellow star – were more prone to random official examination of papers and subsequent awkward questions. Against the ever-present possibility of street arrest, Olia Ginzburg customised garments so that the star could be hidden within seconds whenever danger hovered. She also stressed to her brood the perils of ambiguous utterances being overheard by the wrong person. Too close for comfort already had been an uncle's disappearance into the dungeons of the Gestapo – and it had been necessary for Lucien to be concealed in a woodshed by the headmaster one morning during a Gestapo descent on his secondary school, the all-boys Lycée Condorcet.

At twelve, Lucien was still a well-meaning if uninvolved student, albeit one who'd graduated from the tooth-rotting innocence of boiled sweets to the lung-corroding evil of the untipped cigarettes that he'd be chain-smoking well before he left his teens, eventually tearing the cellophane off up to five daily packets of mega-tar Gitanes. He was soon to promote his first alcoholic black-out, and was bragging to his classmates of having had his hand inside a girl's knickers, even if, in the aeon before the birth pill and the Swinging Sixties, everyone knew that such claims were usually either exaggerations or downright lies.

Lucien and his blazered cronies were inspired to invent some of them when, during morning break and immediately after lessons, they gathered by the railings to pretend not to notice the coltish charms of hoity-toity young ladies from a neighbouring sister school.

Characteristic of pubescent boyhood too was the furtive swapping of dirty jokes and, in the 1940s, passing round selected illustrations from magazines of female lingerie – the hardest visual pornography then available to them. Lucien's stories about his sexual encounters had been fuelled further through the profound effect of his coming across *Lolita*, Nabokov's famous and disturbing novel about a man who has a sexual relationship with his under-age stepdaughter.

Suppressing earlier inhibitions, precocious Lucien was also developing an aptitude for easy acquaintance that came more naturally to Joseph – who was absent for most of 1942, manipulating the eighty-eights in the mid-south, a freedom of movement that owed much to forged documents and the string-pulling of the club entrepreneurs employing him. The following year, Olia and the children were able to join him at 13, Rue Des Combes in Limoges, convenient for commuting to an increasing workload.

The Ginzburgs remained in the city until the Allies liberated France in 1944. The most intriguing of these incomers were from the United States, evoking something akin to submissive wonderment mingled with a touch of scepticism – as if they weren't quite real. Certainly, a gum-chewing GI acknowledging bemused stares with a wave of a fat cigar was more spell-binding than the common-or-garden French squaddie with his peanut wages and in-built sense of defeat. More than ever, North America seemed the wellspring of everything glamorous from Coca-Cola to sub-titled horror flicks about outer space "things" to The Ink Spots whose crooning would enrapture Paris during their European tour in 1947.

Many a Frankish entertainer accepted a second-class status, flattered to breathe the air round those that he'd been used to worshipping from afar, but among those fighting back both before and after the war were the likes of Trenet, Cora Vaucaire, Lucienne Delyle, Lys Gauty, Georges Brassens, the dancing vocalist Mistinguett and, most illustrious to a wider world, Maurice Chevalier. Yet, as a prisoner of war for over two years, Chevalier had been advantaged by an acquisition not only of an engaging "'ow-you-say" grasp of the English language, but also the trademark straw boater and Noel Coward smoking jacket for a one-man show of jauntily urbane characterisations that included mime, comic monologue and songs, a few of them self-written. Before an Eiffel Tower backdrop, he became inseparable from '*Ah Lurve Paris*', '*Zank 'Eaven For Leedle Gurls*' and all the rest of them after he Made It as a caricature Frenchman on stage and screen in the USA and Britain – where few Gallic artists had made much headway.

Being enormous within French-speaking territories, however, could be enormous enough. If unknown internationally, Georgius, the "Chevalier of the suburbs", was guaranteed well-paid engagements for as long as he could stand for an energy and epic vulgarity that matched that of Britain's Max Miller. Both Georgius and Maurice had been well into their thirties before achieving worthwhile recognition, thus buttressing the mitherings of French parents and teachers that, unless you'd been born into showbusiness, it was unwise to see it as a viable career. It was a facile life anyway, a vocational blind alley. Chevalier and his sort apart, no-one lasted very long.

Most middle-class households believed that the very idea of a boy venturing onto the professional stage in any capacity was almost as deplorable as a girl becoming a stripper. Regardless of who was present in living rooms where geometrically-patterned linoleum was the sole hint of frivolity, a parent would often switch off a wireless if it was broadcasting jazz, pop and whatever else had been lumped together derisively as "swing" – because it was an audial representation of the ridiculous, neon-loud and alien junk culture that caused Papa to fly into a rage if his adolescent – not "teenage" – son came downstairs in an American tie.

In the poorer quarters of Paris, his counterpart's sartorial self-expression was less repressed. There, prototype *yé-yé* wore garb that only the American GIs on passes and the boldest French homosexuals would be seen dead in: zoot-suits, "spearpoint" shirts, black-and-white footwear and those contentious hand-painted ties with baseball players or Red Indians on them. Visions of garish excess, they were not unlike Britain's Teddy Boys either with the same brilliantined ducktails, brass rings adorning their fingers like knuckle dusters, belts studded with washers stolen from work – and a musical preference for the less slushy shades of US pop music.

Like the Teds too, they modelled their personalities on hard-man *film noir* anti-heroes like James Cagney and Humphrey Bogart.

Younger ne'er-do-wells Marlon Brando and James Dean were skulking in dark alleyways as these more disreputable French youths prowled the boulevards in swaggering phalanxes with hunched shoulders, hands rammed in pockets, and chewing gum in a half-sneer; their women trailing forlornly behind them. A lone pedestrian would cross over to avoid them as, bored silly, they looked for things to destroy, people to beat up.

In this prelude to rock 'n' roll rebellion, the guitar was associated with Latinate heel-clattering and Romany camp-fires rather than anything remotely teenage. It was an actual Spanish gypsy who Joseph paid to teach his son the instrument as a means to earn money as a busker if times got tough. As well as being portable, it was more attractive than the piano to Lucien with his raging hormones. With mastery of the guitar, he could cut a dashing romantic figure – in his own mind anyway – as the swashbuckling rover of legend: swarthy good looks, stalwart build, neckerchief, lustrous black hair, brooding intensity.

Satisfying only the latter requirement, nineteen-year-old Lucien's whole being was screaming for sex, sex and more sex when he began sniffing round Elisabeth Levitsky. Two years older than he, she was more dauntingly free-spirited than the usual "nice" girl of the late 1940s, "saving herself" for her wedding night.

Elisabeth and Lucien had Russian ancestry in common, but the Levitskys spoke of a genealogical link with aristocracy. Of more pragmatic interest to Lucien was a perk of Elisabeth's job as general factotum to a surrealistic poet named Georges Hugnet. She had access to the flat of her employer's blood-brother, the painter Salvador Dali whose extravagant eyebrows may have raised without the customary affectation had he caught her using his dwelling for afternoon trysts with her new boyfriend.

The trespassers could have placated Dali with the information that Lucien was now a full-time art student under the post-Cubist Fernand Leger and the more genial, if less famous, Andre Lhote, a late contemporary and friend of Cézanne, arguably the father of modern art. Soon to die, Leger had explored – like Dali – film and other media, and was to fine art what the equally elderly Paris-born composer Edgard Varèse was to music in his fascination with the imagery and hidden artistic vocabulary of modern technology and mass-production. While there was pride in Lucien's familiarity with the great Leger, Fernand the person was not especially approachable. Self-obsessed and out of place in a student-centred environment, he was of a type who regarded the imparting of knowledge to others as a distraction from higher cultural purpose. He was, therefore, inclined to show involuntary disinterest in his charges unless any of their ideas could be incorporated into his own body of work.

Though Leger was returning to more figurative painting in his last years, abstract expressionism was all the rage in the early 1950s – especially the lyrical Tachism of the Ecole de Paris. It wasn't done to be both an abstract expressionist and – another major trend – a "kitchen sink" realist. You were either one or the other. Undecided, Lucien Ginzburg experimented with each, revealing vigour rather than subtlety in conspicuous brushwork and nakedly discernible structure. Although he was no Picasso or even a John Bratby, it wasn't laughable for Ginzburg to apply for a post as an art tutor to provide a fixed financial bedrock for married life with Elisabeth.

Their courtship had been interrupted by the War Office who, anxious about the latest outbreaks of terrorism by disaffected colonial subjects in Algeria, sent for Lucien Ginzburg. The dreaded official-looking envelope that hung like a sword of Damocles over every young Frenchman fluttered onto 11b's doormat one dark morning in 1949. The National Service call-up papers within obliged Lucien to join the army for a year – a lifetime when you're hardly more than a teenager.

His patriotic chore began in as dispiriting a manner as it would continue. As he hadn't been brought to the barracks on a stretcher, the induction medical was a mere formality. Next, his hair was planed halfway up the side of the skull with electric clippers, and he was kitted out with a ill-fitting uniform which had the texture of a horse blanket. During basic training, he was bawled at from dawn till dusk prior to a posting to the Ninety-Third Regiment of Infantry in Charras where he – like anyone who wasn't exactly illiterate – was considered officer material, and proffered a commission in the Reserves.

Ginzburg's decision to remain in the rank-and-file precluded any participation in the Algerian hostilities, but the square-bashing, the rifle drill, the boot-polishing and the anti-Semite baiting made the months drag so intolerably that he considered deserting. In any event, he merited a spell in the glasshouse for going AWOL to keep a date with Elisabeth now that they had crossed the impalpable barrier between inferred companionship and declared love.

Soon after he was demobbed, the two had named the day, and were living together firstly in a room within earshot of a jazz band's weekly rehearsals in a deconsecrated chapel, and then in various inexpensive hotel suites – including that once occupied by the poets Verlaine and Rimbaud, and another next door to Leo Ferré, a *chansonier* who sat on the right hand of George Brassens in the Valhalla of French popular culture.

Finally, Elisabeth and Lucien settled into the Maison Des Réfugiés Israelites, 6 Avenue De La République after tying the knot on 3 November 1951. A letter published after his death intimated that Lucien was completely besotted with his bride, and "incapable of thinking about tomorrow".

Gladly, he'd filled a vacancy on the same block at a primary school that catered principally for the children of Jews and survivors of the Holocaust. With its comparatively short hours, teaching art was an easy option. What with a good-looking wife, supportive parents and a spacious flat on a main thoroughfare at the very centre of Paris, the story might have ended happily every after. The pipe between the teeth, the clipped beard and the brown leather elbows on the tweed jacket would epitomise Lucien's adjustment to respectability by middle age.

During lunch hours, he doodles on the assembly hall's upright when not relaxing in the staff room. His income is supplemented by teaching guitar and piano at home and, on other evenings, running "rhythm and improvisation" workshops at the nearby adult education centre. Both participants and onlookers seem to enjoy the sessions in a knowing, nodding sort of way.

He immerses himself in music as other family men might immerse themselves in do-it-yourself, photography or football. Selecting an artefact from an impressive record collection, Lucien likes the tactile sensation of handling an album cover and reading the liner notes, finding much to notice, study and compare. With an observed reverence, he trances out to classical music – though his soul will always be in the jazz that takes him back to a lamented youth.

In real life, Lucien was very much a jazzer of more modern kidney than his father. Rather than snapping his fingers to the plinking and puffing of traditional jazz, he strove to drop buzz-words like "Monk", "Gillespie", "Bud Powell", "Art Tatum" and "Miles Davis" into conversations during intermissions down the Blue Note, Hot Club and like clubs where he watched wistfully as domestic jazzmen like Henri Genes and André Claveau betrayed their inferiority complexes about the Americans who influenced them and everyone else.

During one such evening, Ginzburg fell in with Michel Gaudry, a double-bass player for whom work with Powell and Duke Ellington had been among the summits of his professional life. After much persuasion, his new friend pitched in on piano in a jam session. Though Lucien didn't make a fool of himself amid the subtle bebop cross-rhythms and melodic complexities, he was reluctant as a rule to partake in such blows owing to misgivings about his own capabilities as an improviser. "He had a complex about it," surmised Gaudry, "and the reception he got if ever he risked getting on stage didn't improve this state of affairs. I remember offensive remarks about his physical appearance coming from the front rows. As he was already crippled with nerves, that didn't do much to make things better."

These dubious recreations apart, there was also enough moonlighting time after work and during the long holidays for Lucien, now in the Musicians Union, to supplement his salary by leaning on his father for an *entrée* into the bar, club and dance hall circuit as a semi-professional musical accompanist.

In 1954, he was to start the first of several annual residencies coinciding with the summer recess at the Club De La Forêt in Le Touquet, a resort on the Channel seaboard. However, as Joseph advised him, sometimes the work was unsatisfying in substance, but there was plenty of it within easier reach, whether in the smaller venues such as Club Geneviève and L'Ecluse, a music hall like Madame Arthur's, fashionable Club L'Echelle de Jacob in St Germain des Pres on the edge of the Latin Quarter, or – in your dreams – the Bobino, backing Brassens who surfaced there as often as rocks did in the stream.

More Lucien's mark, perhaps, was the Théâtre Des Trois Baudets, just off Boulevard De Clichy in Montmartre. A converted cinema, it drew students and weekend beatniks – all berets, holey sweaters and bumfluff beards – as well as tourists looking for something less polished than the Moulin Rouge. It may have been because the *clientèle* wanted more than incidental accompaniment to revelry that it was common for Trois Baudets entertainers to be roundly booed if they didn't supply it. Conversely, a grotesque camaraderie could accumulate after an initially gawping crowd tuned into the most unlikely act that an audacious booking policy had procured.

It was a good shop window for anyone who wanted to move up to somewhere more prestigious on the Left Bank like, say, Francis Claude's arty Quod Libet. From there, you could cross the river to his Milord L'Arsoille, capacious and steeped in history. Danton, Mirabeau and other *dramatis personae* of the Revolution had met socially in this selfsame building in 1792, the year that Rouget de Lisle penned 'La Marseillaise'. In those days, the club was called "Le Caveau Des Aveugles" because the proprietor only hired blind musicians since they couldn't see the dissolute goings-on of his illustrious customers.

A small army of big names – including Orson Welles and Jean Cocteau from the realm of the cinema alone – were out in force when, following refurbishment, it was reopened as Milord L'Arsoille in 1950 with a cabaret bill headlined by Michèle Arnaud, a singing comedienne who was to have a bearing on Lucien Ginzburg's life. She was herself destined to win the *Grand Prix De Chanson* at a song festival in Deauville two years later, but her street urchin looks, if endearing, were not then the stuff of enduring stardom as a singer *per se*. Nevertheless, seasons at Milord L'Arsoille were to be Arnaud's springboard to the Olympia, France's premier music hall and a means to a Chevalier-sized world of possibilities.

While it contained a plethora of recording studios and radio stations, Michèle's home town of Toulouse near the Spanish border was beyond the geographical limit that the entertainment industry, centred in Paris, could be bothered to search for new sensations. Yet its talent scouts weren't above making nightly excursions to the dingiest metropolitan clubs to view the human goods displaying themselves in hopes of a rags-to-riches leap to fame.

Tina Rossi from Corsica and Iberian tenor Luis Mariano were among those who had "arrived" already from small beginnings in

Parisian watering holes – while in Club Genèvieve, Brussels' own Jacques Brel was metamorphosing from a clumsy rustic to one more attuned to what record company supremos expected of a singing money-maker. He worked in split-shifts there with Charles Aznavour, a twenty-nine-year-old Armenian soon to come safely into the harbour of celebrity – as would Dalida, a former Miss Egypt, about to be "discovered" by Lucien Morisse, Radio Europe station director and her future spouse.

Dalida's second release, 'Bambino', was to be a huge Yuletide seller throughout continental Europe, but for many an artiste – even one based in Paris – records (if any) were but adjuncts to earnings in the provinces where it was feasible to maintain at least an illusion of professional employment for years on the same bill as fat-thighed dancing girls, red-nosed comics, acrobats, jugglers, trick cyclists and *pierrots* with names like "Spak" and "Bip". This road was generally obscure and quiet, a dusty, wearisome road that didn't look as if it led anywhere important – but there was always a chance that it might. A club in Chartres where you'd always gone down well changes its policy and you don't fit any more, but then you get a fortnight second-billed to The Delta Rhythm Boys further from the kernel of affairs on a trek round Belgium.

It wasn't how good you were, it was who you knew, wasn't it? Les Filles A Papa, a teenage trio, gained bookings because of their better-known songwriting fathers. Theirs was one of the corniest acts in the City of Light, concluding as it did, for gawd's sake, with the three donning masks of their parents' faces. Then there was Sacha Distel, another well-connected showbiz brat, who had become a respected jazz guitarist before his seventeenth birthday in 1950, often sitting in with distinguished Americans visiting Parisian clubland. He played hard in other respects – with Brigitte Bardot and Juliette Gréco, svelte and spectral high priestess of popular existentialism, among his amours. With lost business innocence too, he'd invested wisely in music publishing, switched smoothly from jazz to singing hard-line pop, and was full steam ahead for his first million.

Meanwhile, someone like Jacques Brel's income on aggregate was about a thirtieth of that of a dustman. Frequently, he was worth less than the resident pianist who backed him – and it occurred to many such players that, while you didn't have to like what you did, if you got in with the right people and were sufficiently versatile and understanding about unorthodox talent, you stood a surer chance of a livelihood than any two-bit show-off at the central microphone.

There was token mutiny from Lucien Ginzburg – manifested by his strumming guitar behind a busking singer for several hellish weeks – before he followed in his father's footsteps. For months previously, the dinner register had swum before Lucien's budgerigar eyes in the classroom. After each night's stint at the piano, he'd got home as the graveyard hours chimed, and grabbed what rest he could. Over breakfast, he'd decide how best to keep the brats quiet today.

Battling to stay awake, he couldn't think straight and would struggle through till morning break on raw power, greeting with a snarl any child approaching his desk. Yet, beneath it all, M Ginzburg was no vinegary Fernand Leger, and the children had grown to be fond of him for his slangy turns of phrase and infectious enthusiasm for his subject.

It was no surprise for Lucien to be contacted during lessons to deputise that evening at some dive in Montmartre or a coming-of-age party outside the city limits in the Bois de Boulogne. Inevitably, his double life had burnt the candle to the middle, and it was the day job that had to be sacrificed so that he could concentrate on what was becoming a lucrative career as a musician. So too vanished Lucien's aspirations to be a painter. "The question is to know if we abandon passion or passion abandons us," he'd reflect years after he'd thus allowed himself to be sucked into a vortex of events, places and circumstances that hadn't belonged even to speculation when he was winding up a messy afternoon of *papier mâché*.

Lucien's skills as an artist were to prove useful, however, when he was "resting". Self-employment with its undercurrent of insecurity drove him to painting furniture and colouring monochrome film stills that cinemas sold in those days. This kept the wolf from the door, but vocationally he was on the lookout for opportunities beyond just being an all-styles-served-here sideman to a cache of vocalists on a given bill. While there was money to be made by transcribing scores, arranging and as a rehearsal pianist for stage and television shows, Lucien was aware too that the jobbing tunesmith was as indispensable a part of the music industry.

Unlike most classically-trained musicians – including his own father – he was not self-depreciating about his knowledge and selective liking of entries in the newly-established national record and sheet music sales charts. He recognised too that fortunes could be made by churning out assembly-line pop for the masses – and so it was that Ginzburg applied for membership of SACEM, passing the required entrance examinations in summer 1954 and filing six compositions on 1 August of that year.

The general procedure was that when you'd accumulated sufficient product on demonstration tapes, you would then attempt to place it with suitable artists. Lucien, however, was not a natural hustler, very much the opposite. He didn't have a fast mouth, that cunning intertwining of modesty and self-projection, or an Aaron to his Moses. For three years, he lurked behind the *nom de plume* "Julien Crix", and became so self-doubting about his abilities as a lyricist that in 1955 he delegated that responsibility to others such as Louis Laibe, artistic director of Madame Arthur where, through Papa, Lucien had snared a plum job conducting the house band.

At Madame Arthur's, each act was expected to make use of the band if only for a rumble of timpani as a rabbit was produced from a conjurer's top hat. Usually, fare would embrace something wholly musical. A more rounded entity than the diverse variety associated with the British music hall, a French presentation was more often a series of sketches and songs concerned with a specific and interlocking theme – a "concept" if you like – rather than a parade of entertainers connected only by a master-of-ceremony's loquacious continuity.

With Laibe, Ginzburg knocked together a revue hinged on circuses entitled *Zita La Panthère* for Madame Arthur's 1955-1956 winter programme, making the most of the troupe then present. This included a portly impersonator named Toni Coste, acrobat Paul Alt and Lucky Sarcell, a villainous-looking protégé of Mistinguett, who'd been the first person to sing a Lucien Ginzburg opus – 'Antoine Le Casseur' (about a girl's yearning for a charismatic hooligan) – in public, a fact not greatly appreciated at the time.

Nevertheless, his confidence boosted, Lucien put another number, 'Je Broyais Du Noir' – with lyrics from Paul Alt – in the way of a bigger fish in Juliette Gréco, the thinking man's French actress in whose throaty drawl Philips, one of France's handful of major labels, had perceived recording potential. She was known to scrutinise any interesting up-and-coming songwriter for likely material, but, having heard nothing from her weeks after sending in 'Je Broyais Du Noir', Lucien screwed up the courage to ring her agent to ask if she'd had time to rub a professional chin over it. He was greeted by a curt riposte that Mme Gréco was "too busy" to answer his covering letter. Anyway, if he hadn't heard by now, he must assume that she'd turned down the wretched song. Yet, if dejected, Lucien accepted Gréco's indifference as the prerogative of her sombre glamour. He did not despise her for it, and remained a fan of her music.

As he hadn't experienced any himself, it might have been tempting for him to be sardonic about her success. Gréco was not a run-of-the-mill singing sensation with her intellectual aura and, most pointedly, the detergent-white facial cosmetics – lipstick too – relieved only by the blackest mascara and eye-shadow, and framed by straight hair of the same shade. She covered her figure in a tent-like sweater that tapered into form-fitting trousers, the uniform worn by her devotees, mainly undergraduates in dimly-lit bedsits with Man Ray on the walls.

It signalled something vaguely promising that someone like that could Make It without compromising such a stark image. Lucien could believe, quite genuinely, that he too could be a contender if he was given the works by the publicity department of a company like Philips. He could believe that and yet still respect Gréco. He could jeer and yet his admiration for her was *kosher*.

A word like "*kosher*" was a reminder that, to give himself the best possible chance, he ought to lose his Jewish surname at a time when anti-Semitism – and, indeed, prejudice against immigrants in general, no matter how entrenched – still lingered in the psyche of even the most vehement European foes of the Nazis. Even as late as 1966, Brian Epstein would complain that because he was a Jew, he'd not been included on the Queen's birthday honours list as his Beatles had been. One who was, Bud Flanagan – among Britain's most cherished wartime entertainers – began life as Reuben Weintrop just as Charles Aznavour did as Shahnour Verenagh Aznavourian – and, in 1956, Lucien Ginzburg likewise adopted a stage alias, albeit for reasons that were less to do with his born name's racial implications than it sounding – so he'd explain – like that of a back-street hairdresser. From now on, he was going to be "Serge Gainsbourg": "Serge" as a genuflection to his family's Russian past, and "Gainsbourg" to the primary school pedagogues who always spelled it wrong (in the 1980s, it was sometimes rendered as "Gainsbarre").

Any thoughts about an impending ascent to stardom were tempered every time his shaving mirror told him that he'd never be a Charles Trenet, all dazzling smiles, athletic frame, curly hair and graceful movements. Serge-Lucien was also cognisant that at twenty-eight, he'd achieved little of consequence, and was older than many of those already of national renown as it had become easier since the war for those with good looks and "personality" to jump the gun without years of scrimmaging round the unsalubrious clubs that littered Paris.

Sodden with cynical ruminations, Gainsbourg (who had neither) was drinking an inordinate amount of his pay – on aggregate, about 2,000F (old francs) a night – as soon as he received it. Slapping the bar, he'd spread a sheaf of notes and order a round, motivated less by a wish to carouse as getting up the nerve to regale the sillier females who'd been cow-eyed round the bandstand with his florid vocabulary and rich fund of rude jokes.

He was now being "talked of" with other women, and his cheery flirtations were among factors that had so weakened his emotional allegiance to Elizabeth that the couple had drifted into open estrangement. Long before the *decree nisi* was granted on 9 October 1957, Lucien was back with his parents in their new apartment off Avenue Foch, and waiting, like Mr Micawber, for something to turn up.

It did when Joseph, despairing of his son, was offered a season at Milord L'Arsoille starring Michèle Arnaud then riding her biggest hit, a translation of Canadian singer Paul Anka's 'Diana'. Joseph's diary was full, but perhaps M Claude might be interested in young M Ginzburg? The suggestion didn't much excite Francis Claude, but this Lucien, Serge or whatever he called himself wasn't an obvious no-hoper. It would do no harm, he supposed, to give him a break.

chapter two

Du Chant A L'Une!

Living *la vie bohème* beat teaching, and there were times when he found a mild enchantment in imagining that it might go on forever. Nevertheless, if the year-long Milord L'Arsoille commission was gratifying financially, it was probably another blind alley, and it was nauseating for him to weigh up its cash benefits against his self-image as an artist.

With commendable objectivity, Serge capitalised on, rather than shrank from his vexation by channelling it into the compositions that were now pouring from him, judging by the number registered with SACEM between 1954 and 1957. As it had been with the Great McGonagall, idea upon idea chased so rapidly through his mind that it was all he could do to write them down. Shards of inspiration cut him even during a short stroll to the tobacconist's. Others imposed themselves at bedtime, yanking him from the quietude that precedes slumber. In dressing gown and pyjamas, he'd be surrounded soon by smeared coffee cups, twisted cigarette butts and pages full of notation as he figured out a chord sequence to a fragment of melody. From just a title, a sketchy chorus or perhaps the ghost of a first verse would smoulder into form, and red-eyed, unshaven impartiality and a quality-control peculiar to himself would occupy him until the grey of morning when his mother, half-feeling her way down to the kitchen, would notice the crack of electric light under his door.

His formal training put him a cut above those musical illiterates who had to dah-dah-dah "head" arrangements to a transcriber in days when it was the norm for a singer, unencumbered by an instrument, to front what often amounted to a full orchestra. Nevertheless, the world of pop had widened since the advent of rock 'n' roll, and it became necessary to unlearn many ingrained dos and don'ts. Creative flow was inhibited too by the stylistic clichés and habits of jazz as Gainsbourg grappled with his muse, endeavouring to disguise sources of inspiration in hopes that nothing would remain aggravatingly familiar.

On days when little would come, all he could do was despair or daydream, lying full-length on the bed, hands under head, smoking, smoking. He'd wander over to the window to gaze glumly at the street below. Then in a ritual of thwarted eroticism, he might position himself in front of the wardrobe mirror, and perform to thousands of ecstatic fans that only he could see, feeling no end of a fool afterwards.

It seemed dafter to be anything but pessimistic, but such feelings could be kept at arm's length when boozing after he'd finished at Milord L'Arsoille. Yet he'd pay for its short-lived magic the next day, waking up thick-tongued after another bender, promising himself never to touch another drop but sinking three fingers of hair-of-the-dog spirits within an hour of getting dressed.

One frolicsome evening, he was blessed with the after-hours company of the club's manager and resident star. Until then, Francis Claude and Michèle Arnaud had taken only the minimum notice of the buttoned-up Serge with the perpetual cigarette hanging from his lower lip, but the ensuing conversation coaxed from him the revelation that once music had been but an extra-mural pursuit when he'd aspired to be a painter. Intrigued, the two invited themselves back to Serge's bedroom-cum-studio to see his work. Depreciatingly, he fished out the few canvasses that he hadn't yet destroyed; among them a self-portrait, so heavy with impasto that it stood out in lumps. However, Michèle was less impressed by this than the pencilled lyrics – his own – and music of an opus entitled 'Défense D'Afficher'. He was a songwriter as well then? Could she hear this one?

With their eyes on him, Serge almost shook his head to slough off the hushed, butterfly attention. Nonetheless, he stubbed out his weed, cleared his throat and opened the piano lid. A deep breath and he was into the opening line: "Seven in the evening, it's nearly dark..." He's waiting interminably on some sordid corner for his date to show, sinking into a despondent daze induced by the fixity of gazing at a wall festooned with graffiti and tattered posters as the clusters of passers-by thin. It was quite tough material for the time; certainly far beyond 'Diana' or anything from *Gigi*, 1958's Chevalier film musical with 'Thank Heaven For Little Girls' in it.

Glistening with embarrassment while the 'Défense D'Afficher' coda – the repeated title – died away, Gainsbourg blinked at the keys before glancing up with enquiring eyebrow at his tiny audience, which was nodding and smiling with manifest pleasure. Did he have any more? Why don't we work some of them into the show? Couldn't we make room for Serge to sing one himself?

The following night, a timid songbird was cajoled up onto the stage to play it safe with pretty-but-nothing 'Tour Le Chant'. Gainsbourg's knees knocked, his body swayed, his eyes were screwed shut and his voice was tremulous with terror, but the spectators – who included, so one legend goes, President-in-waiting François Mitterrand – interpreted it as part of the act, along with the vague and self-conscious hand-ballets.

He was hardly an overnight sensation. Nevertheless, there came to be a noticeable if small-scale cult who were entranced by Gainsbourg, and the running order was reshuffled slightly in his favour so that a typical Milord L'Arsoille bill in mid-1957 would place Serge below Arnaud – soon to defect to the Bobino – and Jacques Dufilho, but lording it over two other turns. Moreover, Arnaud endorsed his worth as a composer by slipping his 'La Femme Des Uns Sous Le Corps Des Arbres' – which, in passing, acknowledged North America's growing dominance of world pop – and placatory 'Jeune Femmes Et Vieux Messieurs' in between US covers and her usual chansons from the likes of Ferré and – a particular preference of Serge – Guy Béart.

Unsolicited, a vocal group, Frères Jacques, began performing his 'Le Poinçonneur Des Lilas' – introducing it as "*Le Premier Concerto Gainsbourgeris*" – after Paris at large first caught the writer singing it in person on a local radio broadcast that December. Though catchy, 'Le Poinçonneur Des Lilas' wasn't bursting with Christmas cheer exactly in its narrative about a Metro ticket clipper who finds *"toujours des p'tits trous"* so soul-destroying that he punches *"un grand trou"* in his own skull with a pistol. Yet its rapid-fire delivery and descending woodwind ostinatos conveyed a sound-picture of the rush of travellers, whether pleasure-seekers or lemming-like commuters, down the escalators, not giving so much as a second glance at a dead-eyed face below the regulation *képi.*

A sure sign that Serge might be going places was the insertion of of 'Le Poinçonneur Des Lilas' into the stage repertoire of Phillipe Clay, a vocalist then capable of filling the Olympia, and a request for further Gainsbourg numbers. To Serge's chagrin, none of these was recorded by Clay – though the younger Hugues Aufray, France's foremost executant of skiffle (albeit a craze that was not gripping the nation as tightly as it was in Britain) was able to get one of the remaindered Clay items, 'Mes P'tites Odalisques' (literally, "My Little Harem Concubines"), onto the thirty-three rpm disc mentioned in its very chorus.

It was, nevertheless, Michèle Arnaud's rendering of several Gainsbourg songs during the course of a single performance at the Bobino in 1958 that brought him his first stray paragraphs in the national press, and a laudatory article, ("Serge Gainsbourg Chez Milord L'Arsoille"), in the magazine *Combat*, that dwelt more on his skills as a composer than what was still a curate's egg of a stage act.

During a memorable first conversation around this time, Yves Montand asked Gainsbourg, "What do you want to be? A lyricist, composer or performer?" "I want to be all of them," was the reply. Most preferred other artists – notably Arnaud's – readings of his songs. Yet Serge was willing to continue finding his feet on the boards. He was amenable, for example, to mixing his own numbers with those of others – Ferré, Aznavour, even Cole Porter, Gershwin and Irving Berlin – to thus conform to lingering critical dictates about the necessity of including a generous portion of old favourites and current smashes. An uninterrupted set of your own stuff wasn't then *de rigueur* because what agents, recording managers and like powers that be were looking for was overall competence and versatility rather than individuality.

Whoever had penned the item that elicited it, Serge was quite tickled whenever anyone – especially if female – cried encouragement to him. There were to be episodes throughout his career of favourable reactions to an apparently unlooked-for exposure to the limelight creating false impressions of abilities as an entertainer in a vulnerable mind. Even in 1958, he was able, with a certain logical blindness, to make out that every one of his slots at Milord L'Arsoille and during summer in Le Touquet was a triumph in retrospect.

However, minus the rose-tinted glasses, his customary stage fright did not endow him with that element of lip-trembling pathos that some find endearing. Instead, he had an edgy, ponderous ungeniality that gave the material no assistance whatsoever. In the highest tradition of jazz, a run of Serge Gainsbourg recitals was beset with good and bad nights. When he was bad, he was very, very bad, but his knot of devotees had deduced that, though he was no Chevalier under the spotlight, he was developing an intangible something else.

Whatever it was, it wasn't obvious to record company outriders, voracious for new faces to exploit and discard for a fickle public, and often checking out up to twenty acts in one evening. So what's with this Gainsbourg *schmuck* that's made Michèle Arnaud so evangelical about him? The most immediate impression was that no photographic miracle on an LP sleeve could make Serge's face his fortune. It hadn't helped either when he pulled a lower eyelid down in one circulated publicity shot. No question, he had a clear deficit of – how can we put this? – sex appeal. With his short-cropped Nero haircut, huge ears and beaky nose, he was the man least likely to send *les midenettes* – France's "bobby-soxers" – into paroxysms of screaming ecstasy.

From the disobliging way some of them put it, you'd think they were talking about Quasimodo. With perfunctory kindness, thirty-year-old Gainsbourg was recommended to set his sights on the path of a securer anonymity, ie working to order as a backroom composer with a publishing company. Yet there was somebody important who, on a hunch, decided to take a risk.

Jacques Canetti, a showbiz jack-of-all-trades had, in his capacity as Head of Artists and Repertoire at Philips, "discovered" Brassens, Gréco, Béart, Brel – and Boris Vian, jazz trumpeter and singing writer of satirical pieces of which the most famous, 'Le Déserteur', took the form of a letter from a newly-conscripted soldier to the President of the Republic, and contained the daring line: "If blood has to be spilt, Mr. President, set a good example by spilling yours." Vian was known on the Left Bank as the irreverent author of the novel *I'm Going To Spit On Your Graves*, and journalism that was sincerely loud in its praise for all manner of ingredients in black America's musical melting pot, whether the rural stumblings of the Mississippi delta, Chicago and New Orleans rhythm-and-blues or, via the likes of Chuck Berry and Little Richard, its rock 'n' roll derivation.

In turn, Boris was much admired by Serge – who had seen him perform several times earlier in the year – to the degree that there was a point of comparison when a Gainsbourg demo tape landed on Jacques Canetti's desk. A second opinion was sought from a recording manager, Denis Bourgeois, who chose to assess it on the merits of the songs rather than their singer's looks and personality. He too perceived similarities with Vian – though he recognised too a half-concealed quirkiness in Gainsbourg's offerings that could be made more distinctive in the non-retractable realm of the studio. Bourgeois's opinion was so valued by Canetti that the newcomer was added cautiously to the label's roster with an option on extending the contract if exploratory releases gave cause for hope.

An initial notion was for Vian to collaborate with Serge as perhaps his co-writer or producer – but Boris was now unavailable as he'd been deemed just the one to specialise in jazz and rock 'n' roll on Philips' Fontana subsidiary (and was to die in 1959).

Nevertheless, Alain Goraguer – who bore the same relationship to Vian as arranger Gil Evans did to Miles Davis – was the next best thing. On the evidence of his pipe-and-slippers demeanour, and from lending a cursory ear to *Go Go Goraguer!*, his latest album in his own right, Goraguer seemed outwardly to be one of a kind with André Grassi, Michel Legrand, André Popp and other nonchalantly proficient middle-aged middle-of-the-road bandleaders who had first refusal of virtually all record dates in Parisian recording complexes throughout the 1950s. It was as if French pop couldn't be done in any other way or with any other players than those bound by the rigidity of radio-imposed conservatism and union officials who would spring to the defence of any malicious pedant in the fourth row of violins who yelled a gleeful "time's up!" in the middle of a take.

Yet, its lunatic fringes notwithstanding, Alain loved all roots and branches of jazz with a passion more eager than even Vian and now Gainsbourg (whom he'd already seen and applauded at Le Touquet). He was, therefore, less dogged with veneration for Gallic pop's elder statesmen and correlated respect for the antics of ensembles like Les Filles A Papa. Neither was he going to automatically squeeze Serge into the lushly orchestrated mould of the day: "decent" pop that programme planners for national radio thought the public ought to enjoy.

This used to mean that there was little middle ground between nursery rhymes and Maurice Chevalier. Despite fuller post-war employment giving them the money to spend on records, teenagers were not yet regarded as the industry's most vital target, and were condemned to put up with an inordinate amount of the same music that their elders and younger siblings liked; the first stirrings of rock 'n' roll warranting token spins on the wireless before being brushed under the carpet as another US fad as transient as hula-hoops and the Cha-Cha-Cha.

The title of 'Paris, Tu N'A Pas Change', a mid-1950s smash by Jean Sablon, summed up the stranglehold that its staid overseers had – and seemed likely then to have forever – on France's electric media. Unless you toed a clean, winsome line, you wouldn't have a hit. If you did, the business would take care of you, find you a job when your time was up, and the circle would remain unbroken. There was no reason why affairs couldn't carry on as they should with harmless, ephemeral doggerel to be hummed, whistled and sung imperfectly by the milkman while another ditty was prepared by reworking the same precept with either the same act or a new one with a different angle.

As long as you didn't do anything that the entertainment establishment didn't approve, a gramophone record in the "Top Twenty" could place you in a strong if short-term negotiating position for more remunerative and respectable work in variety, cabaret and even TV shows and advertising. If you'd learnt enough of the ropes, you could muscle in too on publishing, production, artist management and conveyor-belt songwriting.

For Serge Gainsbourg, all this had been received information from the cradle. Raised in a showbusiness family based in Paris, he had had infinitely more contacts than outsiders like Dalida and Brel as well as an instinct acquired swiftly for the manoeuvres needed for that extra push up the ladder – all the way if his time came – and the know-how to sidestep the sly quagmires and downright thuggery of the music industry. However much of a shrinking violet he still was on stage, his professional ups and downs since 1954 had hardened him with the tenacity and confidence to strike any necessarily bellicose stance in negotiation.

For a start, he wasn't going to be a corporation marionette like Dalida. While he would confer with managers and other payroll courtiers, he alone was to accept responsibility for professional decisions, no matter how unwise. There'd be occasions too when he'd take an intense and often unwelcome interest in every link of the chain from editing block to pressing plant to marketplace. Moreover, he was sufficiently long in the tooth not to be so dazzled by transient pop fame to think that he'd last. Always, he'd expect it to end – as it often would.

The first of several career peaks began with the issue of *Du Chant A L'Une!*: nine tracks on one of these new-fangled ten-inch thirty-three rpm long-players – LPs – somewhere between the twelve-inchers yet to come and the seven-inch EP (extended play) that, replete with picture sleeve and usually a title track, was a more common (and economical) release than the single in France. Both were pressed on the plastic forty-fives that had superseded seventy-eights.

With a core combo – vibes, guitar, sax, piano, double bass, brushed drums – assembled by Boris Bourgeois, and a eulogy on the back cover by Marcel Ayme – who had lately translated Arthur Miller's *The Crucible* for the French stage – *Du Chant A L'Une!* consisted of the self-penned stand-bys in his stage set such as 'Le Poinçonneur Des Lilas' and the numbers that Arnaud did too. Overall, it was a listening rather than a dancing album with close-miked voice floating effortlessly over limpid and tasteful cocktail jazz: all the premeditated carelessness and hurried meticulousness inherent in capturing the spirit of the moment with the infallible polish achieved through the musicians' close knowledge of each other's foibles.

Neither Gainsbourg nor Goraguer presumed to dictate nuances to fellows seasoned by countless daily sessions, but ran through the essentials of every number quickly before Serge vanished into the vocal isolation booth. There, in a world of his own, he shifted gear with the composure of a Formula One racer while the band kept effortless pace during an exhilarating evening's labour with a couple of the pieces down in one. It also fostered a sparkling vocal presence that belied the singer's taciturnity on stage – as well as instrumental solos of more open-ended design than you'd expect on what was supposed to be a pop record.

Some items were scarcely in the realm of pop at all. Musically, 'Ce Mortal Ennui' lived only in its nine-note riff and tacit hooklines while 'Du Jazz Dans Le Ravin' was more a recitation of poetry-and-jazz persuasion: the sort of thing you'd hear at *demi-monde* gatherings where table lamps are dimmed with headscarves, and the eyes of cross-legged beatniks are closed in rapture.

Some of the subjects in the lyrics, however, might have brought the party down. Witness 'Du Jazz Dans Le Ravin' as it details blood puddling out of a couple involved in a car crash. Other areas covered weren't everybody's bag either, but a composer of songs about piano removal men ('Le Charleston Des Déménageurs De Piano') and the art of alluring a man in the style of a recipe ('Le Recette De L'Amour Fou') was not to be dismissed easily.

It's good to have a laugh, ladies and gentlemen, but there was also more than a little off-hand breast-beating in 'L'Alcool' – an inebriate spewing out dismal contemplations about his love life. Elisabeth's spectre effuses from the speakers in 'Ce Mortal Ennui' in which a man tires of his lover, but lacks the motivation to finish with her. While the words of 'Ronsard 58' were the work of Serge Barthélémy, a Milord L'Arsoille acquaintance, their misogyny – along the lines of a girl who, though rich in material comforts, will never be more than a little scrubber morally – was endorsed by the sole creator of 'Mes P'tites Odalisques'.

While its contents stepped outside pop's stagnant "moon-June" limits, *Du Chant A L'Une!* was radio-friendly only marginally. Unleashed on Europe's crowded ether, it picked up just scattered plays – mainly of 'Le Poinçonneur Des Lilas' – because the seamier imagery and swear words that pocked the companion tracks did not escape the censorship of the universal aunt that was the French media in the late 1950s. Near the knuckle too, Brassens' 'Pornograph' and Ferré's 'Temps De Plastique' had also been excluded from prudish airwaves, but when one watchdog of decency asked Michèle Arnaud to tone down the sexual innuendo in 'Jeunes Femmes Et Vieux Messieurs' and 'La Femme Des Unis Sous Le Corps Des Autres' when she opened at the Olympia for Brassens, she pondered the request carefully before marching on and emoting both totally unamended.

The restrictions that it suffered guaranteed what could be described politely as modest sales for the Gainsbourg album, but there was no doubt about a critical success that affirmed the respect accorded to Serge as a "musician's musician". Though the Philips publicity machine had subtracted five years from his age, teen appeal didn't come into the equation, be it in *Le Monde*'s sober but supportive analysis or Boris Vian's lavish approbation across two whole columns in the *Canard Enchaine*.

Such a wealth of complimentary coverage was no mean achievement for a first timer – and more than enough to convince Philips to include Gainsbourg on *Opus 109*, a showcase LP with Guy Béart, Ricet Barrier and funnyman Bernard Haller, taped on the evening of 12 November 1958 at Theatre Des Trois Baudets. Through Canetti's agency too, Serge was engaged – rather optimistically – to warm up the audience for Yves Montand at the Théâtre De L'Etoile, and was elevated to second-to-last at Milord L'Arsoille – as if to imply that he was only one rung below whatever hit parade entrant was headlining.

He was also encouraged to tidy himself up a bit by investing in stylish but not too way-out suits or maybe smart casuals for stage wear, and to focus himself on every customer, not the floor or the nearest tables. Had he ever come across the term "back projection"?

The ego massage of these attentions and having records – two spin-off EPs as well – in the shops resulted in slicker performances that prompted a universal cessation of conversation the instant he walked on, and a readier unfurling of considered ovations, especially after *Du Chant A L'Une!* won its maker *Le Grand Prix De L'Académie* – the Frankish equivalent of an Ivor Novello Award.

Into the bargain, Serge was being courted by those he used to canvass. Returning to the concert platform after two years away, Gréco was grubbing round publishers' offices for a suitable means of an interrelated relaunch of herself as a recording artist too. Meeting Gainsbourg not really by chance in the Philips building, she accepted gladly his new 'Il Etait Une Oie' – beneath the lyrical imagery, a naive virgin is seduced and impregnated – as the only previously-unheard item on a planned all-Gainsbourg EP. There was also talk of the more mainstream Pia Columbo releasing her version of 'Défense D'Afficher'.

If heartened by a syndication that consolidated his status as a songwriter, Serge couldn't retire on it, and his income still depended most upon bookings that were about to catapult him into a promotional slog round the provinces with the *Opus 109* troupe. If nothing else, it wrought in him a more workmanlike stagecraft as he did battle with the varying public address systems of far-flung theatres, cinemas, casinos, sports pavilions, village halls and, a new innovation, boarded-over swimming pools.

Driving, driving, driving to strange towns and stranger venues, Serge's first national tour was not all it was cracked up to be. Uncertain about whether he'd even be sleeping comfortably that night, he'd endure shampooing in toilet washbasins, overcoats for blankets and waking up shivering to Haller snoring open-mouthed a yard away. In fly-blown wayside cafes, Barrier would tunnel into a greasy but unmistakably satisfying fry-up while, across the formica table, Gainsbourg picked at some fishy melange and toffee-coloured *pommes frites* with less enthusiasm. All part of a day's work too were flat batteries, overcharging alternators, jammed starter motors and long waits for mechanics who may or may not fix them.

Beyond the pale of Paris, the zigzagging itinerary might have been arranged by someone who thought that a thousand kilometres was merely a few inches on a map. *Plus ça change.* Frequently, there wasn't time to remove stage make-up, and Serge would slip into an uneasy doze with the road buzzing in his ears as the convoy of cars hurtled through the night in order to reach the next evening on time. Admitted to one civic institute's inner sanctum, a local journalist had the rare treat of watching Gainsbourg seizing the first opportunity to shave in a week.

While it circumscribed serious composition, ideas that came to him in inconvenient moments could be formulated after the exhausted vehicles bumped into the service car park, and the occupants lugged their equipment and effects into a darkened auditorium with its chilly essence of disinfectant and a flat echo of yesterday's booze and tobacco intake. Until showtime, Serge might tinker secretively on a battered piano in a backstage alcove, but he couldn't stop himself being dragged into the behind-the-scenes intrigues and jealousies that would come to a head in *prima donna* tantrums you could hear in the galleries and squabbles that ricocheted like shrapnel between any given combination of the principals for all the wonderful-to-be-here vapourings and scripted grinning unzipped as soon they got in front of the footlights.

There was also much competitive tilting for the downfall of the knickers of stage door Jezebels who didn't spoil no-strings frivolity by getting sulkily proprietorial when all a lonely journeyman needed was someone who didn't care. How refreshing it was to be studied unsurreptitiously by prattles of girls innocent of Parisian *sang froid* with its feigned indifference and circuitous enquiry.

Carrying himself with a ruttish swagger onto the boards, Gainsbourg had licence to lock eyes fleetingly with any woman who looked as if she'd give in to nature's baser urges. Fancy-free nowadays, casual procurement of sexual gratification became second nature to him. Bartering in sex could be sealed between performances with a beatific smile, a torrent of desire and an "All right then, I'll see you later".

"Take women for what they're not and leave them for what they are," was a Goldwyn-esque saying to be attributed to Gainsbourg years later when his public image as the most heterosexual of men was in sharpest profile. Yet, during stops on those early treks round France, he would sense being watched by males aspiring to an orgasm at his thrust too – and why not? Ever the iconoclast, he was to confide to a journalist's tape recorder that, yes, he'd once had a homosexual experience, "so as not to remain ignorant".

This may not have been true, but since the breakdown of his union with Elisabeth, he was no longer a lovestruck hand-holder anymore, and wasn't so naive to presume that, with their respective spouses not looking, the married members of the *Opus 109* team weren't on the look-out for illicit diversion from among the tarts that solicited them nightly. This was certainly the case with Jacques Brel whose tired wife had desensitised herself against his known carnal shenanigans away from home. Well, it wasn't as if mistresses and one-night stands were uncommon or even a purely Gallic phenomenon – though it was a Gallic homily that ran: "The chains of marriage are so heavy that it takes two to carry them, and often three."

It would be Gainsbourg who'd introduce Brel to Sophie who'd go from bed companion to the Belgian's full-time girlfriend. The two men had had instant rapport when flung together on the 1959 tour that followed the *Opus 109* expedition. The differences between the reserved, cultivated Parisian and the jovial Belgian *parvenu* only cemented their brusque empathy. A more reflective character by nature, Serge was often content to be a passive listener as his new pal, angry or sardonically amused by everything, gave his lightning-bright imagination its ranting, arm-waving head. Neither did Serge object to being upstaged by the more renowned, more animated Jacques – though he took to heart some of Brel's teasing ambiguities like: "Me, I get it wrong, but you – you are a bluffer."

The cast also included another lifelong friend in the stand-up comedian Coluche. All lads together, there were outbreaks of boorish behaviour, generally in language that would shock a drunken marine, but Serge, Jacques and Coluche passed many a moonlit mile listening to classical music on the car radio. They also understood how to conduct themselves during small-talk with council dignitaries and their hoity-toity children with whom they'd be snapped, shaking hands, in this small town with its sir-and-ma'am propriety or that rural district where the 1950s wouldn't end until about 1966.

There was no company in which Serge couldn't integrate. In university cities like Bordeaux or Reims, young aesthetes comprised a pronounced minority in the audience. They'd detected a certain *épater le bourgeoisie* in Gainsbourg – and heard in *Du Chant A*

L'Une! – and in the take-it-or-leave-it manner he put across its contents on stage – an agreeable uncommerciality that was an antidote to the more mindless pleasures of chart pop on the grounds that the more arduous the effort required to like something, the more "artistic" it is. On these terms, "artistic" meant endless centuries of a film by Cocteau; one of Shakespeare's so-called comedies or the Japanese water-torture effect of listening to some minimalist composer: a cultural duty first, and fun frequently a poor second.

At the turn of the decade, collegians of this kidney were more likely to be "sent" by Lewis, Meade Lux than Lewis, Jerry Lee. With "cool" defined by Jack Kerouac's Dean Moriarty rather than Elvis Presley, LP sleeves strewn artlessly about their "pads" might advertise a pseudo-sophistication that ran from Stravinsky to modern jazz. At a pinch, this took in the likes of Ray Charles whose black skin tipped the balance of a style midway between jazz and pop. Charles could be forgiven anything but that mass acceptance exemplified when he had a global chart strike with 'What'd I Say'.

Such "selling out" was deplored by provincial sophisticates who, sporting sunglasses even in a midnight power cut, allied themselves to Modigliani-like doomed romanticism and man's conquest of a disordered nature through the self-sacrificing detours of art. In sock-smelling hostel rooms where skip-read Genet, Nietzsche, Camus and Sartre looked well on bookshelves, Gréco discs were as omnipresent as posters of Che Guevara would be in the late 1960s – and her new *Juliette Gréco Chante Serge Gainsbourg* EP made it hip to pay observed respects to its creative source. Fustian intellectuals would buy Serge drinks to oil the wheels of prolonged conversation, and to be seen nattering familiarly with a frog princeling from the Queen of Cool's court. In reciprocation, Gainsbourg found less crowded hours with such patrons – particularly those who still breathed an atmosphere of coloured dust, palette-knives and hammer-and-chisel – a stimulating change from the unintelligible platitudes shouted over the racket when unwinding after the show in a nearby bar.

Invited back to, say, a college hall of residence, the tension would flow out of him as the liquor flowed in, and the students would be delighted to discover that he spoke the same jargon as they. Night became morning via dialogue for the sake of dialogue about, perhaps, the transmigration of souls, the symbolism of dreams, what Sartre wrote about the Soviet intervention in Hungary in 1956 and what Camus thought he meant. Then it might drift off into word games, free-association poetry amid asides about the masterpieces that one or other of them was going to paint, the brilliant films he was going to direct, the ground-breaking novels he was going to write.

More often than not, Serge would draw on a cigarette and nod in smiling agreement with whatever futile and pretentious soliloquy was coming to a close. Resting his voice was sometimes the only answer as, unaccustomed to singing so frequently, Gainsbourg's vocal cords would weaken to a gravelly croak, bubbling with catarrh. However, the effect was not always unattractive. Some even considered it gruffly charming as he strained his central octaves past their compass when, with concentration on every word lighting his face, he all but gulped the microphone fed through a horribly distorted PA set-up in some back-of-beyond auditorium that was the antithesis of pop and fame.

"Never again," he muttered to himself as, delivered from the treadmill of the road, he snuggled between the sheets of his own little bed again. Yet he was conscious that unless he pulled another stroke soon, he might be consigned to the oblivion from which he was still emerging. An entertainer was, after all, a commodity to be bought, sold and replaced when worn out just like a scouring pad. Of course, there was the temptation to throw the race before he was beaten. Instead, he investigated the vexing question of not so much how to progress onto the next level, but how to keep a minimally tolerable cash-flow going.

He studied the hit parade as a stockbroker would a Dow Jones index, but it was another medium altogether that threw down a line to him as the ripples of *Du Chant A L'Une!* and its by-products grew fainter. The front cover portrait of the artist had been brought to the notice of assistant director Jacques Poitrenaud who felt that Gainsbourg – assuming he passed a screen test – was suitable for the blink-and-you'll-miss-him bit-part of Leon, an untrustworthy denizen of a peculiar club, in the forthcoming *Voulez-Vous Danser Avec Moi,* a vehicle for Brigitte Bardot who, at twenty-five, was in full bloom as French cinema's "answer" to Hollywood's Marilyn Monroe and Ealing's Diana Dors, and was even mulling over trying her hand as a pop singer on the basis that her screen popularity might translate into hits. Before she even entered a recording studio, her provocative likeness had graced covers since 1952's *Girl In A Bikini* soundtrack LP.

Serge was disappointed that, because they were never in the same scene, he did not get to meet the national *femme fatale*. Willowy, but with the bosom of a well-developed matron and an avalanche of blonde tresses, the pout and the giggle gilded former fashion model Bardot's hybrid of unruly sexuality and doe-eyed ingenuousness. She had been propelled to stardom by 1956's *Et Dieu...Crea La Femme* (*And God Created Woman*), hailed in contended retrospect as a precursor of the New Wave, a term that came to be all-embracing – some would say, meaningless – after its inauguration by such as Chabril, Godard and Truffant with their heavy reliance on hand-held cameras, laconic and seemingly improvised dialogue, and overall aura of don't-care existentialism. Unlike Hollywood and Ealing, the emphasis was on characterisation rather than plot.

The plot of *Voulez-Vous Danser Avec Moi* was certainly less intriguing than the off-screen action. Somehow, the project seemed jinxed, what with the death of principal supporting actress Sylva Lopez after only a few days' shooting, followed by that of male lead Henri Vital later. Yet these interruptions along with the anticipated fraught tempers, rows and walk-outs were overcome, and the movie muddled on to its autumn première and a not uncharitable critical response. *Citizen Kane* it wasn't, but the general verdict of those who noticed him was that Serge Gainsbourg had given an unexpectedly worthy account of himself in his silver screen debut.

If not as natural an actor as, say, Charles Aznavour or even Elvis Presley, he'd proved able "to other be" more effectively than most pop musicians who fancied themselves as cinema attractions. Brel, for instance, had been wooden as the star of a 1956 short, *La Grande Père De Monsieur Clement*, but just as Gréco, Bardot, Catherine Deneuve, Jeanne Moreau, Marie La Fôret and Isabel Adjani plugged gaps between their celluloid ventures by flirting with pop, so Gallic chart names like Brel and Hugues Aufray were used expediently to spice up the credits and guarantee a flick some additional interest.

Testifying to more intrinsic virtues than pop celebrity not yet stabilised, Serge at least was prepared to take direction, was open to criticism and advice, and was ever ready to pick up tips from on-the-job expositions by more experienced thespians. Punctual at rehearsals with all his lines learnt, he came to be accepted within the profession as a reasonably good Bad Guy. He didn't mind either remaining in ignorance about the often flimsy threads of the dashed-off Italian-French epics that made up the bulk of his film appearances into the early 1960s. Interchangeable screenplays mingled stories from the Old Testament, Ancient Greece and the Roman Empire with a lot of chaps dressed in sheets, Messalina-type man-eaters in plunging gowns, gladiatorial combats, persecuted Christians, sub-Cecil B de Mille reconstructions of Mount Olympus or the Circus Maximus, and crowds of extras for various Sermons on the Mount and processions of plumed legions with SPQR standards.

In 1959 alone, the sharp-eyed would spot Serge in *Hercule Contre Samson, Le Révolte Des Enclaves* (as a centurion) and Pietro Francisci's *Ercole E La Regina Di Lidia* – which, with more of its budget assigned to publicity than its actual making, reached English-speaking movie-goers as *Hercules Unchained*. At any rate, it was dire.

Better were *nouvelle vague* domestic efforts like *L'Eau A La Bouche*, on at a cinema near your continental pen-pal in spring 1960, for which Gainsbourg and Goraguer knocked together a soundtrack EP that shifted just over ten thousand copies on the strength of its title track, a bongo-pattering samba that was the only vocal item amongst bland pseudo-jazz instrumentals pruned down from the incidental music.

As it was (and would be) with most movies in which Gainsbourg was concerned, only specialist film societies showed *L'Eau A La Bouche* outside France. Nevertheless, from this small beginning, he not so much much dipped a toe as plunged headfirst into aspects of film beyond simple acting. He hadn't a clue how to go about most of these once he'd taken them on. Nevertheless, with enviable application, he'd learn what he could *in situ*, get a clearer picture from the confusion, and unknowingly banish many preconceptions and invent new ones. As if it was the most natural thing in the world, he'd be "spotting" uncut sequences with a stop-watch, arguing with a set designer about scenery, fretting about character development, deliberating over camera angles, and making suggestions to the director about pacing and the evolution of the story.

chapter three

Le Temps Des Yoyos

Tenacity was rewarded – sort of – with more behind-the-scenes film work such as *Les Loups Dans La Bergère*. Very much of its time, Gainsbourg's soundtrack is interesting for documentary rather than recreational reasons in its xeroxing of the clichéd bongo-pattering "party sequence" music that dates both a type of "modern times" continental movie made over and over again, and most of Gainsbourg's output on disc into the early 1960s. In one ear and out the other, sanitised nods to cool *Kind Of Blue*-period Miles Davis (notably in 'Generique' and 'Fugue') were fused with passages that at different times might have reminded the rare Briton who heard them then of Max Harris's whimsical theme tune and incidental music to *The World Of Gurney Slade* (a surreal television series starring Anthony Newley) and the Latin-flavoured big band ebullience of Edmundo Ros, freighted like *Les Loups Dans La Bergère* with generous employment of rim-shot staccato, the ching-a-ching-ching ride cymbal and the trills, tootles and rasps of brass and woodwinds.

Edmundo's swollen baritone – like you'd imagine a human camel would sound – was not dissimilar either to that of Gainsbourg on the sung version of 'Cha Cha Cha Du Loup'. It had emerged as something of a trademark on the album that preceded it by a few months, the enigmatically titled *No 2*. Musically, this had pre-empted 'Cha Cha Cha Du Loup' in 'Mambo Miam Miam' and, if undercut with a breath of the Orient and startling horn arpeggios, 'L'Anthracite'. Apart from the language, nothing from *No 2* and *Les Loups Dans La Bergère* would have been out of place on the BBC Light Programme which, with its easy-listening executive brief, was usually a much of a muchness to anyone twiddling the dial for anything exclusively teenage. When it was clear that rock 'n' roll was here to stay, the Corporation had permitted *Saturday Club*, a weekly two hours of uninterrupted pop, but most of the time, the Light Programme washed over any adolescent within earshot, who made as much attempt to distinguish between individual items as a shopper does between wedges of supermarket muzak.

If anything, French popular radio addressed itself even more to those who'd satiated their appetites for musical adventure. This policy was a deliberate cultural disenfranchising of *le yé-yé*, now fully developed into a Gallic species of pop fan given to outbreaks of barracking at concerts, and treading warily amidst official disapproval by a government just as aghast as all right-thinking European adults had been at the noise, gibberish and loutish excesses of the rock 'n' roll epidemic spreading from the States. Efforts to ban this latest *yé-yé* subversion had been less tacit after Bill Haley And The Comets performed at the Olympia in 1958.

Thirty-three-year-old Haley and his paunchy dance combo were not the most suitable envoys of rock 'n' roll – but they had been the first to visit France, and the fans went as crazy as fans could go. In the ear-stinging pandemonium, there'd been jiving in the aisles and the slitting of the upholstery of tip-up chairs – many of them snapped off their spindles. Patented too by their transatlantic cousins was the stylised delinquency that had been enacted after the show when hundreds of over-excited ticket-holders let off steam in an orgy of brawling and vandalism that had concluded with ten being rushed to hospital and over fifty arrests.

The country had not found its first encounter with *gen-u-ine* US rock 'n' roll easy to forget. It might have appalled the old and square, but all but the most serious-minded of their children had been entranced by the trash. Lost in dreams and half-formed ambition, some decided to try rock 'n' roll themselves, and thus submit themselves to an infinity of incomprehension, deprivation, domestic uproar and derision – especially derision because the results, particularly vocal, were generally more genteel and embarrassed than even Pat Boone's white market emasculations of Little Richard and Fats Domino. The spirit was willing, but a French rocker tended to be raucous not passionate if he ever got as far as shedding enough of his inhibitions to cut up rough.

Another problem was that rock 'n' roll had developed into an English-language music, and would remain so for all time. Even on static-ridden radio, French reproductions of US hits did not, therefore, sound anywhere near as accurate as they might have done at the tender mercies of British artists. The problem was mostly the clipped solemnity born of someone singing in a language not his own over accompaniment shining with complacent polish and bereft of transcendental edge or thrilling margin of error.

There was, therefore, no immediate *bona fide* domestic riposte to Elvis Presley as there was in Cliff Richard, luminary of British television's teenage pop showcase, *Oh Boy!*. This didn't bother French impresarios anxious to turn a hard-nosed centime with as much of this racket as the traffic would allow for those feeble-minded enough to pay for it. It was obviously a perishable commodity, so why waste time trying to get this Elvis person to tour when our own boys were already doing the job? The answer was that teenagers were so affronted by most indigenous pop that coin-operated sounds were preferable to such an act if it was booked for a local club. It, rather than the juke-box, was the intermission, an opportunity to go to the toilet, talk to friends, buy a drink. If anyone cared enough to pay attention, it was for the wrong reasons as perpetrators struggling to scale the heights of their aspirations, afforded glimpses of high comedy to their audience.

Worse, French rock 'n' roll was unexportable, even when a contagious backbeat was grafted onto the universally traditional as was the case with the first homogenous try at rock 'n' roll in a 1958 adaptation of the nursery rhyme 'Billy Boy' by Danyel Gérard, a vocalist under the aegis of Lucien Morisse who had stretched his managerial tentacles beyond Dalida to become a Parisian equivalent of UK pop svengali Larry Parnes.

National Service led Gérard to be overtaken by newer icons more skilled at copying the Americans – notably Johnny Hallyday whose singing and passable mastery of the guitar had gained him a virtual residency at Le Golf Drouot, Paris's foremost *yé-yé* hangout. Hallyday's first national radio broadcast in 1960 incited Vogue, one of Philips' most worrying rivals, to hasten him into the studio for a single.

Pathe-Marconi, seeking to provision itself with an "answer" to Hallyday, grabbed a refrigerator salesman named Richard Anthony to sing principally renderings of US smashes for home consumers; among them Buddy Holly's 'Peggy Sue' and Lloyd Price's 'Personality'. Likewise, Les Chats Sauvages left a wound in the charts with 'Est-Ce Que Tu Le Sais' ('What'd I Say') as Sylvie Vartan did tentatively with 'Say Mama' (as 'Il Revient') from Gene Vincent. Les Chausettes Noires scored too with 'Be-Bop-A-Lula', the number most associated with Vincent, so popular in France that he'd find himself there time and time again over too many years of dogged touring.

Before lead singer Eddy Mitchell went solo, Les Chausettes Noires recorded 'Johnny B Goode' ('Eddy Si Bon'), signature tune of Chuck Berry, the US rock 'n' roller that most awed Serge Gainsbourg for the neo-Gallic equality of lyrics and melody – and, sub-consciously perhaps, for the *Lolita* tinge in songs such as 'Sweet Little Sixteen', 'Little Queenie' and 'Sweet Little Rock 'N' Roller'.

There'd been a shadowy link with these – and The Big Bopper's 'Little Red Riding Hood' – in Gainsbourg's sinister likening of himself to the Big Bad Wolf in 'Cha Cha Cha De Loup'. Far removed from Berry, the Bopper – killed in the same 1959 plane crash as Buddy Holly – and, indeed, classic rock in general, Serge seemed, in one of the bilious clichés of music journalism, to have Grown Old With His Audience – if only because of the conversational flow of the issues he'd tackled. Indeed, it was as if he'd always been old.

Meticulously detailed scorings were allied to clever – too clever for the commonweal – librettos on *No 2* that, say, played on words in 'L'Anthracite'; went back to nature in 'Adieu Creature'; dealt ostensibly with eating in 'Mambo Miam Miam' ('Mambo Yum Yum'!), and, in 'La Claqueur De Doigts', mocked a finger-popping hipster as sexually frustrated as the character in the album's finale, 'L'Amour A La Papa'.

With three years on Berry and not much younger than Bill Haley, Serge was never cut out to be an icon of *le yé-yé*. Neither was he sufficiently well-established to be on a plateau of showbusiness where a chart entry is a mere sideshow. Selling records and keeping a weather-eye on the latest trends was to remain a constant preoccupation.

He finished 1960, for instance, by meeting mainstream pop halfway with 'Laissez-Moi Tranquille'; obscure lyrically, it bounced along to an arrangement reminiscent of a watered-down Lord Rockingham's XI, *Oh Boy!*'s house band of slumming jazzers. 'Laissez-Moi Tranquille' was the most played track from 'Romantique 60', an EP with a sleeve fraught with symbolism: Serge with a bouquet of flowers in one hand, and a gun in the other. "To those who love my songs," he wrote, "I give the flowers. The others get shot."

Like every other of his releases thus far, it sold steadily enough in Switzerland and Italy as well as French territories to make it a worthwhile commercial exercise – and for Olympia booking manager Bruno Coquatrix to add him as "special guest" to a bill topped by Jacques Brel. This and another Olympia appearance supporting Juliette Gréco coincided with the issue in spring 1961 of a third LP, *L'Etonnant Serge Gainsbourg*. Marking time artistically, it reworked old compositions like subdued 'Les Amours Perdu' which in its contradiction of enjoyable melancholy reached out to self-doubting bedsit diarists oblivious to the callousness of the man in 'En Relisant Ta Lettre', correcting the spelling in his girlfriend's suicide note.

The majority of subscribers to French teenage magazines like *Special Pop* hadn't read the books necessary for comprehending *L'Etonnant* tracks like 'La Chanson De Maglia' – from Victor Hugo – and the 'Le Rock De Nerval' instrumental – inspired presumably by the tormented Gérard de Nerval, a precursor of the French surrealist poets, who hanged himself from a Parisian lamppost in 1855.*

A bard better equipped to cope with the century into which he was born, Jacques Prévert's way with words had been put to use as a screenwriter for film director Marcel Carne. Acknowledging a kindred spirit for a lyricism that veered from ridicule to 'Les Amours Perdu'-esque wistfulness, Gainsbourg sought the sexagenarian Prévert's ready permission before paying homage by opening *L'Etonnant* with 'Chanson De Prévert' – which, after it was "covered" by Gréco, surfaced as one of the most popular items in the Gainsbourg portfolio.

With whom was it popular? Serge's devotees – if that is the word – were still of a type more likely to browse in bookshops than an Eddy Mitchell fan. Scholarly dispositions also dictated the finding of much to intrigue in label and sleeve information on records – such as the frequency in which the Gainsbourg name cropped up in the bracketed writer's credits beneath song titles like made-to-measure

* *De Nerval was also to be the subject of 1974's 'Dream Gerrard' (sic) by Traffic*

'L'Accordéon', his first Gréco A-side, in accordance with her wish to "sing about France as if it was a foreign country" as she had already in Ferré's 'Paris Canaille'.

Commissions from further afield included material for Petula Clark, a star in Britain since her teens. After a French duplication of one of her hits by Dalida in 1957, Petula herself was invited over to perform at the Olympia. Marrying into her record company's promotion department, she was as well-known in France as she was at home by 1961.

Other feathers in Gainsbourg's cap included songs for Catherine Sauvage, Zizi Jeanmaire (to be immortalised years later in Peter Sarstedt's 'Where Do You Go To My Lovely'), up-and-coming Greek chanteuse Nana Mouskouri – and Brigitte Bardot who'd been grabbed by for a one-shot forty-five by a new label named after its founder, Eddie Barclay.

By 1962, she had defected to Philips, and was becoming as much of a legitimate pop star in Europe as Elvis Presley had become a legitimate movie actor in the United States. Like Elvis too, her later films were less distinguished than her first. Never mind, she could play a bit of guitar, had a limited but tuneful soprano – and, like Maurice Chevalier, didn't pronounce initial aitches. "She had a unique voice," estimated Barclay, "half little girl, half siren. She didn't sing as much as she talked a song. To be fair, hers isn't a great voice, but she had a terrific talent for putting a song across, and she took her recording career seriously."

So would English topless model Samantha Fox after a Top Ten breakthrough with 1986's 'Touch Me (I Want Your Body)'. Its lyrical determination had been patented a quarter of a century earlier by Brigitte in 'Invitango' with couplets such as "I invite you to the lewdness of this tango/where I will come to know the feel of your body against mine". It was crude stuff against the sensitivity of *Le Mépris*, arguably Bardot's finest (and most controversial) film, but, though not incisive insights into the human condition, her output on disc didn't pretend to be anything more than well-crafted piffle at a time when pop was at its most harmless and ephemeral.

Resorting to stretching out vowels and splitting up words to ensure that lines ended with the required root syllable – a process that he'd re-employ time and time again – sound mattered more than meaning in Gainsbourg's initial jobs for Bardot. On her eponymous

debut album, he contributed jogalong 'Je Me Donne A Qui Me Plait' –
and 'L'Appareil A Sous' with a backing track that – in a lower key –
would have suited Bobby Vee, Bobby Rydell, Bobby Vinton and all the
rest of the insipidly handsome boys-next-door with bashful half-smiles
that constipated the hit parades of North America and, whether in
person or transmitted through domestic heart-throbs in the same
mould, everywhere else.

With success in this trite new medium granting her an even more
splendid certainty about everything she said and did, Brigitte began
shovelling out a greater proportion of recordings that were intrinsically
self-referential statements written on her behalf, and often taken from
accounts of her life in the popular press. Part of the national furniture
by now, her television showcase on New Year's Eve was as expected an
annual event as the incessant playing of Brel's 'Au Printemps' on the
radio every 21 March.

Serge Gainsbourg still hadn't breathed the air round Bardot, but he
was in thick with others of comparable renown. Petula Clark was to let
him use her flat for a filmed interview; his name was in the same sized
type as singing actor Claude Pascal on a poster advertising one
evening's bill at a new Parisian nightspot, and he was engaged by Sacha
Distel to provide and perform a new song each week throughout the
latest run of that clean-cut smiler's *Sacha Show* series.

His first offering was to be for a New Year's Eve special with Petula
Clark and Jean-Pierre Cassel, but he was poleaxed by an ear infection so
severe that he was obliged to pull out. By way of consolation, Serge was
granted a spot on a spectacular presided over by Cassel, an entertainer
who, like Distel, thrived on a picaresque charm – and he was able to
fulfil that winter's remaining *Sacha Shows.*

Such pragmatic big-name approbation gave Gainsbourg
expediential leeway to speak of Petula, Claude, Sacha, Jean-Pierre and
other of his glittering chums on chat shows and – generally before the
first commercial break too – on variety presentations where he might
undergo self-humiliation in comedy sketches.* All this boosted
attendance figures at his still-regular Milord L'Arsoille residencies.

He was leading what the economist would call a "full life" – for even
off-duty hours were mortgaged to the cliquey ordeals of conviviality
presided over by initiates of that inward-looking caste that was Parisian

---

* *Such as he did on* Rendez-Vous Avec...*with Jacqueline Jouser, mother of Antoine De Caunes,
destined to host Channel Four's* Eurotrash *magazine series in the 1990s*

showbusiness. This closed shop bred many insecurities, but the cardinal sin was to show them. That visible desperation is too nasty a reminder of the impermanence of stardom and wealth was a pervading thought that kept Serge on his toes when mustered to pick electric guitar in an impromptu "supergroup" – that included Guy Béart – at the fortieth birthday celebration of Raymond Devos, a television humorist who might have been Spike Milligan's French blood-cousin.

In the midst of the hysterical chatter, rehearsed patter and smug backslapping that attends such galas, the atmosphere would be laced with an essence of fine tobacco and expensive shampoo, and you'd pass up to a dozen entertainment legends along a single staircase of pearly cleavages, toupees, bow-tied tuxedos and cocktails like melted crayons. Jacques Tati would be snapped sharing a joke with Juliette Gréco, and Alain Delon would unzip himself in an adjacent urinal to Johnny Hallyday in the gents. Don't look now, but isn't that Françoise Sagan the novelist? That chap who I can't quite place...I've seen his picture on the front of a long-playing record that my daughter at art college has on instant replay on her gramophone.

Following his spell on the bandstand, Gainsbourg dared a careful walkabout, trying not to look as if he was making an effort. He ended up at a table on the periphery of small-talk monopolised by Edith Piaf. Money was seated before Serge in this bossy little madam who was a French cross between Vera Lynn and Judy Garland. Not one for luvvie platitudes, she soon wormed out of the new arrival what he did and how much use he could be to her. In turn, Serge got a contact address from Piaf and mailed her some songs the very next day. This, however, wasn't prompt enough because forty-eight-year-old Piaf had had the removed eyes of a dying woman – which she was. At the funeral in Paris weeks later, the crowd attending was so huge that some of the celebrity mourners were pushed into the open grave.

Had he been that close too, Gainsbourg would not have suffered the pitiless *woompf* of flashbulbs reserved for institutions like Brassens, and even Aznavour. Yet figures for *L'Etonnant Serge Gainsbourg* and, cumulatively, its vinyl predecessors had been just healthy enough to warrant Serge's first headlining tour. But while it embraced dates as far away as Algeria – despite a recent earthquake and the on-going animosity towards French imperialism – box office receipts were never remarkable – sometimes as low as a fifth capacity – except at Milan's Piccolo Theatre where, astonishingly, it was standing room only.

This did not, however, yield latent showmanship in Serge Gainsbourg. He had not begun to press on the nerve of how far he could go, and was still susceptible to episodes of petrified inertia. Consequently, there wasn't much backchat and encouragement of audience participation – in fact, little evidence at all of natural warmth and force of personality. Nevertheless, the quality of his songs (and their familiarity to his audience, no matter how small) often won the day to sustained cheering.

Spontaneous salvos of applause would be provoked by specific couplets emoted either without embroidery – so as not to jar their elegance – or extemporised like a jazz vocalist after he got the knack of slipping comfortably from suppressed lust through lazy insinuation to intimate anguish, sometimes mingling humour and gloom in the same line. This was also the ace up the sleeves of Aznavour – whose voice was beyond remedy after youthful years bawling headlines as a newspaper vendor – and laconic Brel who likewise reinforced his appeal via untutored phrasing, eccentric breath control and intonation that was the antithesis of plummy *bel canto* nicety.

Serge's diction and range had been knocked out of true by endless cigarettes – and he was now so heavy a drinker that there'd be a tumbler of bourbon handy in the wings (though onstage perspiration diminished its effect). After the show, he'd be inclined to bond with others with a taste for liquor – and marijuana too according to a freshly-concocted libretto, 'No No Thanks No'. On the road, he'd sleep it off in cat-naps during a punishing booking schedule that might involve a *soirée* in Calais on Friday with Saturday night somewhere in the Alps.

This restless existence of travel, music, booze – and women – did not turn Gainsbourg into a name sufficiently big for paparazzi titbits to yet splash vivid and scandalous hues on his personal life. As far as his diehard fans were concerned then, the depths of his depravity were chain-smoking and a fondness for drink. Paramours (with whom he was photographed but rarely) were not brought to notice by a press who weren't particularly interested anyway – except if a third more famous party was involved, such as film actor Claude Berri who was romancing his Italian leading lady Laura Betti at the same time that she was walking out with Serge.

Richer and closer to matinee idol stamp than Gainsbourg, Berri seemed the better bet to Betti. Now that the tour was over and a trough loomed with regard to television exposure, he wasn't altogether sure that he even wanted to make another record. It had been just over a year since *L'Etonnant*, and it seemed that he was on the wane again – even in Paris now that Francis Claude had retired from managing Milord L'Arsoille, and Serge, spurred perhaps by misplaced loyalty, had quit too. Apart from SACEM payouts for nothing that had been a big smash, there were only one-nighters and joining his father on the trivial round of northern casino residences in Cabourg – backing Jenny Alpha (no, I'd never heard of her either) – and back at Le Touquet.

Drowsily mooching to the newsagent's near his parents' home where he still dwelt, there were times when it was as if he'd never made those records, sang that encore or stood before showbusiness nobility. Fast comes the hour when fades the fairest flower. Let some other poor sod have a turn. Let someone else be milked dry and used as a disillusioned scapegoat. To hell with the record industry's short-sightedness, its mental sluggishness, its cloth-eared ignorance! Who needed the time-serving incompetence, the fake sincerity, the backstabbing and the contradiction of excessive thrift and heedless expenditure? In what other sphere of the most corrupt business could a dam burst on such a deep river of embezzlement, arm-twisting and concealment of guilty secrets?

Sour grapes aside, each week's new Top Twenty hammered home the futility of a thirty-five-year-old wasting any more time and energy playing pop stars – or a thirty-five-year-old who hadn't really Made It settling down as one of these "quality" entertainers whose flop records were excused as "too good for the charts". As they always will be, youth and beauty were all that was needed to shift sub-standard product. These days, it was possible to get away with merely being young. After all, he considered, what else had done the trick for this "Sheila" that everyone was talking about?

Raised in a corner sweet shop, she'd been plain Anna Chancel before she'd got herself noticed hollering Petula Clark numbers in Le Golf Drouot, and handed a Philips contract on a plate. With mathematical precision, a shrewd translation of Tommy Roe's 'Sheila' put this ordinary-looking teenager at the top of the hit parade. She also had central roles in many vacuous movies that would supplement a stunning array of further Number Ones. Swiftly numbering tens of thousands, her fan club consisted mainly of schoolgirls like herself, who aped her beehive hairstyle and wore a brand of Sheila attire bespoken by a chain of Sheila boutiques.

She was a fraction too late for the Twist, the "most vulgar dance ever invented", according to *Melody Maker*. What more did it need to shake the world? The Twist lingered longest in Europe where the Letkiss and La Yenka were the continent's donations to a *mélange* of variations: the Fly, the Gorilla Walk, the Mashed Potato, the Jerk, the headache-inducing Shake, the Hully Gully, the Hitch-Hiker, the ungainly Turkey Trot, the Madison, the back-breaking Limbo, the Pony, the Slop *ad nauseum*. Les Chakakas, a Belgian septet, even contrived to sneak into insular Britain's Top Fifty with the opportunist 'Twist Twist' – and a demobbed Danyel Gérard regained lost ground with 'La Leçon De Twist'. Yet it was Johnny Hallyday's million-selling bi-lingual cover of Chubby Checker's 'Let's Twist Again' in 1961 that had convinced most folk that this fair-haired youth was to France what Cliff Richard was to the UK.

Others who came into their own with the Twist and its spin-offs included Sylvie Vartan (with 'C'Est Le Mashed Potatoes'), Les Playboys and Les Twisters. Through 'J'Irai Twister Le Blues' and an untranslated 'Let's Twist Again', Richard Anthony proved a sound investment for Pathe-Marconi – as did Claude François who had drummed in a Monte Carlo jazz unit before ambition drove him to Paris where he was seen demonstrating the Twist in the Caramel Club, and groomed for the hit parade via the expected native reproductions of such as 'Venus In Blue-Jeans', 'The Hully Gully' and an 'If I Had A Hammer' that was behind counters a mere week after Trini Lopez's US blueprint.

Up until the mid-1960s, it was an unusual French chart single that didn't have an explanatory "(Slop)", "(Mashed Potato)" or whatever printed between the title and the composer's name on the label – so that the cats would know with what permutation of the Twist they were supposed to cut a rug. One of four forty-fives from her LP issued for juke-box use and promotional purposes only, Brigitte Bardot's

'L'Appareil De Sous' was rated as a "Twist".

On the basis of the title, the committee that passed judgement on these matters had no need to furrow its brows over semi-instrumental 'Requiem Pour Un Twister', the single lifted from Serge Gainsbourg's fourth album. However, you could only Twist to it if you were desperate. Rather than the eight-to-the-bar on a shut hi-hat that was the essence of the required beat, 'Requiem Pour Un Twister' – like nearly all drumming on Gainsbourg recordings into 1964 – adhered to the scuffed skins and suspensory *tssh-t-t-tssh-t-t-tssh* sibilance of opening and closing hi-hat cymbals that makes you think more of being slumped mute, immobile and unapproachable, at a table in the nicotine-clouded half-light of a jazz club than doin' the Hippy Hippy Shake with all o' your might in some packed-out ballroom where pubescent hormones raged till way past bedtime.

Serge compounded his cool with liberal garnishings of electric organ, purring and fluid, that held sway over *No 4*'s obligatos and lengthy instrumental interludes – though an apposite trombone permeated 'Black Trombone'. Yet, to be brutal, the album bored most teenagers of the day to tears. For all its attention to detail – such as the guiro on 'Baudelaire' – it was of a strata of jazz so polite that it borders on lounge muzak.

On Gainsbourg's first all-vocal effort too, it wasn't always easy to cling to lyrics either. Counter to the *chanson* tradition – in which tunes are sometimes little more than a repeated series of notes used to carry lyrics that might be weakened by stronger underlying elaboration – Gainsbourg was far closer to Anglo-Saxon pop than Ferré, Brel, Aznavour *et al* in that his words could not be (or ever would be) as easily divorced from musical settings or stand as comfortably alone as printed stanzas. Reading them in cold blood, the impression is that many seemed to have been created with an ease as devoid of ante-start agonies as a McGonagall poetic gem – like those in, say, 'Black Trombone' in which (like his songs for Bardot) meaning did not take precedence over phonetics (with lots of lines ending in "onne"). Then there was quasi-monotonal 'Quant Ta T'Y Mets', but if it was repetitive, at least it was brief with words that rolled off Serge's tongue without pomp. Likewise, he made unaffected meals of 'Les Goémons' – likening his loves to seaweed thrown up by the waves – and 'Requiem Pour Un

'Twister' with its narrative about the death of drunken Charlie.

More subjectively, Gainsbourg presents himself as 'The Intoxicated Man' in tipsy musings that take on a breadth of gesture that is simultaneously personal and universal when its trace elements of Franglais and Zola's *L'Assommoir* embellish the hallucinations and descent into a sozzled black-out. Booze has always been the most common and acceptable stimulant in both pop circles – demonstrated by the public personas of generations of stars from Dean Martin to Shane McGowan – and the general populace. As exemplified by the old English air, 'John Barleycorn' and the 'What Shall We Do With The Drunken Sailor' sea shanty, it was also the earliest to be celebrated in song.

Random instances from the past fifty years include 'Cigarettes, Whiskey And Wild, Wild Women', 'A Pub With No Beer', 'White Lightning', 'Red Red Wine' and any number of gutbucket Mississippi and Chicago blues items. More pertinent to Gainsbourg, Brel was to address alcohol in 'Amsterdam', 'La Chanson De Jackie' (borrowing "pink elephants" from 'The Intoxicated Man') and 'La Bière' – while Aznavour would be propping up the bar, spewing out dismal observations, in 'Two Guitars' before his torpor dispels and he becomes active and restless as the tango speeds up to *allegro con fuoco*.

Deviation of tempo on *No 4* was so insignificant that there was a sense of hear-one-and-you've-heard-'em-all as outlines dissolved between tracks to the degree that it was almost the sound at any given moment that counted more than individual pieces. With Philips wondering how long they could maintain moderate success with moderate records of uniform blandness, Gainsbourg fanned out beyond his customary place of work, the Blanqui complex in Paris, to investigate New York and, ultimately, London for newer technology and minds more attuned to contemporary sound.

Nothing European was up to US standards, but, as he couldn't afford to record in the Big Apple, *Les Anglaises* were the most viable second-hand option. After all, France had dropped territorial defences to import British pop talent by the ton. Doug Fowlkes And The Airdales were wowing 'em at Le Golf Drouot, and Vince Taylor, a vocalist from Middlesex in artistic debt to Gene Vincent, had taken up virtual French citizenship after he'd headlined at the Olympia.

On disc, there'd also been stronger signs of UK resistance to chart

Americana than abroad in such as gorblimey 'Come Outside', a Number One for Mike Sarne and Wendy Richards, and, also in 1962, The Tornados' 'Telstar' which, unbelievably, also topped the US *Hot 100* where few European acts had ever made much headway.

Therefore, puffing fretful duty-free Gitanes, Gainsbourg in London waited for the native hirelings to tune up. In Alain Goraguer's stead was Scottish bandleader Harry Robinson, 'Lord Rockingham' himself, calling them to order for four titles that would constitute a 1963 EP, 'Vilaine Fille'. Its highlight turned out to be 'La Javanaise', dripping with massed violins and discharged in an easy-listening croon – playing relentlessly on the letter "V" – by Serge in Aznavourian mode.

In the apocryphal period between a post-army Presley's Italianesque ballads and the first stirrings of Beatlemania, 'Vilaine Fille' aligned more with current fashion than any previous Gainsbourg release. Correlated with this sharpening of commercial profile was a sea change in Serge's acting career as he floated free of *Hercules Unchained*-type historical yarns and sailed into the latter half of the twentieth century for virtually every other film in which he'd be involved.

Via the advocacy of its second male lead Joe Turner*, Gainsbourg was given a silent cameo as a pianist in *Strip Tease* – for which he penned a title song intended for its star, Christa Paffgren (later Nico, featured *chanteuse* with The Velvet Underground). Her Germanic contralto, however, proved too guttural, so it was passed to Juliette Gréco as her second Gainsbourg A-side. The rest of his *Strip Tease* music was instrumental with 'Some Small Chance' dribbling limpid pools of vibraphone and subdued Light Programme horns, and 'Wake Me At Five' breaking the mould with not the slightest vestige of cocktail jazz in its neo-bolero turnaround on blaring brass, snare drum, timpani and rock 'n' roll guitar, albeit one shorn of any "blue" notes.

With scarcely a pause, Gainsbourg plunged into another low-billed role for the same director, Jacques Poitrenaud, in *L'Inconnue De Hong Kong*, a comedy starring a disinclined Dalida. After the shooting, the cast endured plummeting, fused lights and rocking fuselage when the aeroplane back to France was caught in a typhoon. So unnerved was Serge that he came close to cancelling a deserved fortnight's holiday in Greece before the return flight to Paris and more film work.

In some cutting room or other, he entered, with deceptive

---

* *Though a black American too, Turner was not the blues shouter of the same name, but a jazzman long resident in Paris*

casualness, the life of film editor Babeth Si Ramdane. Neither of them knew then to what extent or for how long their professional undertakings would interweave, but decades later, she'd still be fitting images to his ideas, even turning down better financial offers to so do.

A less enduring but vital principal of the *dramatis personae* of Serge's musical career was Michel Gaudry who'd recall that "he often wound up in late evening in the Mars club where I was appearing with the guitarist Elek Bacsik. One day, he asked us to do a recording with him." As adept as Gaudry at both improvisation and reading dots, Bacsik, a Hungarian, was omnipresent on jazz radio where his version of Dave Brubeck's 'Take Five' had evolved into something of a party piece.

Prior to the Gainsbourg record dates beginning in November, Elek and Michel warmed up by backing him in concerts on three consecutive Tuesdays at the Théâtre Capaines near the Olympia. If nothing else, the two jazz shellbacks were impressed by the attendances of Gréco, Béart, Clay and Sagan as well as all the expected fabulous nobodies for whom the main event of the evening was to see and be seen during the intervals when they'd thread through to the corner where Serge had wedged himself, rehearsing mentally what they were going to say by way of congratulations, and the smart way in which they were going to say it. The professionally-minded Gainsbourg would smother bemusement at the tongue-tied gaucheries, and suppress a temptation to scribble a sarcastic remark when requested to autograph a dog-eared *Du Chant A L'Une!* or well-thumbed 'Romantique 60'.

Smiling indulgently as their paymaster was thus pestered, Gaudry and Bacsik were to be the nucleus of a permanent backing unit for Serge – who'd found a perpetual turnover of personnel on previous outings prohibitive – after assisting with what would be *Gainsbourg Confidentiel* – Serge's first twelve-inch LP, his final overtly jazzy offering, and, so Michel Gaudry remembered him declaring, "the last record I make before buying myself a Rolls-Royce" with more confidence than he could possibly justify.

Produced by Claude Dejacques, formerly Vian's console midwife, *Confidentiel* got underway with 'Chez Le Yé-Yé', title track of the EP that had been the album's taster weeks earlier. There was a lyrical reference to a current hit – The Crystals' 'Da Doo Ron Ron' – and, though as indistinct as a trace of vapour in the sky, it was possible to discern Chuck

Berry's 'Roll Over Beethoven' in the introit to its twelve-bar blues chord pattern, but that was *Confidentiel*'s only musical concession to being anything more than a *No 4* holding operation.

It's probable that my own musical palate has been too coarsened by the decades of pop that have flown by since my grandmother bought me Adam Faith's 'What Do You Want' in 1959. Nevertheless, I can't write anything very constructive about *Confidentiel*. Adjectives like "soporific", "dull" and "mind-stultifying" spring to mind as I struggle to remember 'Negative Blues' as having flecks of guitar half-chords, and 'Elaeudanla Teiteia' as the one where he sings a staccato chorus, over and over again.

Give it credit, the looser abundance of *No 4* had been stripped away in favour of a sparser ensemble with no gratuitous frills or 'La Javanaise' grandiloquence – but listen consecutively to *No 4*, *Confidentiel* and 'Comment Trouvez-Vous Ma Soeur', the movie soundtrack EP that came next, and it all becomes interchangeable on today's car cassette deck with your eyes on the road ahead. Yet we mustn't forget that when vinyl was the only format (and LPs too big to steal), buying a record was more of a commitment. A mighty peculiar teenager might save up maybe three weeks' paper-round money for *Confidentiel* – and he'd make sure he got his money's worth by playing it until it was dust – or at least long enough to comprehend trifles like the harp shimmering across the solitary melodic notion that was the film's 'Eroticotico!'.

If there'd been words to 'Eroticotico!', an educated guess is that they'd have been about sex – an area investigated too on *Confidential* in 'Negative Blues', 'Chez Les Yé-Yé' (another *Lolita*-type ditty) and 'Le Talkie-Walkie' (grim amusement when girlfriend forgets to switch it off during a romp with another man). Nonetheless, it wasn't only the meat that mattered. Serge could get quite moony too. In 'La Fille Au Rasoir', she likes being tickled by his electric razor, but can't hear his protestations of affection over its buzz. Lost love rears up in 'Amour Sans Amour', 'Sait-On Jamais Où Va Une Femme Quand Elle Vous Quitte', 'La Saison Des Pluies' and the nostalgic 'Les Temps Des Yoyos', but elsewhere he longs for the high life in 'Maxim's' and alludes to his New York trip in 'No No Thanks No'.

A more direct and euphoric recollection of the city jumps out from the subtle tonal shifts of 'New York USA' on his second album of 1964.

Treacly slickness was less prized a musical commodity on *Gainsbourg Percussions* in its perceptible drift away from the more exquisite eruditions of yore – though it could be as stubbornly chromatic. Moreover, a lazy bebop hi-hat couldn't be prevented from underpinning 'Coco And Co' with its superimposed night club ambience that bolstered commentary about the jazz combo playing there.

These digressions aside, *Percussions*, as its creator explained, was meant to convey "an explosion of laughter, the exoticism of the choir" – namely twelve African females behind his lead vocal in a manner that indicated a stark awareness of Miriam Makeba, Queen of African *chanson*. The only other melodic devices were guitar and woodwind – saxophone or flute – over a pot-pourri of polyrhythms from an array of congas, bongos and more minor percussion as well as a standard drum set (struck with sticks or brushes as appropriate). For good measure, jungle sound effects were mixed into 'Là-Bas C'Est Naturel'.

Symptomatic of a more intense engrossment with rhythm, 'Joanna' was an unconscious evocation of 'Tie Me Kangaroo Down Sport' in a pulsation pertinent to the surprising lightness of elephantine Joanna's dancing feet. More typically, self-explanatory 'Ces Petits Riens' was 'Girl From Ipanema'-ish in construction on an album that was more Stan Getz than Rolf Harris.

Percussions, however, was among the first audacious creaks of a door that would open wider on a treasury of what would be termed "world music". From these caskets, Malcolm McLaren, Adam And The Ants, Peter Gabriel and other post-punk cultural burglars would help themselves. Yet Gainsbourg did not incorporate wordless tribal chanting and further non-European elements into the new LP in the same organic fashion as chartbusting South African John Kongos would in the 1970s, via uncompromising socio-political lyrics that paralleled a heady flavour of the Transvaal in backing tracks that anticipated the fusions of fellow Boer Johnny Clegg.

Percussions was too "clever" to be a pop hit. Smirking in the direction of his jazz cronies rather than, say, Nigerian "high-life" executant Fela Ransome Kuti, Gainsbourg ensured that there were plenty of tricky round-the-kit fills and a trumpet reacting to underlying chords rather than the more obviously melodic aesthetics of 'Quand Mon 6.35 Me Fait Les Yeux Doux', an up-tempo contemplation of imminent mortality that bit too hard for much airplay. Soloing that pressed beyond the one verse at most that was normal on pop items pervaded tracks like 'Coco And Co' in which Serge is barely able to control his in-joking mirth at times.

He mutters more than sings 'Pauvre Lola' – which is punctuated by bursts of merriment from one of a chorale that, like Ray Charles' Raelettes, leant as much on the negro spiritual's exhorter-congregation interplay as a *Missa Luba* mass from deep in the Congo on the likes of 'Marabout' – notable for the *omnes fortissimo* reiteration of its title and the falling modulation at the end of each line – and 'Tatoué Jérémie', a call-and-response narrative about someone with tattoos in unlikely parts of the body.

'Tatoue Jérémie' was more unacceptable an opus for mid-morning radio than 'Quand Mon 6.35 Me Fait Les Yeux Doux', but it was possible to yowl *Percussions* from the rooftops on a hectic promotional tour that took in press calls as well as stage appearances. Dragging enigmatically on a cigarette, Serge gave unblinking copy to those few hacks that could be bothered, clarifying the record's remoter lyrical by-ways, and staring back in curiosity if prodded about his private life.

It had been too costly to take the choir with him, so a mere two singers approximated the breathtaking mass harmonies on *Percussions*. Yet Serge made more of a show of it than might have been expected in the light of disappointments like only a hundred turning out to see him in Brussels' cavernous Théâtre KO. Moreover, he was a generous front man, permitting musicians a longer leash than on record, and never failing to direct adulation towards them.

In its exhausted aftermath, he tried to assimilate what good had come from this latest public journey. There'd been no significant rise in sales for *Percussions* or the back catalogue – and, for want of anything better, he'd let its new management talk him into a month back at Milord L'Arsoille. Finally, to crown this crestfallen return to base, Serge Gainsbourg had got married again.

chapter four

Baby Pop

She was Françoise Antoinette Pancrazzi, known as "Béatrice" – because, like Serge, she detested her born name. Like him too, she'd been battle-hardened by divorce. Unlike him, however, Béatrice was beautiful. To some, it had been inconceivable that a pocket Venus like Béatrice had even spared Serge a second glance. Gossip may have assumed that it was the same fascination expectant mothers felt sometimes for an unsavoury morsel of food, but celebrity, however qualified, can be a powerful aphrodisiac – and Gainsbourg was still of enough interest for press photographers to loiter at the ceremony.

Though she too was of aristocratic stock, Béatrice was very different from impetuous, bohemian Elisabeth. If rather possessive and prone to bouts of sulking, she was supportive of any feasible means of advancing Serge's career, shouldering many of his day-to-day trials and tribulations while he hunched over the new Steinway grand piano – her wedding gift to him – that was installed in his parent's place where he chose to remain most of the time while Beatrice continued to live in her old flat, a stone's throw from La Madeleine and within earshot of central Paris's unremitting churn of traffic.

It was an unorthodox arrangement and perhaps not the soundest foundation for wedded bliss – particularly as a man so busy is apt to be an inattentive spouse. Yet Béatrice had been tolerant when overworked Serge was unable to unwind sufficiently to enjoy whatever brief leisure could have been theirs before the arrival of a daughter, Natacha, in August – in between *Comment Trouvez-Vous Ma Soeur* and *Percussions*.

Instead, he tended to keep Dracula hours, taking breakfast in the late afternoon to fuel himself for frowning over scrawls of music and words until gone dawn. Streets away from the squalling baby and connected disturbances, the breadwinner could sink into depressions and have neuroses in peace, and sleep off an accumulation of fatigue that would climax with forty-eight hours oblivion after a giddying week of writing all night and spending each day that followed in the studio.

As a recording artist, he was beating a calculated retreat. Why should he knuckle down to another album predestined to traipse a dismayingly familiar path to the bargain bins? Weighing up the negligible cash benefits of all that effort against his self-picture as a singing composer, he elected not to compete against both the Johnny Hallydays on his own patch and the British beat groups that were deluging overseas Top Tens now that Swinging London had surfaced as the planet's prime purveyor of pop music.

In 1963, 'Dominique', the fated Singing Nun's only hit, had been the most overt Gallic challenge to the traditional enemy's domination of international charts, but out of the sub-cultural woodwork were crawling legion outfits like Triangle, Les Sunlights and Les Cyclones who'd had their quiffs sculpted into Beatle moptops, and had seized upon attributes of the new cross-channel idioms that felt the least uncomfortable.

From Gerry And The Pacemakers' portfolio alone had come respective translated copying in 1964 by Claude François and Richard Anthony of 'How Do You Do It' and 'You'll Never Walk Alone'. Sheila cashed in with Manfred Mann's 'Do Wah Diddy Diddy', and nineteen-year-old Françoise Hardy, visualised by indolent columnists as a "new Gréco", with an EP, self-penned but titled 'C'Est Fab' to signify breadwinning affinity to British beat. Sylvie Vartan went the whole hog with 'I'm Watching You', a French Number One sung in English and recorded in London with members of the city's Nero And The Gladiators – just as Richard Anthony had borrowed Adam Faith's backing Roulettes for his version of Unit Four Plus Two's 'Concrete And Clay'.

These *sacré* guitar groups were giving the music publishing houses and production companies of Paris a nasty turn, but certain entrepreneurs saw this as merely a slow moment, and were preparing to bare their teeth to the invasion. Among these was the mercurial Denis Bourgeois who'd launched Bagatelle, an enterprise that was to melt Serge Gainsbourg into its caress by suggesting that he write songs for France Gall, a sixteen-year-old singing *wunderkind* under the wing of Alain Goraguer. He'd perceived Sheila-sized potential in this diminutive, blonde child of Robert Gall, a tunesmith rated by clients like Aznavour, Hugues Aufray and his own France, launched into the hit parade with his 'Sacré Charlemagne'.

A friend of the Gall family, Serge was then bogged down with the music for *Les Plus Belles Escroquies Du Monde* – a movie confined to French regions – having withdrawn from a race against Michel Legrand for *Les Parapluies De Cherbourg*, a screen operetta starring Catherine Deneuve, sub-titled *The Umbrellas Of Cherbourg* in Britain and North America. The France Gall project was a welcome change of activity, especially as the most immediate event on her horizon was to do with her selection as Luxembourg's entry in the Eurovision Song Contest, the mother of all such festivals in that it amassed an annual television viewing figure of millions from every competing country from Finland to Greece. Even though two-thirds of the US *Hot 100* had been British in origin the previous year, every one of that island's nations still deigned to take part. In 1965, the competition had yet to plumb the artistic *bing-bang-biddley-bang* depths that would reduce it to one of the most important dates on the calendar for the connoisseur of *kitsch*. All the same, instant familiarity had always been the key to success. Applying a decade's songwriting craftsmanship to the task in hand, Gainsbourg came up with 'Poupée De Cire Poupée De Son', a catchy musical trinket that seemed as likely to win the day for the duchy as anything else. Nevertheless, Serge couldn't help but insert a *soupçon* of characteristic cynicism in lyrics about a pop idol whose attempts to elicit sympathy for an emotionally deprived if cosseted lifestyle only brings to the fore how little anyone considers not only what her personal aspirations might be, but whether she even had any.

This would translate as 'A Lonely Singing Doll' in a timely cover by Twinkle, a London dolly-bird, after France Gall's Eurovision triumph in Naples on 20 March 1965. Alain – who'd conducted the all-purpose orchestra – and Serge, a spectator who appeared outwardly to have no stake in the outcome, had struggled not to lose their cool as each candidate's tally of points was announced, but had combusted with elation when the final result brought them forward beneath the vast proscenium to receive the golden statuette.

Striking while the iron was lukewarm, 'Baby Pop', another Gainsbourg opus for Mme Gall, was rush-released before 'Poupée De Cire Poupée De Son' had yet to drop out of Top Twenties all over Europe. In hard financial terms, it proved as lucrative via snippet exposure in a TV commercial for a new cosmetic of the same brand name. The young singer of 'Baby Pop' was as unknowing of its underlying sniping at the brittle fabric of fame as she'd been of that within its predecessor. A third Gainsbourg composition, 'Les Sucettes', would be parroted deadpan by Gall, ignorant in her maidenly innocence of its none-too-subtle smuttiness until someone opened her shocked eyes to it, causing her to withdraw from public life for weeks.

France's blushes were mitigated by the income that her association with Serge had generated. The teaming-up was, of course, symbiotic as he too was able to transfuse his bank account with the first mammoth royalty cheques he'd ever received. Always a dutiful son, Gainsbourg's prosperity also granted Joseph and Olia a dotage rich in material comforts such as the holiday villa he bought for them. For other nearest and dearest, he was the fount of expensive birthday presents and, had they so desired, a second-hand renown as relations of the Eurovision victor.

As the sunshine and showers of his working life had attested thus far, showbusiness was a fickle mistress, ready to fling him back to Madame Arthur obscurity at the drop of a seventy-eight. With this worrying psychological undertow, Serge sought to ensure that he'd recoup more than golden memories when the game was up. His eyelids might grow heavy during meetings with his accountant with their complicated expositions containing phrases like "convertible debenture" and "tax concession", but he'd started investing in antiques and, more guardedly, in fine art such as disturbing 'La Chasse Au Papillons' by Dali – with whom he was ruminating about collaborating on a ballet.

A similar creative liaison between Stravinsky and Dylan Thomas had likewise run aground on a sandbank of debate over action. Nevertheless, Gainsbourg was back in demand as a fashionable songwriter, just as he'd been after *L'Etonnant* – but in macrocosm. As well as Distel, Bardot, Michèle Arnaud – after a long vinyl silence – and other previous customers, orders came in from Dalida, actress Valérie Lagrange – and Claude François who was provisioned eventually with 'Hip Hip Hip Hourrah' as the B-side of a smash hit two years later. Claude's long wait was indicative of the length of the metaphorical queue to Serge's door. Too much work was a good problem to have – and it gave him deep pleasure sometimes to turn down a supplicant like patronising Philippe Clay who offered to record an entire album of Gainsbourg material as long as his magnanimity was acknowledged by a share in the songwriting loot.

More regrettably, Serge couldn't help Eddy Mitchell and Johnny Hallyday either, but he found time for Régine, another *chanteuse* of Gréco persuasion, who he heeded for her advice and caustic efficiency when prodding financial handlers about matters from disregarded record company percentages to the smallest petty cash fiddle. Theirs was to be a long term artiste-composer partnership that was tailored to facets of Régine's stage personality and drawn from mutual points of view and a shared sense of humour, whether expressed in 'Si T'Attends Qu'Les Diamants Te Savant Au Coi' ('If You Wait For The Diamonds To Jump Onto Your Neck') or comic 'Pourquoi Un Pyjama A Rayores A Fleurs Ou A Pois' ('Why Pyjamas Are Striped With Flowers Or Dots').

To outsiders, Serge's methodology appeared slapdash and tardy – like a painter dabbing at a hanging canvas minutes before the gallery opens. There were numerous instances of him walking into a session with nothing prepared beyond, say, a chord sequence or some half-finished lyrics. While the engineer was occupied with some tedious mechanical process with tape spools, switches and faders, Gainsbourg might be on the other side of the glass-fronted booth, collating the rest of the words or at the piano, teasing a melody from nothing more than a riff. Sometimes, he'd give it up as a bad job, but often he'd catch the lightning, and a musical structure would shine through with increasing clarity as the studio clock dictated short cuts and the ditching of more and more clutter.

All that remained to be done then was the fairy-dusting, editing and mixing – and that could be delegated to someone such as Goraguer or Dejacques. Serge didn't always stick around for anything like that – because there were only so many fantastic playbacks of, say, Valérie Lagrange's rendition of 'La Guérilla' that could be endured in one sitting by a man jellified with exhaustion.

Worse, long hours hacking records out of a solid lump of acetate meant that it wasn't all smiles in his private life. Béatrice didn't talk anymore, and Serge was hardly ever around to listen. Even when he was there physically, his mind was back in the subterranean depths of Studio Blanqui or over in London where he'd worked with Arthur Greenslade, a studio veteran of greyer eminence than Harry Robinson, on items that included the topical 'Qui Est "In" Qui Est "Out"', title track to the EP that was Gainsbourg's only release in his own name in the whole of 1966.

This latest sojourn in England was from late 1965 to the following February when he took rooms in La Cité Internationale Des Arts, established by the writer and political activist André Malraux as stop-gap housing for artists of all types and nationalities. As well as its low rent, communal facilities and a handy location in the middle of Paris, Serge enjoyed the interaction with others of his kind so much that he contrived to stay for nearly twice the regulated time of a year.

Such a development dampened further Béatrice's optimism that somehow they'd be a proper family one day. Yet she clung onto a belief that, for all his workaholism, vocational frustrations and resulting worn-out moodiness, her husband was worth keeping. Neither was Serge himself immune to twinges of conscience about why he wasn't content with his doting wife and a little girl who adored a neglectful Papa who was now almost permanently away from an abode that he treated as what was coined a "crash pad" in Swinging Sixties parlance. He'd storm in at five in the morning, and leave again after midday on rising for a dressing-gowned *petit déjèuner* and a hand-squeezing departure to get up to Béatrice knew not what. Persevering, she seldom complained about him as he did that she didn't understand him – the stock lament of the maudlin drunk to a barmaid. An increasing alcohol intake was staying the phantoms of encroaching middle age whilst floating his marriage into a choppier sea as his visits to Béatrice's apartment all but ceased, and he seized opportunities to get tipsy without any disgusted reprimands.

"He's not funny," was his own reply to "How would you describe Serge Gainsbourg?", put to him by *Special Pop*. Principally on the strength of his professional alliances with teenage icons, he was apparently one of few older artists held in borderline regard by post-Beatles record-buyers – though reaction to his handful of public appearances in 1965 contradicted this.

Second-billed to Barbara – another contender for Sheila's crown – he left a nationwide tour after five engagements of cat-calls, barracking, slow handclaps and his own verbal retaliations. More typically, he was totally ignored. There was no escaping it: he was doomed before he so much as opened his mouth. He could have sung like a nightingale and gyrated like Mick Jagger, but, with the looks and maturity of a pop sensation's manager rather than a pop sensation itself, he was a bit, well...you know. Who could scream and tear her hair out over someone who was as carnal as a favourite uncle? A back-handed compliment was that boys who came to slobber over Barbara didn't mind their girlfriends liking him. Yet a solitary snigger could set the whole house off and then it'd be murder until the curtain came down.

So unnerved was Serge by this episode that it was to be many years before he hazarded stepping onto the concert stage again – but he didn't need to bother then because of the reanimation of his acting career. These days, he was spilling over onto the small screen as, say, a tramp in *Des Fleurs Pour L'Inspecteur* police serial, and a lunatic in another series, *Vidocq* – in which he was required to bellow an "impromptu" ditty chorused by forty other asylum inmates.

While he acquitted himself admirably on these occasions, his most consistent money-spinner would always be his music. The "paradox" of his output was discussed in *Diapason*, a more adult publication than *Special Pop*. In so many words, it argued that he seemed to operate ambiguously with chart-directed candyfloss for the likes of France Gall that had a sufficiently sophisticated edge to convince the snootiest critics that these and his excursions on the boards were necessary to provoke commissions for work of more substance.

In Geneva during Gainsbourg's first headlining tour back in 1961, onlookers had included director Pierre Koralnik, recipient of many prizes for ground-breaking television. It was a *soirée* he hadn't forgotten five years later when, at Michèle Arnaud's suggestion, he invited Serge to compose a comedy musical as the first in-colour outing on France's new second nationally-networked channel. Accepting the challenge, the perpetrator of 'Baby Pop' came up with *Anna* from the unlikely source of an earnest story-within-a-sermon by the seventeenth century prelate Jacques Benigne Bossuet. Lightened-up, its loose updating had shades of John Boorman's *Catch Us If You Can* in 1965 with The Dave Clark Five, in that an advertising agency employee is so taken by a photograph of a model that nothing would do but he must look for her far and wide. The moral message was that it was a search for something he already had – for the girl was none other than his bespectacled secretary.

A sub-plot had been on the cards briefly whereby Marianne Faithfull*, Mick Jagger's pop singing English paramour, fresh from the cast of Chekov's *Three Sisters* at the Chichester Festival, was approached by Koralnik to be a wayward foreign foil to the refined Anna – played by twenty-six-year-old brunette Anna Karina, ex-wife of Jean-Luc Godard – and female lead in most of his flicks until the divorce a few months before the screening in January 1967. To her went the singing of Anna's only hit song and tie-in forty-five, 'Sous Le Soleil Exactement', a stop-start ballad of a milieu that also encompassed Brian Hyland's morose 'Sealed With A Kiss' and 1964's 'Remember (Walkin' In The Sand)' from The Shangri-Las. Unhappily for all concerned, 'Sous Le Soleil Exactement' did not warm up sales for the – now very collectable – soundtrack album or forestall condescending reviews that, while praising the visual effects, wrote it off as not much fun. While Serge was to protest in retrospect that *Anna* was "French rock ahead of its time", even he was to agree that the music hadn't lasted particularly well.

* *Whose 1967 B-side 'Tomorrow's Calling' – alias 'Hier Ou Demain' – was an Anna opus excluded from the soundtrack album*

That contemporary pundits thought even less of it put the tin lid on a notion of turning *Anna* into a cinema film after matters had got as far as lining up a cameo by Eddy Mitchell, and Goraguer putting Gainsbourg in touch with Michel Columbier, an arranger and conductor whose expertise in the field of TV commercials, so Alain felt, qualified him to assist with the intended score. Whether or not Columbier anticipated more than a practised but detached professional relationship, he became fascinated by what he saw as his new collaborator's ancestry nurturing a sense of melody that did not lend itself to precise transcription any more than the most lowdown blues did. Apart from skin pigmentation, what was the difference anyway between the Russo-Jewish serf and the negro slave of *Uncle Tom's Cabin*?

Serge and Michel complemented each other very well, and were to continue working together when the trail had gone cold on the *Anna* movie. A more hidden benefit of the aborted project was Serge striking up a friendship with Willy Kurant, the televised portrayal's photographic supervisor, who would still be summoned for technological donkey-work on Gainsbourg projects for long after the three month deadline for *Anna* was up.

While attending to *Anna* by day and the rest of his crowded schedule by night, Serge billeted himself on Koralnik, thus losing further contact with Béatrice and the circular arguments and cliff-hanging silences that drove him out of her door and back to studio, saloon or film set.

Sometimes, heartache followed him there too. In August 1966, he had a minor role in a dubious little flick entitled *Le Jardinier D'Argenteuil*, attractive to him mainly because it entailed a trip to Columbia. The novelty of this working holiday wore away swiftly, however, when Serge was arrested after he was blamed for the carelessly discarded cigarette that had ignited a fire in a restaurant. Under police interrogation, he was unable to recollect completely the circumstances that had brought him there. Regardless, he faced up to his accusers and persisted with a denial of arson until some backstairs fixing had the charge quashed possibly because of the odd silence of material witnesses.

He flew from Columbia under a cloud to furnish *Le Jardinier*

D'Argenteuil with its incidental music before servicing likewise four more films of no great merit, one after the other, finishing with *Les Coeur Verts*, a documentary short about urban youth – for which he stumbled upon the melody that the world would come to know as 'Je T'Aime...Moi Non Plus'.

chapter five

L'Horizon

B ack-to-back film music stretching over a year into the future was a sure sign of stagnation. The France Gall well was drying up too. She was now more knowing, and could no longer be dealt with as a budgerigar that doesn't understand what it is saying. She understand that "LSD" was nothing to do with pounds, shillings and pence in 'Teenie Weenie Boppie', a cautionary tale that struggled in 1967's spring charts. A real comedown by previous standards, 'Teenie Weenie Boppie' pitched France into a pop netherworld from which she was not to emerge until she became conjoined, both professionally and personally, with Michel Berger, a singing songwriter who had evoked screams in a support spot to The Kinks at the Olympia.

However temporarily, the older Gainsbourg had lost the knack if not the inclination to make up a yuk-for-a-buck. The title of a new composition, 'Boum Badaboum', was also its main lyrical thrust. Neo-dadaist in its calculated mindlessness, it was just the ticket for the Eurovision Song Contest – which, in 1967, was teetering on the brink of its descent into drivel hinged on hooklines like snatches of kindergarten babble: 'La La La', 'Boom-Bang-A-Bang', 'Ding-A-Dong' *ad nauseum*.

'Boum Badaboum' was to be the gauntlet that Monaco threw down via Minouche Barelli, daughter of the conductor of the orchestra in Monte Carlo's famous Casino. Though Minouche gave of her best, 'Boum Badaboum' swallowed dust behind Sandie

Shaw's 'Puppet On A String', and was a flop on a global scale as Serge knew it would be in his heart of hearts – though his mother had begged to differ, and had wept with disappointment at its failure. Nevertheless, 'Boum Badaboum' didn't fare as badly as an entry sung by Michèle Arnaud's son Dominique Walter – which scraped up just one vote. Feeling sorry for the lad, Serge offered him his services, but Dominique was one of these unfortunate individuals like Henry VI or Richard Cromwell, groomed but unsuited by nature to follow in the footsteps of a more capable parent. Perhaps for the sake of his mother, Gainsbourg persisted with Dominique for several record releases, even putting more profitable work from Johnny Hallyday and Sheila on ice to help young Walter find his feet in showbusiness.

With any illusions about an impending climb to stardom shattered, Serge's protégé threw in the towel and carved an infinitely more satisfying niche for himself in the petroleum industry. More promising on paper was the yoking of Gainsbourg with Marielle Mathieu, a Parisian teenager with an urchin cut and stage presence like a less *outré* Piaf, but this too was a vocational cul-de-sac, ending with Serge passing Marielle's unissued recording of his 'Desesperado' to Dario Moreno, a tenor of Engelbert Humperdinck bent.

All that France at large knew of Gainsbourg then was mostly what it saw in the so-so films, and perused in stray tittle-tattling paragraphs in showbiz gossip columns – though he did rear up on the front page of *France Soir* in a story about a lorry driver attempting suicide by driving his sixteen-ton vehicle into the Seine. Serge was among a party in a nearby café who sprang to the rescue, dragging the fellow out of the water and standing him a stiff drink before the police and ambulance arrived.

Overseas, Gainsbourg's impact was felt only by all but anonymous insinuation via the likes of 'A Lonely Singing Doll' – and even then, certain of his more acerbic lyrics – like Brel's – were sterilised, truncated and, in some cases, so warped that they bore as much resemblance to the originals as a Marx Brothers film to its screenplay. Yet Serge was untroubled by the havoc wrought on them as long as the assorted and incoming monies settled into the complicated but fixed financial channels leading to his purse. The battle might not have been worth fighting anyway as, more often than not, a Londoner's literal decoding of, say, a conversation between two Parisians would be as confused as a Parisian's would be when earwigging one between two Londoners.

To an English-speaking world, the very name "Serge Gainsbourg" meant nothing except to those who derive deep and lasting pleasure from studying raw data on record labels. They'd note "Gainsbourg" among credits for translated items by Twinkle, Petula Clark and Dionne Warwick, but few troubled to find out more. How could they anyway? You'd have some hunt for mentions of any Gallic names whatsoever in music journals like *Melody Maker* or *Billboard* because no-one from France except Chevalier had yet got far in Britain and North America before the mid-1960s.

Richard Anthony had crept into the UK Top Twenty in 1964 with a credible reading of The Everly Brothers' 'Crying In The Rain' – though his attempts to capitalise on this small beginning damaged his domestic standing until 1966's 'Fille Sauvage' (The Rolling Stones' 'Ruby Tuesday') brought him back in from the cold. Yet a heavily publicised visit to Britain – which took in an appearance on ITV's *Ready Steady Go* – did not belittle Johnny Hallyday in the tear-filled eyes of the hysterical female fans who jostled with nigh on 200 press photographers outside the church on that sad morning in 1965 when Johnny emerged with his bride, Sylvie Vartan.

Other red-letter days for Sylvie that year were her spots on the *Royal Command Performance* and across the Atlantic on *Hullabaloo* and then *Shindig* with Paul Anka, writer of her 'I'm Watching You'. She was, however, unable to work the same chartbusting miracle abroad with a voice that sounded unsure and wooden – but not winsomely so – to Anglo-Saxon ears.

Nevertheless, starring in his own US television spectacular, Sacha Distel was clasped to North America's bosom without alienating his grassroots following at home. He was fighting essentially the same battle as the crassest pop act that wished to get off the Gallic treadmill and rake in the dollars. Grasping too that this was the market that counted most, Marielle Mathieu's eventual inroads into the domestic Top Twenty were a dry run for the States – though her repertoire would remain invulnerably French no matter what tongue the actual lyrics she sang.

A minor territory like France would cease to matter financially if, like Mathieu and Distel, you were on a winning streak in this hugest sales area of all. Nicole Croisille, a jill-of-all-trades on the Parisian stage, landed a cabaret residency at Chicago's Playboy Club where she was bruited as being in the same league as Judy Garland. She then proceeded to take Uncle Sam's fair land for every cent she could get for the rest of a career that touched its apogee in 1966 with her hand in *Un Homme Et Une Femme*, the first French film soundtrack album to breach the *Hot 100*.

Despite himself, Jacques Brel had impinged upon the United States almost by stealth after a substantial cult had snowballed from a target group containing more people who read books than the fans surrounding the voluptuous Croisille – and Charles Aznavour who was striding further than either of them after 1965's *His Love Songs In English* LP bound him to fulfilling decades as one of Gaul's leading musical ambassadors. In that boat already were The Swingle Singers, a choir that had been assembled in 1963 by Ward Lamar Swingle, former conductor of Les Ballets De Paris. Addressing themselves to jazzy arrangements of the classics – particularly Bach – their wordless style had the unprecedented effect of predetermined mass scat-singing.

Like Aznavour and The Swingle Singers, Gainsbourg was not the stuff of teenagers, though young marrieds might put his old albums on the turntable during dinner parties. Yet he was esteemed by Harry Robinson, Arthur Greenslade and other foreign indwellers of the record industry who been around him when, with piano and notebook within reach, he was possessed by an impulse that might have impinged itself at an inconvenient moment in, maybe, a lift, the cross-channel ferry or during a business lunch.

Sometimes, he would write at the speed of a train, while on more pedantic occasions, he'd stand over Greenslade at the keyboards, slinging in whatever occurred to him as an arrangement was pieced together to, perhaps, 'Elisa', a instrumental theme for yet another movie – *L'Horizon* – that rested on a crafty renewal of the simplistic tonic-to-dominant cliché beneath a string section that gnawed at it as a lead guitar or saxophone might have done. Back in Paris, he and Michel Columbier had listened as intently to each other as a nascent 'Elisa' had ripened. Typically, after demonstrating a four-bar fragment of melody, Gainsbourg's admission that "I don't know what to do after that" had sparked off a chord change and the rest of the line from Columbier. Then one or other of them would play it again and again until the flow chart of ideas unfolded further.

That the *Un Homme Et Une Femme* soundtrack had been described by one reviewer as "a series of expensive commercials" was a testament to Goraguer's businesslike wisdom in introducing Gainsbourg to a creator of jingles. The pair were grappling once more with their joint muse over autumn 1967 when Jean Gabin, venerable star of *Le Jardinier D'Argenteuil* made a specific request for Serge to both act in and, with Columbier if he liked, provide the music for his next film.

La Pacha is memorable as an arena for the earliest manifestation of Gainsbourg inserting a highly offensive word in a song – offensive enough for radio to have nothing to do with 'Requiem Pour Un *Con*'. What else did Philips expect of an A-side that was a – probably unknowing – brutalisation of William Blake's 'The Sick Rose' in its crowing and unveiled celebration of male sexual domination? Not so shy-making were the lyrics Gainsbourg layered onto 'Elisa' that, nonetheless, belied its sinless Chevalier-esque bounce. Advisedly, he revised them for Zizi Jeanmaire to sing on a TV show, mainly by changing the location from "the jungle of my hair" to a theatre of war. What war was unstated in a libretto that might be construed as being as multi-purpose as the contemporaneous 'It's Good News Week' by Hedgehoppers Anonymous or Barry McGuire's 'Eve Of Destruction'.

If they realised that Gainsbourg was the brains behind it, Zizi's 'Elisa' bolstered his standing with the blossoming hippy sub-culture despite his smart if open-necked attire and the defiantly shortish hair of an incorrigible old jazzer. Indeed, he was, he supposed, active after a dispassionate, *artiste*-like fashion in publicly supporting pacifism, ecological preservation and left-wing popular opinion – and he had no qualms about burdening the listening public with 'Requiem Pour Un Con' and other tracts the old and square found disagreeable.

Because they expose a point of view, all lyrics are political by definition – even 'Boum Badaboum' – and governing bodies had sound reason to envy the pop celebrity's easy manipulation of young minds, lending credence to the homily, "I care not who makes a nation's laws as long as I can write its songs". 'Eve Of Destruction' had struck the right chord because, firstly, "protest" was all the rage then, and secondly – and perhaps more crucially – "it's a great sound", enthused Jonathan King, composer of 'It's Good News Week' and, as far as I'm concerned, as near as you'd get then to Gainsbourg's English equivalent. A hybrid of playfulness, deliberated tastelessness and a doubtful retraction of outspoken contempt for what he called "the very lowest common denominator in the pop audience" would make King wealthy as, both under his own name and as *eminence grise* behind others, he foisted over a decade's worth of the most shallow chart ballast upon those he had once despised openly.

"Since when has pop been a vehicle for sincerity?" he'd argue. Yet 'Eve Of Destruction' got the elbow on all Los Angeles radio stations because those then looting and rioting in the city's most run-down district were more likely to take heed of McGuire's feigned emotion than informed opinion in a newspaper.

The former New Christy Minstrel's doom-laden one-size-fits-all global smash set in motion a "golden age" of protest, but it had been Bob Dylan – whose younger self had also been Living In The Shadow Of The Bomb – who had been infinitely more responsible for both restoring the United States as the tuning fork of pop, and jolting its under-used brain into reluctant, quivering life. Reading the signals, France's pop practitioners – a good few of them not quite getting the point – had weighed in late as usual.

Hugues Aufray had been among the first to jump on the protest bandwagon with his *Aufray Chante Dylan* while the single most messianic symbol of hipness was still singing through his nose about war being wrong. Like, people get killed, you know. Other Gallic entertainers of Aufray's stamp dipped into Dylan's songbook, and quoted his lyrics as if they were proverbs. Moreover, though it meant sweating a bit over words, SACEM members – even Eurovision entrants – were putting their minds to fifth-form sermons and biting indictments of society rather than the tried-and-tested travesties of love.

Judging by 'Desesperado', Jeanmaire's 'Elisa' and even 'Teenie Weenie Boppie' rather than 'Boum Badaboum', moon-June was not Serge Gainsbourg's way by choice, and so it was that, in spring, 1967, he booked what was now his customary London studio behind Marble Arch to record 'Torrey Canyon'. It echoed Barry's McGuire's view on 'Eve Of Destruction': "It's not exactly protest. It's merely a song about current events" – namely the giant oil tanker that, colliding with a reef off the spreading panorama of Cornwall, released a slick that covered nearly three hundred square miles, the most widespread pollution threat to the channel coastlines and their wildlife ever known.

Rather than diving to the heart of the situation as Dylan might have done, Gainsbourg annotated the voyage to the disaster – but the difficulty with topical ditties is what becomes of them when they are no longer topical or the topic isn't very uplifting. Serge's treatment of a serious subject was fine, and it had started to imprint itself on listeners' memories more than 'Chatterton', a "shopping list" effort about time-honoured suicides, on the same EP. However, pop obeys no law of natural justice, and 'Torrey Canyon' was a virtual non-starter owing to its delayed release date and the public's newer preoccupation with food shortages traceable to the summer's Six-Day War in the Middle East in which Israel, antagonised by Egypt-under-Nasser's closure of the Straits of Tiran to shipping, had routed swiftly the armies of Nasser and allied Arab republics. While the trouble was brewing, a cultural attache from the Israeli Embassy appealed to Gainsbourg as a fellow Jew to write a military march to blast from the radio as the troops massed. Metaphorically touching his cap, Serge knocked together the suitably bombastic 'Le Sable Et Le Soldat': David versus *"les Goliaths venus des Pyramides"*.

Days later, 'Torrey Canyon' rather than 'Le Sable Et Le Soldat' prompted the prefecture of Brittany to wonder aloud if he'd care to compose a hymn – to be translated immediately into Breton – for the sailors of the region, now that France's fishing limits were on the point of being extended to twelve miles. Can we have it in time for an outdoor service in Rennes tomorrow?

chapter six

Blow Up

While Serge Gainsbourg was catering for the patriotic whims of the Israelis and Bretons, a British movie, *Blow Up*, was on general release throughout Europe. "Modern" enough to seem dated now, *Blow Up*'s portrayal of the euphoric, anything-goes – many would say "nihilistic" – spirit of Swinging London was a little bit antiquated even in 1967. Carnaby Street and "Mod" was out by then; the junk shops of Portobello Road were prospering amid a passion for Victorian military uniforms and olde tyme whimsy, and flower-power was wafting in from San Francisco, a city that was overtaking used-up London as the Mecca of the young and groovy.

A few steps behind, Parisian boutiques could still charge inflated prices for imported garb that enabled what some still called the *yé-yé* to mimic London's fading Mod conformity: corduroy jackets with narrow lapels and a faint fecal odour; denim shirts with button-down collars; Cuban-heeled "Beatle" boots; thigh-hugging hipsters in Billy Bunter check; ties ranging from knitted plain to op-art slim-jim to eye-torturing kipper, and, sartorial epitomes of the 1960s for the ladies, "kinky" boots and the skirt that was immortalised in 'Mini Mini Mini', a tardy 1967 hit by a Jacques Dutronc, ex-guitarist of Les Cyclones.

Rather than berets, heads would be covered with a cap like the one John Lennon wore in imitation of Bob Dylan in the previous year's Beatles celluloid vehicle, *Help!*. Lambrettas with a dozen mirrors each phutted in Parka-ed cavalcades through the underpasses of the *peripherique.*

Trying as hard to keep up, there were film-makers who felt that Swinging London ought to be captured for posterity while it was still there. Peter Whitehead's first full-length feature film, *Tonite Let's All Make Love In London,* documented the phenomenon in uncertain transition after an evocation at its very cusp in *Help!*.

Overseen by Michelangelo Antonioni, the artiest director of the mid-1960s, *Blow Up* was somewhere in between. It was a slow-moving two hours without much of a plot, but one of The Yardbirds smashed up a guitar, Vanessa Redgrave took her bra off – and female pubic hair was seen by British movie-goers for the first time, courtesy of the thespian listed as "Blonde" in the closing credits.

Her name was Jane Birkin. Hers had been a privileged girlhood divided between Chelsea's Cheyne Gardens and a residence near Freshwater on the Isle of Wight where the whole brood took long, sunny holidays, and the children – Jane, elder brother Andrew and younger sister Linda – spent much of their adolescence. In hopes of improving the French she had grasped with incomplete success at school, Jane was also sent to live for several months with a Parisian family. As Edith Piaf dwelt in the same apartment block, she and Jane may have passed another on the stairs.

Had they exchanged more than just greetings, Piaf would not have taken the teenager for anything other than English. Furthermore, had Edith been able to distinguish between different British accents, she'd have had Jane down correctly as upper class if only for an urbane elegance that suggested that, on her native turf, her vocabulary was freighted with PG Woodhouse-esque phrases like "jolly good" and "right-ho!".

Gap-toothed and tomboyish, "Jane was a little girl who wanted to be a little boy," according to her mother, the comedy actress Judy Campbell. Jane's father was Commander David Birkin, a hero of Dunkirk. Though he was minatory when appropriate, Birkin's flexibility about King's Regulations was reflected in his children's liberal upbringing, and in his support for a gregarious wife's career and her rubbing shoulders with such as Noel Coward, Ralph Richardson, Cicely Courtney and others visible in British-made happy endings on celluloid that were the antithesis of Hollywood's neurotic *film noir*.

These connections may have oiled the wheels for Jane's first big role at sixteen as a deaf mute opposite Richardson in Graham Greene's *Carving A Statue*, and assisted Andrew's *entrée* into a world of the cinema behind the cameras. Indeed, he was on location work for what would become *2001: A Space Odyssey*, Stanley Kubrick's most abiding essay as a director, when Jane, just turned twenty, had been in the throes of *Blow Up*.

Her willowy curves and avalanche of wavy hair had put her in a league that was wide enough to contain bosomy Jean Shrimpton, skeletal Twiggy, lissome Pattie Boyd and like regulars of *Vogue*, *Seventeen* and the fashion pages of Sunday supplements. With the relative girth of middle life, Boyd would later confess to possessing "a couple of mini-skirts which I still try on if I can get into them, but, God, I can never believe we wore them so short". To carry it off, models had needed to be slim-waisted as never before. It was also mandatory "to look childishly young, naively unsophisticated," pontificated Mary Quant, Jean and Pattie's *haute couture* Diaghilev, "and it takes more sophistication to work out the look than would-be sophisticates ever dreamed of."

Just as it had been fitting for Pattie to snare a bit-part as a lisping schoolgirl in Dick Lester's *A Hard Day's Night*, so Jane Birkin, on "discovery" by Shrimpton's photographer David Bailey – himself as outrageous and well-known as a pop star – found herself in quasi-cameo roles as a dolly-bird in seminal Swinging London flicks like Lester's *The Knack* until *Blow Up* seemed to round off her work experience at the most populist end of the British film industry.

At this point, Jane, had she wished, could have urged her agent to negotiate a recording contract. Just as it was with almost any given French screen actress who'd taken pot-shots at the charts, so a combination, perhaps, of personal vanity and a desire to maximise public exposure had already caused the likes of Diana Dors, Lynn Redgrave, Susan Hampshire, Hayley Mills and Honor Blackman to preserve their warblings on disc; Mills racking up a

US Top Twenty smash with 'Let's Get Together' – and, if a flop first time around, 'Kinky Boots' from Blackman (with her Avengers co-star Patrick McNee) was polished up to be a freak hit over Christmas, 1990.

Hardly any of these English roses could sing, but when has that ever mattered? Nevertheless, because marriage and the impending birth of a daughter, Kate, had put Jane Birkin's showbusiness ventures on hold by the time *Blow Up* came out, the world was to be spared – for the time being – a rather querulous treble that did not cling as certainly to a tune as it would in a then-unimaginable future.

Jane's husband was *Oh Boy!* veteran John Barry, a Yorkshireman thirteen years her senior, who, even before the sundering of his John Barry Seven in 1964, had been as dependable a composer of celluloid soundtracks as Serge Gainsbourg was in France. Since then, however, buffs of the genre had begun speaking of him in the same sentences as Malcolm Arnold, William Walton and Ralph Vaughan-Williams. Yet the distinguished if much younger Barry's roots were as much in jazz and pop as the classics, having had early efforts as an arranger broadcast by Johnny Dankworth before the formation of the Seven with himself as its trumpeter and vocalist.

In tandem with Lord Rockingham's XI, the combo had been resident on *Oh Boy!* prior to notching up Top Forty entries in its own right and as the bedrock of its leader's trademark "Stringbeat" (ie violinists plunking pizzicato) layering on hits by Adam Faith – whose 1960 movie, *Beat Girl* was John's first film score. Jumping at similar chances, Barry's name was to be as synonymous with James Bond movies in its way as Sean Connery's by the time he and Jane Birkin became an "item".

Bond was an unstoppable cinema attraction all over Europe, but most peculiar to France was a craze for films based on cartoon characters from magazines like *Pilote, Spirou* – and the more censorable *Barbarella*, made flesh-and-blood for the silver screen in 1967 by Roger Vadim with a cast that included *Blow Up*'s David Hemmings and the third Mrs Vadim, Jane Fonda.

The first had been Brigitte Bardot who had also embarked on

a third espousal – to Gunther Sachs, an aristocratic German who led a pampered life buoyed by his family's engineering fortune. His match with Brigitte in 1966 had hit trouble almost immediately, and parting was less than a year away when she alighted on 'Comic Strip' – complete with POW! WIZZ! ZONK! interjections – from Serge Gainsbourg's 'Torrey Canyon' EP to be short-listed for her next New Year's Eve televisual extravaganza.

So far, she had had no direct contact with Serge – and wouldn't have if it was up to Béatrice. His wife wasn't keen on him being around good-looking females of even the most unimpeachable reputation, let alone one like Bardot's. Hadn't venerable *Le Jardinier D'Argenteuil* star Jean Gabin – and him with a known eye for a pretty woman – been appalled to be cast opposite what he called "that thing that always goes around naked" in an earlier movie?

Because of their unconventional living arrangements, Béatrice could be no Beryl Formby who watched her henpecked George, the Lancashire music-hall entertainer, like a lynx and ruled him with an "iron petticoat", but it was noticed that Mme Gainsbourg had started materialising at her husband's various places of work. On a Christmas Eve edition of the TV show, *Dim Dam Dom*, it was reported that Béatrice had been hovering out of lens range on Serge's "nativity" sketch with Chantal Goya, straight from the set of Godard's sexy *Masculin Feminin*.

Such baleful omnipresence was among factors that was destroying a marriage that, as in the 'Ce Mortal Ennui' scenario, muddled on beyond an irreversible erosion because Serge hadn't sufficient incentive to end it until, to speed up the inevitable divorce, he accepted responsibility for the breakdown, and paid the price of stiff financial ordinances pertinent to a daughter to whom he was forbidden access unless her mother was in attendance too.

It was too late to cancel the decree absolute, but concern for Natacha's well-being as well as conflicting emotions – hurt, anger, loss and dependence – towards each other overflowed to such an extent that the couple decided to give it another try, but within weeks,the interminable old grievances peeped out over the horizon, building rapidly from a trace of vapour to Wagnerian thunderstorm.

By autumn 1967, Serge had shaken off marital fetters for the second and, for all he knew, last time. What had changed from a joy to a burden had fallen away just as he spotted the tell-tale signs of another slump in his professional life. On every front, friends and rivals, new and old, were forging so far ahead of him that it seemed fanciful to imagine that he'd ever catch up.

Though Brel had downed tools as a working *chansonier* after a farewell tour, he missed the limelight enough to take the lead part of Don Quixote in a sell-out Parisian production of *Man Of La Mancha*, not long after Aznavour's record-breaking run of almost seventy standing-room-only engagements at the Olympia. If further from the public eye, Michel Legrand was going beyond altogether now that *Les Parapluies De Cherbourg* was lifting him off the domestic treadmill to the glossier Hollywood highs of *The Thomas Crown Affair* and an Academy Award – the first of many – for its 'Windmills Of Your Mind' theme.

Of French pop's newer elder statesmen, Claude François remained adored as "Clo-Clo" by teenagers whilst addressing himself to their parents most ably via a greater proportion of largely self-composed ballads. One of these, 'Comme D'Habitude', was to be the means of his deepest penetration overseas when English lyrics by wily Paul Anka transformed it into 'My Way', a cabaret warhorse for every third-rate Sinatra after it became Ol' Blue Eyes' signature tune, holder of the record for the longest stay in the British chart, and a royalty-earning nest egg for its creators through revivals over the years by artists as diverse as Elvis Presley and The Sex Pistols.

Domestically, Jacques Dutronc had muscled into Gainsbourg's area by composing for others – notably Zou-Zou (a former Twist exponent) and Françoise Hardy. Dutronc might have been contented with his lot had not he and Jacques Lanzmann, editor of the soft-porn *Lui* magazine, chortled at the same jokes. Setting simple melodies and clever hook-lines to Lanzmann's rapid-fire lyrics – specifically designed to be funny – Dutronc's calling as a kind of Frankish Benny Hill hit its stride after a Top Ten entry with 'Le Vagabond' had paved the way for chart-topping 'Et Moi Et Moi

Et Moi' (which became a national catch phrase). Later efforts like 'Mini Mini Mini' were better known beyond France but LP tracks such as 'Hippy Hippy Hourrah' and 'Cactus' (with a nonsensical chorus) were more typical Dutronc-Lanzmann fare.

Jacques invited professional suicide if he cut the cackle. Because he didn't mind making a monkey of himself on stage, he was unlikely to steal female fans from Danyel Gérard, even if the latter's appeal had palled after he got engaged. Nevertheless, Gérard had ploughed back his earnings into a remunerative production company, and had also come up trumps as commissioned songwriter with Marie La Fôret's 'Les Vendanges De L'Amour' and Herve Villand's 'Mourir Ou Vivre' among his chart triumphs.

More recent arrivals included Marie-Paul Belle, Michel Polnareff, hirsute Antoine – modelled on a Bob Dylan who'd "gone electric" two years earlier – and Salvatore Adamo who'd Hit The Big Time in 1966 with three chart strikes in succession. Like Distel, Adamo's conservative image garnered a large middle-of-the-road audience but, with a shy smile that belied personal tragedies known to his fans, his appeal also antedated that of the US school of singer-songwriters of the early 1970s – especially when, after a 1967 trip to the Middle East, he penned 'Inch Allah' and 'On Se Bat Toujours Quelque Part', anti-war singles more specific – and potent – than Gainsbourg-via-Jeanmaire's 'Elisa'.

Johnny Hallyday was still chief among Gallic pop luminaries for whom songwriting was more incidental, having checkmated old rival Richard Anthony at every turn, especially in South America where an attendance of tens of thousands at a Hallyday show in Argentina was not unusual. Neither was it strange to hear Johnny keeping fervidly abreast of whatever was happening in more vital markets as exemplified by selections on his *Olympia 1967* LP like 'In The Midnight Hour', 'If I Were A Carpenter', 'Hey Joe' and Los Bravos' 'Black Is Black'.

Meanwhile, Sheila's rags-to-riches story was being serialised in *France Soir*, and tit-bits about her amorous entanglements were to become more riveting to her followers than her latest record.

Serge Gainsbourg could never have guessed, but, both

personally and professionally, he was about to sail a more roller-coaster sea than any of them, when sucked into a vortex of events, places and circumstances beyond his wildest dreams before being dragged down into a undertow deeper than he could ever have imagined.

chapter seven

Contact

When the firm behind *Special Pop* published a 390-page pop encyclopedia in 1967, Serge Gainsbourg was deemed worthy of an entry. If his – and Legrand's and Aznavour's – weren't as voluminous as those of, say, Hallyday, Anthony or even Dutronc, at least they had one. Brassens and Brel were too unhip for inclusion – or maybe so indifferent to the adoration of schoolchildren that their respective agents couldn't spare the time to mail requested publicity photographs and career summaries.

In a way, being placed between Billy Fury and France Gall – and to be even classed among the overtly pop acts that festooned such tomes – may have been detrimental to Serge's standing as a songwriter still held in awe by such discerning artists as Gréco, Hardy and Marianne Faithfull. In truth, he hadn't quite fitted anywhere in that watershed year. Not for him was either psychedelia or the schmaltz that, paradoxically, also enjoyed a boom with Petula Clark, ex-palais crooner Engelbert Humperdinck, sixty-seven-year-old Louis Armstrong and others of their syrupy stamp groping into European Top Tens to nestle uneasily among the freak-outs of The Move, The Jimi Hendrix Experience and The Pink Floyd.

Gainsbourg was worn out with the realisation that he was stuck in the same rut he'd been in for years. With record companies interested only in consistently successful signings, his very name had become a millstone round his neck. All that seemed to be left was limiting the scope of his artistic goal levels by meeting popular taste at least halfway, not turning difficult, and sticking to the formula if or when he racked up a hit for himself or, more likely, another France Gall. The constricting future that beckoned meant plodding a well-tramped path from maturity to dreary repetition.

An intermittent winner of small prizes in the lottery that was showbusiness, he was too old to either continue daydreaming or to shake a frustrated fist whenever the image of someone like Aznavour flickered from the television. It was a bane of Serge's existence that such contemporaries were doing what they wanted to do rather than just making the most of every crumb of opportunity tossed in their direction.

True, casting directors still went out their way to find him if they wanted someone to play an ill-favoured villain, a sinister underling or any similarly creepy part. He reached a zenith of sorts when *Paris-Jour* announced that he was to be the Marquis de Sade in one TV drama, but more his mark was as prime suspect in a episode of *Dossier De L'Agence O*, a detective series.

He'd been on location in Provence in a role of like magnitude in the feature film *Le Sacré Grand Père* when Béatrice appeared with news of a second pregnancy. The seed had taken hold during the weeks prior to the final estrangement, and the birth of a son, Vania, in 1968's cold spring did not effect any reconciliation.

By then, Serge had outstayed his welcome at the Cité des Artists, and, on wheedling a loan from Eddie Barclay in lieu of some forthcoming film music, entreated his father to look over and report on likely-looking properties, preferably in the university district. In the interim, however, he elected not to return to the parental home. Instead, he rented temporary accommodation that, if he'd been closeted there for more than a few hours, would untidy itself to look as if someone had chucked a hand-grenade into it.

The onset of the arthritis that was to harry Olia for the rest of her days made Serge not like to accept her offers to clean up after him. Moreso, he discouraged visits from Béatrice, even though she'd cast aside her piques and jealousies and accepted the agony of losing him – not that he'd ever really been hers. They scarcely met anymore, but, for a while, he would demonstrate in little fondnesses, the respect that was the due of the mother of his children.

There was yet no evidence of any steady girlfriend, but he seemed on a perpetual lookout for an unsteady one in fashionable clubs-cum-discothèques from which a showbusiness elite and their hangers-on could select a night out: "night" defined as round midnight till when milk-floats braved the cold of sunrise. Scrutinised through spy-holes and not found wanting, you'd hold court with only your equals contradicting you in a forum attractive for its strict membership controls and firm stipulations that no photographers were to be admitted. Close at hand would be an ash-tray, a glass filled at regular intervals – and, depending on status, an abundance of gold-diggers with raw physical beauty their only asset. They were on the spot with the promptness of vultures to chew upon and spit out useful men that trusted them.

Gainsbourg knew the type well and was wary. Nevertheless, the calculating lust for them was as strong as it had been on the *Opus 109* tour when the world was young. He was still partial to variety, and his bouts of promiscuity did not embrace different editions of the same woman any more than his two marriages had.

Whirring Nikons did not, however, herald the comings and goings of Gainsbourg and his fleeting attachments like they did those of Charles Aznavour and his gorgeous new wife. With his school janitor looks and diminutive height, Aznavour was no Distel or Adamo. As he kept telling everyone, "Everything about me is common. I am ordinary like real people. The romantic Frenchman's image is a problem for me. I am not a heart-throb. I am the man next door. The public may see me with Brigitte Bardot in my arms for a TV show, and that is good, because if I can make it, so can they."

The jackpot of all lotharios, Bardot would arrive at showbiz *soirées*, and a murmur would reach a crescendo that she had entered the building. This wasn't television or a picture in *Paris-Match*, "BB" was actually within, asserting her magnetism in abundance as newer stars and their acolytes droned round her like a halo of flies.

With deceptive casualness, Serge Gainsbourg had entered her life at last in October 1967, the month that he and Béatrice gave up hope altogether. Brigitte's ebbing marriage to Gunther Sachs had reached the stage where, two old friends who used to be lovers, they made light of each other's more discreet infidelities; understanding that, sooner or later, one of them would find someone else. Yet, while Sachs had been open-minded about the sex scenes in her films and the attendant publicity, he drew a line when the gutter press fleshed out her dalliance with club owner Luigi Rizzi: "Look, if a man opens an international magazine and sees a picture of his wife naked, with a naked man, don't you think there are grounds for divorce?"

Gunther was to have even more legal ammunition before long. It began innocently enough with his Brigitte and her general factotum – and, until recently, boyfriend – Robert Zaguri approaching Gainsbourg to direct his professional attention towards her fourth New Year's Eve spectacular – to be broadcast internationally this time. In the first instance, she said, could he crank out "something with a motorcycle".

A potentially lucrative fish had bitten, and Serge's response was as impressively swift as it had been to the Breton anthem brief. Overnight, he penned 'Harley Davidson', a rock 'n' roll variation on the eternal triangle that involved the vehicle favoured by the dreaded Hell's Angels brotherhood. With a liberally employed collage of snarling engines, squealing tyres *et al*, 'Harley Davidson' was shot in a garage two days later; Bardot in jackboots and a leather mini-skirt clothing long legs that straddled a bike and conjured up visions that a natural reserve forbids me to detail.

It was one of up to twenty segments pencilled in for a production that pioneered (in Europe anyway) the use of videotape with mimed playback, the inadvertent template of the method still applied for promotional clips in 1990s pop – though in late 1967, it was simply a means of bypassing the false economy of holding up proceedings for the laborious development of cheaper cine-film. Another breakthrough was that *Le Bardot Show* was to be the first prime-time TV special featuring a French singer to be networked in the USA, an advance as momentous in its fashion as Elvis Presley's televised comeback was to be the following summer.

In a profit position before its completion, let alone release, *Le Bardot Show*'s creators could well afford the means to turn their every whim into audio-visual reality. When Bardot told Zaguri about an exhibit in the Musée D'Art Moderne in Paris that she wanted to be central to a routine in which she was to wear a metallic-look dress, nothing would do but that Gainsbourg must be set to work on an apposite song. This time, it took him two nights to finish 'Contact' which wasn't much when reduced to the acid test of just voice and piano, but it was made stratospheric with generous echo on its vocal hook, and nagging riffs on organ and – a contemporary touch-up – monotonal electric sitar, all suspended over a plain four-to-the-bar cowbell.

Sounds marvellous, eh? Brigitte said as much when she and the composer unloaded their trays on the same table for lunch during the shooting of an edition of the *Sacha Show* devoted to her. Even at his lightning speed, it had been too late for Serge to contribute material, but Bardot wondered how he felt about being her male foil where necessary on New Year's Day, sort of Peter Sellers to her Sophie Loren. Gainsbourg wasn't sure he'd heard her properly until the weight of her proposition – the biggest break of his life – crashed down on him.

As well as getting in on the act in front of the cameras, Serge was required to present and adapt more songs to suit the sets and Miss Bardot's wardrobe. Thinking on his feet, he pondered whether there was a 'Goodness Gracious Me' – 1960's fortune-making comedy duet by Sellers and Loren – somewhere as he sifted through his swelling SACEM stockpile for 'Bubble Gum' and, another co-written by Alain Goraguer and recorded on the same two-year-old Bardot single, 'L'Omnibus' with a euphonium carrying the bass line. A similar ambulatory 'Hello Dolly' rhythm undercut 'Comic Strip. On the cards as a Bardot solo item even before 'Harley Davidson', it now had a *Barbarella*-like BB in dark wig, surrounded by speech balloons and punctuating the newly-enrolled Gainsbourg's straight-man vocal with baby-doll interjections.

The ultimate selection of seventeen sequences also included Bardot as a hussar in front of Buckingham Palace; as a nymphet regretting a lost July in St Tropez, and as herself inside La Madrigue, her remote and rambling Riviera farmhouse, "an interior of great charm and simplicity," beamed the London *Evening Standard*'s Sam White, one of few British journalists to review an uncut *Bardot Show*, unseen there generally until an abridged issue on video nearly thirty years on. White enthused too about a piece he understood to be titled 'I Feel Strange Desires Creeping Up The Back Of My Kidneys' that "is done with enormous charm and talent". He continued to almost grasp the wrong end of the stick – though the stick still existed – in observations that "she is naked or half-naked a good deal of the time, first as a modern motorbike-riding Lady Godiva, then she is transformed into a fur-clad panther of a woman. Then again she is Salome, dressed in diamonds and then a kind of Superwoman with long, straight brown hair, pink tights and a heavy chain around her hips."

In passing, he mentioned "the singer Serge Gainsbourg" who'd been to the fore as a shoulder-holstered Clyde opposite Bardot as his moll, exchanging lines in 'Bonnie And Clyde'. This was unvarnished opportunism in the wake of the supplanting of flower-power in Europe by slouch-hatted, tailboard-riding gangster chic, thanks in part to records like Prince Buster's 'Al Capone' and the bio-pic that inspired 'The Ballad Of Bonnie And Clyde' that, riven with machine-gun sound effects, had revitalised Georgie Fame's flagging career. Undulating with murky strings, Gainsbourg and Bardot's semi-spoken take on the mythologising of the pre-war bank robbers had a suspensory menace absent from Fame's winter Number One.

Essentially, both were narratives rather than analyses of the criminal couple's relationship – but whatever the Gainsbourg song lacked in romantic sub-plot, the *Bardot Show* crew detected a friskiness between Serge and Brigitte that was a public surfacing of an off-duty affair. From their first conversation, each had cherished a caprice to entice the other into bed.

As well as the wasp-waist, firm breasts, flawless complexion and other obvious attributes, sending frissons through Serge's being was her disarming directness and a refusal to be an adjunct to him that was so different from the more run-of-the-mill French female who, lost in a man's silhouette, was tolerant of machismo values and a dual code of conduct that condoned his unfaithfulness but not hers or those of his other girls.

Brigitte's frankness about desiring men as men desire women was nutshelled by Simone de Beauvoir: BB was, she said, "as much the hunter as she is the prey". While it lasted, each of her conquests would believe that he was the only person that was important to her – but before he'd even dried his tears, many a broken-hearted former sweetheart pulled himself together sharply enough to go into rhapsodies to cheque-waving tabloids about how adventurous Bardot was between the sheets.

Her latest flame, however, would be more dignified when it was over – or, at least, spare the particulars. To soul-mates that came after her, however, he was to dissect her character, albeit with rueful affection. "He told me that Brigitte was always so easily shocked," Jane Birkin would recall, "and that amused him. He also used to say that she is very straight. Contrary to what many people think, he used to tell me [that] Brigitte is an innocent who plays the little girl: 'Bri-Bri is thirsty'; 'Bri-Bri is hungry'; 'Bri-Bri needs love'. She was so vulnerable, so distressed – and yet at the same time, she has always been dangerously beautiful."

What did one who rivalled Raquel Welch as the media's most physically ideal woman see in Serge Gainsbourg? An educated guess from one with a different set of hormones is that it was probably the same sorcery that had bewitched – still bewitched – Béatrice: the comical monstrosity of a clown.

When Serge was in a jovial mood, he made Brigitte laugh a lot. Then, on switching from wine to spirits, he might be meditative prior to plunging into orgies of maudlin reminiscences: either that or, on rarer occasions, his talk would get louder, his eyes brighter and his behaviour more manic. When he awoke the day after pouring a larger than usual quantity of drink into himself, Bardot had asked him why. "Because I was heady with your beauty," he'd explained, fixing her with a penetrating stare and not a flicker of irony. After a silence you could almost hear, she spoke: "Write me the most beautiful love song you can imagine."

Pragmatism ruled, however, and that night he tied loose ends of 'Bonnie And Clyde' firmly before considering his new love's demand. This wasn't something that could be dashed off like perhaps 1964's 'OO Sheriff' had been for Petula Clark, even though songwriting had long been a knack to him, like making a paper aeroplane. It could also be a chore, sometimes a boring job like any other boring job, especially after the structure and boundaries of a given piece was established and the donkey-work stretched before him.

For a while, he couldn't come up with even the skeleton of anything for Brigitte, just infantile vibrations hanging in the air. What he needed from Béatrice's Steinway was a tune with a poignant yet light quality on which he could hang the right words. The melody from *Les Coeurs Verts* opened the vista to a lyric derived from a reported dialogue between Picasso and his fellow Cubist Braque, and a carefully polished one-liner from Dali: "Picasso is Spanish, moi aussi; Picasso is a genius, moi aussi; Picasso is a communist, moi non plus" ("me neither").

'Je T'Aime...Moi Non Plus' surfaced as a mordant 'Goodness Gracious Me' with eroticism laid on with a trowel instead of humour, when Serge and Brigitte recorded it in a midnight session in December 1967. Neither Michel Columbier organising the musicians nor Denis Bourgeois in the control room betrayed either arousal or distaste as an easy-listening accompaniment seeped incongruously beneath grunts, whispers and half-sung lines like one that translated as "You are the wave. I am the bare island. You go, you go and you come between my loins."

Wait! There's more! "I see you, I want you, I come between your kidneys," groaned Gainsbourg, triggering an antiphonal "I love you. Oh, I love you," from Bardot. While they simulated lingering *carezza* rather than a hammer-and-tongs knee-trembler with clothes on, there was no doubting the sincerity of another utterance, "*L'amour physique est sans issue*" (there's nothing to beat physical love).

At least Serge managed to "hold myself in check", but the planned 'Je T'Aime...Moi Non Plus' single was to have "Not to be sold to minors" across its picture sleeve. This, nevertheless, wasn't good enough for a shocked Gunther Sachs, still standing on his dignity as BB's official husband. Baulking like a gymkhana pony refusing a fence, the lady herself panicked too, and persuaded Barclay to cancel the release and try to get 'Je T'Aime...Moi Non Plus' – Sam White's 'I Feel Strange Desires Creeping Up The Back Of My Kidneys' – removed from *Le Bardot Show*.

The master tape was not destroyed, but locked in a safe where it would lie as unforgotten as The Rolling Stones' 'Cocksucker Blues' and *The Troggs Tape* – an illicit recording of a cross-purposes studio discussion riddled with swearing – would be. Years would pass and, though no-one could cite precise sources of information, an erroneous legend would persist that 'Je T'Aime...Moi Non Plus' was nothing less than four minutes thirty-five seconds of Bardot and Gainsbourg in actual sexual congress in the vocal isolation booth.

On the radio in January 1968 and to those he'd allowed to listen to a test-pressing in private, Gainsbourg protested that this was not so. No-one was sure whether to believe him or not, and the consequent notoriety had mixed blessings. BB almost expected to yawn and stretch to camera shutters clicking like typewriters but new to Serge as an occupational hazard was the paparazzi intrusion that would precipitate unbroken press visibility for as long as he lived.

Yet his association with Bardot had helped draw supplicants for songs to him like wasps round a jam-jar. Among them was Jeanne Moreau – begging for an entire album – and Jean-Louis Barrault reminding Gainsbourg of a long-promised collaboration on a musical that had already been given a working title, *Kidnapping*. The allure of such solicitations was no competition against Bardot as Serge couldn't restrain himself from sneaking away from work-in-progress to be with her whenever possible, the ecstasies of their mutual infatuation keeping him there. Late for a spot before a television audience in *Tilt Magazine*, "Every time I put my shirt on, she takes it off," was his excuse – and a perfectly adequate one, he laughed, for any red-blooded male. Who wouldn't be sensually enslaved by just one pout of BB's languorous lips.

Gainsbourg's professional priority was Bardot too. Other commissions had to wait. On a first-come-first-served basis, he supplied Régine with more songs – including 'Capone Et Sa Petite Phyllis', an inelegant pun on the venereal disease that carried off the scourge of Prohibition. The reins were also loosened sufficiently to enable Françoise Hardy to have 'L'Anamour' and 'Comment Te Dire Adieu', and even for him to compose an orchestra-drenched main theme to *Manon 70* starring Catherine Deneuve, who'd had a son by BB's cast-off Roger Vadim, and was an actress as bankable – and, some would murmur, as ravishing – as BB.

A contract settled before Bardot's coming was Serge's role as a journalist in *Vivre La Nuit*, a movie that was too sentimental as the just-premièred *Le Sacré Grand Père* was too patriotic for a year bracketed by strike-happy upheavals and New Left *événements* filtering through France. "Revolution is this year's flower-power" – so Frank Zappa, leader of The Mothers Of Invention, had summed up 1968 when, with Vietnam the common denominator, kaftans had been mothballed as their former wearers had trailed along with the crowd on its way to genuinely violent anti-war demonstrations and student sit-ins.

These had been stoked up by the likes of Daniel Cohn-Bendit ("Danny the Red") and Olivier Rolin, known as "Antoine" to his Maoist pals at university. "He was one of the most violent of the lot," reckoned Jane Birkin after she got to know him. "They put him in prison for four years for blowing up a building. I think he kidnapped the head of Renault too.

"Serge didn't seem particularly interested in what was going on," Jane would aver too. "Perhaps it was because he was twenty years older than the students." For him, the most signal effect of the festering unrest in the streets was the disturbance of an evening meal at Régine's – but down in Cannes, a political rally disrupted the screening of *Wonderwall*, an oddity of a film that was to fade rapidly from general circulation, having been condemned as "a right load of codswallop" in *The Times*. It was about an elderly scientist who spends his leisure hours peeping obsessively through a hole in his wall at the antics of a young model in the flat next door. The spectacle of her naked mirror-posing, wild parties and athletic sex life is so alien to him that reality dissolves – as does the plot – until his fantasies become concrete when he saves the girl from suicide.

She was played by Jane Birkin, type-cast since *Blow-Up*, and present in Paris in May 1968 at the height of the trouble: "The man who had engaged me to be in his film had his Porsche blown up while we were all inside a club. The *événements* had begun – so the movie was postponed for a month, and the next morning, I was put on an aeroplane back to London. I missed it all – which is why I've never wanted to miss anything since."

chapter eight

69 Année Erotique

F or his part in *Voulez-Vous Danser Avec Moi*, Serge was to be listed
in the "filmography" but otherwise author Peter Evans felt it was
unnecessary to mention him elsewhere in an otherwise thorough
1972 biography of Brigitte Bardot* – who had ended her amour with
Gainsbourg within weeks of the transmission of *Le Bardot Show*. It
had been, according to Jane Birkin, "a little fling. It was nothing that
lasted very long, but when it was over, Serge was hurt."

"That woman has flattened me like a hot iron," howled a
prostrated Gainsbourg. He'd never reconquer her, but Brigitte
couldn't help liking him and wanted him to think well of her. An
eventual new start on civil terms would evolve into a deep, lifelong
friendship, but while the dust had yet to settle on the affair, "They
didn't see much of each other," affirmed Birkin, "even though they
were only a few blocks away in Paris." Nevertheless, they stayed in the
picture about each other's activities – as Bardot did on running into
Mr and Mrs Ginzburg in the street on 18 June 1968, the very day of
their golden wedding anniversary.

Brigitte had approved of the house that Joseph Ginzburg found for
his son along Rue de Verneuil, a few doors away from Juliette Gréco.
As well as ornaments accumulated by the new owner over the years,
colour portraits of BB had been much in evidence until he replaced
them with Marilyn Monroe in sombre monochrome. Reflecting his
jilted melancholia too would be black-and-white tiles throughout a
reception area that was empty apart from a sofa and the Steinway.

---

* Bardot: Eternal Sex Goddess *(London, 1972)*

Other than a bright and airy kitchen and a nursery facing the courtyard garden, dark mahogany filled the rooms, and total blackness covered walls and ceilings all the way up to a studio with a skylit window.

At any given moment for not quite a year, some part of the place would be an uninhabitable no-man's-land of planks and rubble during extensive refurbishing. If Serge wasn't one for marshalling the contracted builders or even doing more than pass the time of day with them, they'd still dine out on the jaw-dropping information that the TV star and former beau of BB was just like any other ordinary bloke who'd come into a bit of money, and was taking the sudden upward turn of his celebrity in his stride. Amusing rather than annoying then, it was rare if Gainsbourg was allowed to eat a restaurant meal in solitude. As well as autographing table napkins while masticating a croissant, he'd be accosted to do the same when hurrying across the Rue de Verneuil pavement to a ticking-over taxi: his only direct contact with the Great Outdoors nowadays.

From the back seat during stop-starting drives through Paris, he'd look without instant comprehension at newsagents' windows displaying magazines like *Marie-Claire*; their front covers promising articles about him inside with "Why Beautiful Girls Fall For This Ugly Man" a prototypical headline. The most eye-catching shelves in bookshops too were lined with the first of more Serge Gainsbourg biographies than anyone could ever have been imagined as well as a limited edition of his lyrics, divorced from their musical settings and presented like printed poems, in commemoration of his fortieth birthday.

He was cropping up more on television too. No longer an also-ran guest in front of some other entertainer's audience, he starred in his own prime-time special on 28 March 1968, even if it was one that jammed the switchboard with complaints about him sucking on a slovenly cigarette during instrumental interludes of a revamped 'La Nuit D'Octobre'.

The unseen millions were to be denied, *La Naissance D'Une Chanson*, centred on the singing smoker's return to Arthur Greenslade's London to record 'Initials BB', a sceptical requiem for the fizzled-out romance. Mains leads from both audio and visual equipment were fanning out in all directions across the hollow chamber when he arrived with a number that was nearer completion than it had been when he'd boarded a train at the Gare du Nord for the cross-channel ferry. This purposely pedantic journey had bought time for him to tease a song out of just a title. Though most of the frames were to cascade onto the cutting-room floor, every unforgiving minute of the trip was chronicled on film as, in railway carriage and afloat, 'Initials BB' bloomed from a snippet of chorus and a four-note verse motif to a John Barry-esque complexity attractively aswarm with careening strings, baroque horns and the cooing of a female choir.

This short documentary was remaindered. So too was *Mister Freedom*, a celluloid send-up of comic-book super heroes with Gainsbourg as "Mister Drugstore" and compiler of a soundtrack that included the irreverent overhaul of 'La Marseillaise' that may have contributed to the flick's non-distribution. Another venture that came to grief was a musical based loosely on a children's story from which was salvaged 'Bloody Jack', a number given to Zizi Jeanmaire to sing in another film that would earn Serge the usual pin-money.

This hat-trick of failed projects brought Gainsbourg closer to the chasm into which he would plunge unless he pulled another stroke of *Bardot Show* magnitude. A contradiction of enjoyable depression overcame him when he re-ran the tape of 'Je T'Aime...Moi Non Plus'. That Brigitte had put the kybosh on it was money down the drain – because it was a surefire hit if ever he heard one. At the very least, it would be a serviceable demo if he remade it with someone else.

To this end, overtures were made to known French *chanteuses* until the idea occurred that someone like Marianne Faithfull or Jane Birkin might do. Yes, it could be quite sexy, a breathy English voice stumbling over the words. What's more, Faithfull was presently on country-wide cinema screens with Alain Delon in Roger Vadim's semi-pornographic *Girl On A Motorcycle*, and it was even more in character for *Blow Up* Birkin, then flitting between London and Paris during the protracted pre-production of *Slogan* – for which Serge had been sent a script with a view to him agreeing to his first top billing in a movie.

Written by its director Pierre Grimblat, *Slogan* in starkest outline was that "Serge", a Parisian film-maker receives a prize at the Venice festival (as Grimblat was to do in imminent reality) where it's love at first sight between himself and "Evelyne" (Jane Birkin). His intentions are honourable – or would be but for a pregnant wife who finds out what's going on, thus sparking off a sequence of psycho-sentimental adventures that culminate with Evelyne going off with another chap.

While Gainsbourg dithered – and *Slogan* was up in the air anyway because of the *événements* – he prefaced his walk with destiny with two less taxing movies, *Eroticissimo* and *Paris N'Existe Pas*. Nevertheless, allowed a degree of control over casting and the evolution of the plot, Serge's eventual acceptance of the role of his namesake pointed the finger at Birkin as the chosen one for the new 'Je T'Aime...', ideal in any case as the *Slogan* love theme – though he was mildly resentful that she was less renowned in France than he'd been given to understand. For her part, Jane procrastinated over the record as he had over the film. While flattered at being asked, the content of 'Je 'T'Aime...', she gasped, "made you go a bit sweaty under the collar".

Thus the wheels of the universe creaked, budged, stuck, budged again; then, with much agonised shuddering, began to come together as Jane Birkin, smarting from her recent divorce from John Barry, went home to mother in Cheyne Gardens whilst waiting for the interior designers to finish her just-purchased abode in nearby Cheyne Walk – where, incidentally, Marianne Faithfull and Mick Jagger were near-neighbours.

As a relatively well-off single parent, Jane could afford a nanny for two-year-old Kate: hence the engagement of Christine Burridge, a naive teenager from the north-east who, like Phileas Fogg's servant Passepartout in *Around The World In Eighty Days*, had any expectations of a settled existence shattered when, within days of arrival at Cheyne Gardens, she was told to prepare Kate for an immediate flight to Paris. If overwhelmed by the speed of events, Christine was not intimidated by her famous employer: "Jane was only about a year older than me. She wasn't a boss. She was a friend. It was a very easy relationship. She was surprised at becoming a sex symbol, but she had presence. She was busy, but she always had time for Kate. The whole reason why we were in Paris was because she wouldn't leave Kate in London."

Ensconced with Christine and Kate in Hotel Esmeralda on the heavily-policed Left Bank, how could Jane have visualised that she was about to become a bigger star in France than she ever had been back home? A year earlier when she was riding along on the crest of *Blow Up*, nothing may have been further from her mind. It had been feasible – as Jane would say herself – that if she and John Barry hadn't parted, she'd have ended up as a housewife.

For the same reason that she might have quit acting altogether, she was to theorise that "perhaps people leave home because they're a little afraid of the competition". Precedents in the realm of pop included British one-hit-wonder Vince Taylor who, concentrating on the possible, had become a huge attraction as France's very own Gene Vincent rather than continuing to joust vainly against the Cliff Richards in the UK Top Twenty. Likewise, lack of UK interest in The Downliners Sect, Greater London contemporaries of The Rolling Stones, was at odds with impressive chart strikes in Scandinavia where they were briefly ahead of The Beatles, circa 1965.

If destined to last far longer than the Sect and, arguably, Vince Taylor in her particular foreign field, Jane Birkin did not get off to an auspicious start when she met *Slogan*'s male lead just before the opening shoot. As in the most hackneyed romantic novel, hackles rose during the star-crossed lovers' first encounter; Birkin begging to differ when Gainsbourg expressed doubts about her command of French. While conceding that her timorous prettiness measured up to the requirements of Evelyne – "Not bad at all, *zat leedle* English girl," he confided to Pierre – there was no immediate sexual tension between them when their eyes met through his cigarette smoke.

On location in St Tropez, Grimblat's concern that the spirit of bad grace had not evaporated combined with the ongoing anarchic mood to necessitate a heart-sinkingly familiar postponement of filming and the scattering of its retinue like rats disturbed in a granary. Gradually, however, the tempest dropped in every sense. Though his lips might not have moved upwards yet, Serge's eyes began smiling almost gently upon Jane who would discover herself shivering with delight. Her reaction was not lost on him during off-camera conversations when they each let slip more about themselves. Among public signs that a courtship was in progress was Gainsbourg, mixing business with pleasure, squiring the former Mrs Barry to a London performance of *Hair*, the hippy musical that had garnered much press attention for the nudity that closed the half before the interval, and spurred its investors to discuss with the composer of *Anna* the possibilities of him adapting it – under the provisional title of *Poil* – for a season at the Théâtre De La Champs-Elysées.

These negotiations came to naught, but every subsequent day of Serge's visit drew Jane and he more inescapably into the same radiant current of feeling. From having simply intrigued her, Gainsbourg's hold on Jane tightened after she tapped the vulnerability within this Fascinating Older Man's brash outer shell. "I soon realised," she would recount, "that all the things I'd taken to be aggressive were actually the self-protection of someone infinitely over-sensitive, terribly romantic, with a tenderness and a sentimentality which people don't see. One day, he told me he was a 'counterfeit bastard' – and it's true." This had been evidenced when, on his return to Paris, her new boyfriend fired off an immediate telegram of undying adoration to Cheyne Walk – and, over the next decade, its recipient would treasure it amongst talismans of such import as her mother's rabbit's foot, and one of Kate's baby teeth.

Like it had been with Bardot, Serge was taken with a disarming self-possession that would not permit him to be bothered by a past that had produced another man's child and displayed Jane naked to the world. Nevertheless, jealous imaginings wracked him when, prior to the resumption of *Slogan* in Venice that September, he followed Jane back to St Tropez where she had slotted in the stop-gap *La Piscine*, a movie demanding her submission to on-screen kisses with ubiquitous photogenic hunk Alain Delon.

Birkin, however, wasn't as troubled by Brigitte Bardot's kindly offer to put up Christine and Kate in her Cote D'Azur villa, far more comfortable and private than a hotel less luxurious than the Biblos where Serge and Jane had booked themselves a suite large enough to contain a grand piano. Indeed, a sister-like harmony was to pervade Birkin and Bardot's dealings with each other, even when they were flung together unclothed in a bedroom scene in a mid-1970s movie. "I lay there next to her," said Jane, "and looked over her every inch and couldn't find a single flaw. Then to make me feel good, she told me, 'Your nose is prettier than mine.' It isn't, but it was sweet of her to say so."

Any emotional misgivings by Jane over Bardot being the muse for 'Je T'Aime...Moi Non Plus' were outweighed by its commercial potential, albeit bolstered by the composer's burgeoning if inflated reputation as a Don Juan. "Imagine it," he bragged, "I've jumped all the most beautiful girls in France."

At least he had the tact to re-record the number rather than simply wiping Brigitte's vocal off the old backing track. Fluttering around his husky sentience – the sound of a man who has been sprinting – Jane's cavy-like peep – dreamy sighing rather than BB's more earthy approach – was oddly appealing in its conveyance of such brush-strokes of enunciation and inflection that a fractional widening of vibrato could be as affecting as another's most anguished wail.

Supervised by Jack Baverstock, a Philips house producer more *au fait* with beat groups, much else was accomplished during the studio time remaining at the same London session in November 1968. Taped with the same brisk finesse as 'Je T'Aime', '69 Année Erotique' had lyrics that, to paraphrase Willie Dixon's 'Back Door Man', the men know but the little girls, they don't understand – and a melody made more captivating by a bass guitar counterpoint and, typifying Gainsbourg's "English" period, "holy" organ and close-miked vocals.

More specifically, just as Bach's 'Minuet In G' had run through 1965's 'A Lover's Concerto' by The Toys, and Beethoven's 'Moonlight Sonata' through The Shangri-Las' 'Past Present And Future', so a Chopin prelude did in 'Jane B', earmarked as B-side to 'Je T'Aime...' – though the words, remembered Christine Burridge, came from a source less cerebral: "Serge looked at her passport – 'Jane B(arry). English. Age...' and so forth – and that was his inspiration to start. She's been found dead by the roadside and someone's reading out these particulars."

Jane's excitement about her disc debut was tempered by anxiety about how her nearest-and-dearest would react. *Blow Up* had passed muster with her parents, but this might press a little too hard on the nerve of their broad-mindedness. Better safe than sorry, she let her mother get the gist of 'Je T'Aime...' – very nice, dear – but lifting the gramophone needle before the acetate span to the racier bit.

"I don't know. What do you think?" was the attitude during Philips' upper echelon's weekly scheduling conference as the more time-serving recording managers tried to gauge the Head of Artists and Repertoire's opinion about proposed releases before committing themselves. They battled for control of their features during 'Je T'Aime...' before agreeing to the its issue on forty-five (on the Fontana subsidiary).

Unheeded had been someone's argument that it would be better for the firm's image as purveyor of decent music for decent folk if 'Je T'Aime...' could be consigned to one of these worth-the-whole-price-of-the-LP tracks on a Gainsbourg-Birkin collection that, as it turned out, would be a rushed job, a cobbling together of songs previously recorded by such as France Gall and Françoise Hardy, a couple from *Anna* and new ones that included the ragtime '18-39' and 'Orang-Outang' which harked back fleetingly to 'Ford Mustang', a fast cross-breeding of tango and march from *Le Bardot Show*. Too late for selection was Serge's half-completed *Lolita*-esque narrative about a character called "Melody Nelson".

While Birkin was as omnipresent and as increasingly coercive a "constant companion" as Bardot, she had also replaced her predecessor artistically as main transmitter of Gainsbourg's compositions in the studio. After fulfilling existing contracts – like 'La Fille Qui Fait Tchic Tchic' for Michèle Mercier – he cut back on writing for anyone other than Jane and himself. As late as 1975, 'Rocking Chair' had been intended for Isabel Adjani after she and Gainsbourg had been on the sofa on the same TV chat show. As his work with Birkin had fired her adolescent ambition, Adjani was to be most disappointed when Jane commandeered the song and kept it under wraps for three years before putting it onto one of her own solo albums.

By then, there was less lust in Serge than when he'd first clapped glad eyes on Birkin, but 1969 had, indeed, been an erotic year for them. Three was often a crowd as their public canoodling went beyond the bounds of acceptable ickiness. There they were, flaunting their shame before the snip-snapping media at first nights, exhibition previews and at dinner in Maxim's, sharing a joke with Dali.

Getting it slightly wrong, *France Soir* had screamed "MARRIAGE SURPRISE FOR SG: FOR HIM SHE LEAVES HER HUSBAND!" in November 1968 after receiving the distressing news that Gainsbourg and this English hussy were living together along Rue Des Beaux Arts in the gabled Hotel d'Alsace – where Oscar Wilde had met his Maker in 1900 – while decorators put the finishing touches to the Rue de Verneuil residence.

There were, however, no old-fashioned looks when the two shared the same bed *chez* Birkin when Jane took Serge to London to meet the family. However strange a choice this Frenchman may have seemed at first, parents and siblings could not help but warm to the breezy vitality of a man in middle life who was as besotted as he could be with a beautiful girlfriend eighteen years his junior – and Mr and Mrs Birkin came to like Serge enough to raise no objections when Jane – not a subscriber to Nietzsche's personal credo that marriage was incompatible with a life of steadfast creativity – announced that she was going to wed the boy. It was, perhaps, just as well that Gainsbourg was going to make an honest woman of her because, shortly after 'Je T'Aime...Moi Non Plus' left the pressing plant in June 1969, so began the concept of Serge and Jane as a Scandalous Couple on a par with John Lennon and his soon-to-be second wife Yoko Ono who had eroded The Beatles' magic for the ordinary fan via the cover photographs – John and Yoko doe-eyed and bare, front and back – of 1968's *Unfinished Music No 1: Two Virgins*. Well, Lennon had a penis, hadn't he? Who'd have thought that a Beatle could possess one of those? To say things most people didn't want to hear, the Lennons had made their lives an open and ludicrous book with Bed-Ins, Bagism and further bewildering pranks considered indecent even after Britain's recent abolition of stage censorship. With a relaxed and assured Gainsbourg's active encouragement – "I am not ashamed to show my wife naked" – Birkin posed, chained to a radiator, for a spread in *Lui*. Lending *Slogan* more fighting weight in the box-office was Jane rolling up for the premiere in a see-through mini-dress, split to the navel but revealing nothing new.

As shy-making was a measure of soul-baring in interview with either or, more often, both of the stars, but boosting *Slogan* most of all was 'Je T'Aime...Moi Non Plus' which, on 11 October, ended Creedence Clearwater Revival's three week reign at Number One in Britain during a rich season for singles originated in France. Though 'Je T'Aime...' was the first foreign language song ever to head the UK list, it finished as runner-up to Frank Sinatra's definitive version of

Claude François and Paul Anka's 'My Way' as the islands' best-selling forty-five of 1969.

"A London taxi driver told me he'd had three children to that record with Serge," Jane would laugh thirty years later. Yet the passage of 'Je T'Aime...' into the hearts of British consumers had not been without incident. With that same summer's 'Wet Dream' by Max Romeo and 'The Ballad Of John And Yoko', The Beatles' worst single, it suffered airplay restrictions and, on the BBC, an outright ban applauded by the Vatican. Furthermore, just as EMI had washed its hands of *Two Virgins*, so Fontana, afflicted with dilatory moral opprobrium, deleted 'Je T'Aime...' just after it entered the Top Ten. Bereft of such scruples, Major-Minor, an independent label launched in the mid-1960s with backing from pirate Radio Caroline, took up the slack and was rewarded – for one week only – with its sole domestic chart-topper, despite an arrangement – retitled 'Love At First Sight' – by Sounds Nice, an innocuous instrumental duo, slinking into the lower reaches of the Top Thirty.

In France alone, the Birkin-Gainsbourg blueprint shifted a quarter of a million after Disc AZ bought the rights from Fontana and rechristened it 'La Chanson De *Slogan*'. Other companies likewise reaped fat harvests in Belgium, Denmark, Norway, Switzerland and Sweden. A further symptom of 'Je T'Aime...' mania was a rash of spoofs and "answer" discs such as 'Soul Je T'Aime...' by Sylvia with Ralfi Pagan; the troilistic 'Up Je T'Aime' by balusters of British comedy Frankie Howard and June Whitfield; 'Ca' from Jacqueline Maillan and Bourvil, a Fernandel type, and a send-up by "Jane Firkin & Surge Forward" on a flexi-disc free with 1969's Christmas edition of the satirical magazine *Private Eye*. Beyond Europe, 'Je T'Aime...' incited furore in hot-blooded Roman Catholic Latin America, but advancement in the all-important USA was sluggish and slight. Even when the artists themselves were brought over in March 1970 to meet the press in New York and Chicago, the nation shrugged its shoulders and, though the most controversial single yet released penetrated the *Hot 100*, it went flaccid in *Position Soixante-Neuf*, if you'll pardon my French.

chapter nine

Gallic Symbol

Had '69 Année Erotique' been released first, it might have been the million-seller rather than 'Je T'Aime...Moi Non Plus'. It meant little outside France – where it wasn't as huge a hit as its predecessor, but a hit all the same. Nevertheless, there was no element of surprise this time round as the public, in expecting to be shocked by Birkin and Gainsbourg, weren't particularly. If self-referential '69 Année Erotique' was designed to touch up the couple's reputation for outrage, it merely entrenched them further in a tolerable if specialist niche (like Maurice Chevalier and Vince Taylor were in theirs) and facilitated an absorption into mainstream, even traditional, pop – for the song's suggestive title was belied by a pleasant mid-tempo tune and an arrangement so middle-of-the-road that one television director sounded out Serge about a re-write – as '70 Année Fantastique' – to welcome in a New Year that was to embrace Brigitte Bardot's biggest chart strike in 'Tu Veux Ou Tu Veux Pas?' ('Do You Want To Or Not?'), containing a key couplet that translates as "You want to or you don't. If you do, that's all right. If you don't, too bad".

On its way up, 'Tu Veux Ou Tu Veux Pas?' collided with 'Je T'Aime...', falling from its perch even in the most far-flung European hit parade – and that, as far as most non-French territories were concerned, was that for Serge Gainsbourg, one-hit wonder and one-trick pony. Never mind, had he so desired, he could live fairly cosily into old age – by investing wisely and exercising thrift – on the consolidated fruits of its success if he let go, stopped trying to prove himself. Serge was forty-two now, but, though most of his hair was still on his head, he looked older – as old as a man who'd been drinking every day for the past quarter of a century. This didn't work against him because, even more than the British, the French like their entertainers to be survivors, and Serge was nothing if not that. Like an old nag put out to grass, he could have settled down as a television and radio "personality", dispensing bonhomie in commercials, situation comedy or as participant or even genial host of celebrity panel games.

He could put on quite an exuberant front when required. In the aftershock of 'Je T'Aime...', he'd provided good copy: plain speaking – delivered in thickened French when abroad – as he countered inane and impertinent enquiries as reiterant as a stuck record. Exhaling a cumulus of nicotine with a sigh, his features would pinch in careful consideration of each question put to him. Even when little of any significance emerged from his lips, Gainsbourg's surrounding cortege hushed when he answered, exchanged knowing smirks, and laughed when he laughed at his own polished-up impishness.

There were other times, however, when he shot his mouth off without thinking. With Jane at an Yves St Laurent catwalk display, he found himself microphone in hand and alcohol in nervous system. Instead of routine banalities, he created a painful scene by blurting that the models were uniformly repulsive. This idea of a joke occasioned titters that became a subdued laugh and then a delirium of appalled joy with sly glances at St Laurent who had stiffened, stared hard at Gainsbourg and looked as if he was about to do something.

The next day an offended telegram was biked to Rue de Verneuil. Piling on the sarcasm, Yves was "sorry to have made you come just to see repulsive things". When the enormity of what Gainsbourg was told he'd done the night before sank in, a shame-smitten letter caught the next post.

That his stupid remark *per se* had been undeserving of the ensuing thigh-slapping mirth was indicative of how much the Gainsbourg phenomenon had consolidated – and that he was now inhabiting a world more exclusive than that of the Raymond Devos birthday shindig, and more cultivated than that of a Mars Club jam session, *circa* 1961. Yet he did not begin huntin', fishin', shootin' or like recreations recommended by those born into privilege – or then develop so voracious a zest for the social whirl that he found it necessary to hide rings under the eyes with the mirror sunglasses that were becoming a standard celebrity party accoutrement. The circles under Serge's eyes were, in any case, almost as distinctive a personal idiosyncrasy as Chevalier's perpetual boater or President de Gaulle's nose.

These and other lines on his face had been deepened by overwork rather than too much fun. Who knew when the bubble – even one as big as 'Je T'Aime...Moi Non Plus' – would burst like it had so many times before? Of all the lessons he'd learned over two decades in the music business, the most important was that you had to seize the moment and cash in for all you were worth – like Chubby Checker had with the Twist – balancing caution and thrift with opportunism and the visible free spending that went with the job of being a star.

While there was no guitar-shaped swimming pool in his back garden, head waiters would conduct Gainsbourg to the best table in Montparnasse diners where only the likes of Dali, Fellini, Hemingway and Bardot could afford to clatter cutlery on plate. With the ease of a rail commuter, he'd jet first class from Paris to a working lunch in London and back again in less than a day, brushing past the handful of freelance photographers loitering at both airports to click shutters at lucrative big name subjects.

At the taxi rank, it was a lucky driver that picked up Serge Gainsbourg – for, within the parameters of his oscillating fortunes, he'd always been known as a generous tipper of chauffeurs, porters, chambermaids, dustmen *et al*. Since the 'Je T'Aime...' windfall, he'd donated a generous sum to a cycling club team – who renamed its championship team after him – and, moved by a newspaper account of a *gendarme* killed on his beat, sent a cheque to the widow. On the assumption that he now had wealth beyond calculation, many hands outstretched to him belonged to scroungers who positioned themselves to wait outside studio, restaurant – and Rue de Verneuil, now a target for graffiti and marathon vigils by journalists and fans sinking into a languid daze induced by the fixity of gazing at the door and windows.

Serge's wallet, nonetheless, would often hold less hard cash than any beggar may have imagined. Small change was as unnecessary to him as eyesight to a monkfish because menials took care of minor purchases, and he never had to prove his identity to sign bills for the larger amounts he paid for paintings by Dali, Paul Klee – and the English surrealist Francis Bacon who, on being noticed by Gainsbourg and Birkin in a restaurant, was persuaded to autograph a 100 franc note to be framed and hung on their living room wall.

Of more intrinsic value would be the 1928 model Rolls-Royce purchased by Serge. Impressed by its tarnished splendour, but not qualified to take it on the public highway, it tickled him to sit in the front seat and smoke, thus using an expensive car as a mere ashtray. It would not emerge from its garage until he sold it ten years later – though he kept the radiator cap for old time's sake as the vehicle, nicknamed "The Spirit Of Ecstasy", had figured in the lyrical scenario of *Histoire De Melody Nelson*, a planned "concept" album – and to be, theoretically, the first LP attributed to Gainsbourg alone since *Percussions*.

He was under more pressure – from Pierre Koralnik – to complete another film soundtrack, *Cannabis*, an indifferent Cosa Nostra-drug trafficking thriller starring himself, Jane and, from the cast of *Hair*, Paul Nicholas. Also, Gainsbourg had had a pen pushed into his hand to sign a contract that lumbered him and, again, Jean-Claude Vannier with responsibility for the soundtrack for a second 1970 movie, *The Horse* – and solely himself with the labour of refashioning and elongating as incidental music a children's song for *Un Petit Garçon Nommé Charlie Brown*, a cartoon of the US comic strip, *Peanuts*. The number that needed his attention had been written by Rod McKuen, a Californian who was Jacques Brel's principal lyrical conduit to the English-speaking world.

Significantly, the *Cannabis* tie-in album bore only one *bona fide* Gainsbourg-Vannier song, and the *Charlie Brown* effort was, frankly, banal – though perhaps that was almost the point. For Gainsbourg, the process of composition was more difficult these days. He'd try to stimulate his muse by drugging himself with challenging books – Defoe, Baudelaire, Rimbaud, JK Huysmans, Leon Bloy (no, I've never read anything by him either) – often several at a time. Once, he'd had non-stop inspiration, but now, if he wasn't careful, he'd hear himself going through the motions with detached efficiency, exploring buzz-words and musical formulae over and over again like an alchemist of old repeating the same experiment, week in, week out, in vain hopes of making gold.

While the same old themes developed new properties and thus steered clear of actual stagnation, Gainsbourg suspected that he'd bitten his talent down to the quick. More and more, he'd suffer writer's blocks as he slumped over the piano keys. Hours would trudge by without a trace of melody or lyric. All the particles of song would sound the same. Languor would set in, and Serge's mind, bathed in tedium, would drift off to the refrigerator, the TV, the drinks cabinet and bed.

The spirit was willing, but he lacked – for the time being – both financial motive and the hunger to create. Moreover, he'd been told by his doctor to take things easier after the onset of respiratory difficulties, groggy awakenings unconnected with alcohol, and a visage that stared vacantly back at him from the bathroom mirror with the sapped parchment-like pallor of one who eluded sunlight and, if left to his own devices, was prone to nourishing himself only with snacks for days on end.

As yet, nothing specific could be diagnosed apart from the clinical depression – constant slight headache, irritability, knotted-up stomach, drop in energy, loss of appetite and all the rest of it – that was common enough amongst forty-something men. All Serge could do was slow down, relax and let time do the rest. Nevertheless, expecting the worst, he couldn't forestall the foreboding that afflicted itself on him as he built up a damning picture of his state of health before placid denial that there was anything to worry about. Maybe he was panicking unduly.

Yet, with a relief that he did not articulate, at least a token adherence to Seneca's *pars sanitatis velle sanari fruit** maxim had him eating regular meals, sticking to daylight hours and gladly devoting more time to Jane and his and her respective relations: visiting a seldom-seen Liliane in Casablanca, and, in spring 1970, appearing with Joseph on *Mon Fils Avait Raison*, a series of studio interviews with fathers and their famous sons involving questions like "Did you have any influence on his career?". The Ginzburgs and Birkins were on amicable terms, and Serge, Jane and Kate were to spend that Christmas in England, inviting brother Andrew over to Paris in the New Year.

* *The wish to be well is the first step towards health*

If no longer a beginner in the movie game, Andrew Birkin welcomed opportunities both to converse with and learn from his sister's fiancé, and, through him, to study and compare the masters of French cinema first-hand – for Serge and Jane were now mixing with directors of the calibre of Poitrenaud, Grimblat, Claude Berri, André Cayatte – and Alain Resnais, maker of *Hiroshima Mon Amour, Last Year In Marienbad*, 1968's *Je T'Aime, Je T'Aime* and other widely distributed but elusive – and typically French – character dramas liked by film buffs but not by anyone who wanted only to be told a story.

Though a real-life incident when Jane (to her eternal embarrassment) bled over Alain's immaculate white sofa might not have been out of place in his *Providence* in 1977, Birkin and Gainsbourg were to make no films for Resnais – and only one for Cayatte, *Les Chemins De Katmandou*, with Jane as a "hippy chick", Renaud Verly as the hero and Serge as the short-haired, moustachioed Bad Guy. The appeal of this unremarkable movie mattered less to Jane and Serge than the all-expenses-paid trip to a location in Nepal – where they were snapped in a rickshaw, starry-eyed with love – and the chance to break the journey back to France with a stay in India.

For their services, Jane as female lead was paid one fee and Serge – whose name was in smaller letters on foyer placards – another. As it would be with Madonna and her first husband Sean Penn, Birkin was the drawing card and Gainsbourg part of the package. Already there had been rumblings from one French tabloid that "It's impossible to see Jane on the screen without having to suffer Gainsbourg".

Even if room hadn't been found for him in the cast, Serge would be around, watching Jane act on a monitor screen, and monopolising her during the lengthy intervals as cameras were repositioned. Most of her roles were in comedies shot in France, but 1971's *Romance Of A Horse Thief* required four months in Yugoslavia, the nearest that director Abraham Polonsky could get to turn-of-the-century Poland without the complications of crossing too far beyond the Iron Curtain for this object lesson in how a product's lack of substance could be concealed with a large budget and employment of the famous; among them Birkin, Yul Brynner and Oliver Tobias (another *Hair* veteran).

At a loose end whilst waiting to play his tinier role, Serge negotiated headlining parts for himself and Jane as World War II Resistance fighters in a domestic production, *19 Djevojaka I Mornar*. Things started to go wrong from the first day. Agitated debates with director Milutin Kosavac would have crew and supporting actors exchanging nervous glances as they sloped off for another unscheduled coffee break until the flare-up subsided to a simmering huff.

One day, it scaled such a height of vexation and cross-purpose that Gainsbourg, to illustrate that he'd had more than his fill of Kosavac and his wretched country, lit a cigarette with a Yugoslavian bank-note – roughly the equivalent of an outstretched arm salute with finger across the upper lip in Germany. A deathlike hush ensued for an eternity of seconds. There was no answer to such an insult – not in words anyway. Police arrived and, during the subsequent discussion, it was thought prudent for Gainsbourg to catch the next flight out as soon as his contracted participation in *19 Djevojaka I Mornar* was over.

It wasn't all smiles back home either. On 22 April, Serge had been shaken from his dreams by a telephone call from sister Jacqueline with the news that sudden heart failure had just taken their father on a seaside holiday a bare week after his seventy-fifth birthday. After the funeral, Joseph's beloved and duteous son took care of all the expenses – including that of the interment in the same Montparnasse graveyard as Baudelaire and, later, Sartre – rather than by the coast, too far for Olia as she became increasingly more immobile with arthritis.

No requiem would be composed for Joseph Ginzburg. Instead, Serge cried his tears, then cartharsis and a dull ache signalled a return to work. First on the agenda was the ballad he'd written for *Romance Of A Horse Thief*. Unavailable to a record-buying public, 'La Noyée' – a kind of French 'Carrickfergus' – was borne by Gainsbourg's own Floyd Kramer-like descending inversions, crushed notes and syncopations on a convenient piano during a taped chat with a journalist in 1972. 'La Noyee' was, he said, tailor-made for Yves Montand, bruited as a second Chevalier since the old fellow's easeful death on New Year's Day. Montand didn't consider it suitable, but Juliette Gréco would be only too pleased to record 'Le Sixième Sens', the last song Gainsbourg penned specifically for her. In Serge and Jean-Claude's backlog of commissions too was sorting out musical tableaux *à la Bardot Show* that would consume both sides of Zizi Jeanmaire's forthcoming in-concert album from the Casino de Paris.

This resurgence of songwriting activity for outside parties may be rooted in the return to artistic form that washe *Melody Nelson* project. It can been seen now as bridging a gap between late 1960s *magnum opi* contemporaneous with *SF Sorrow* by The Pretty Things – the first "rock opera" – and *Sgt Pepper's Lonely Hearts Club Band*, and, with *Tubular Bells* setting the syncretic and expensive standard, the "works" of the mid-1970s: albums as a continuous unity teeming with interlocking themes, leitmotivs, segues, "second subjects" and all that.

Over seven tracks (two of them nearly eight minutes long), *Histoire De Melody Nelson* hung on a specific and recurring mood that was more far-reaching than simply stringing together an assortment of ditties about cars as The Beach Boys had done in 1963. Like *SF Sorrow*, The Kinks' *Arthur* and The Who's *Tommy*, *Melody Nelson* was technically a song-cycle rather than an opera.

One of the most detailed sexual fantasias since the poet Guillaume Apollinaire's posthumous *Ombre De Mon Amour* in 1948, it began with a person much like the composer in a Rolls-Royce. He knocks Mme Nelson, a fifteen-year-old redhead, off her bicycle. This extreme if unintentional method of introduction leads to a passionate affair with attendant entanglements connected to the age gap between the protagonists. An arrangement to meet in a hotel – in Christine Burridge's home city of Sunderland of all places – is thwarted by Melody perishing in a plane crash when the automatic pilot misreads the dial panel.

In cold print, it seems a flimsy foundation for fifty minutes of needle-time, but, swathed in scorings for a fifty-piece orchestra, sight-reading pop musicians and a choir of seventy, the forceful gusto of its quirky grandiloquence convinced most reviewers that it was irrefutably a more credible and integrated classical-rock fusion than Deep Purple's over-ambitious *Concerto For Group And Orchestra* of the previous year. Granted a sneak preview, one critic's claim that it was "the truest symphonic poem of the rock age" had triggered meetings about a post-Christmas television spectacular based on the album, perhaps not the most suitable viewing for a nation sleeping off its seasonal revels. Just as Apollinaire portrayed his mistress Marie Laurencin as a child-woman with a skipping rope, so Gainsbourg had

Jane Birkin in mind as his eponymous nymphette – despite the advance of a pregnancy disguised on the blue front cover of *Melody Nelson* alongside a Serge now unashamedly as stubbled and unkempt as he was behind closed doors.

He hadn't stood any nearer either his razor or a comb that January at MIDEM, the annual international music industry exposition in Cannes. Provoking more comment, however, was his intended second single of 1971, one-riff 'La Décadanse'. For all its implications of shadowy thighs and lewd sniggering, the new album's 'Ballade De Melody Nelson' forty-five had been less obvious an attempt to reconjure the 'Je T'Aime…' commercial magic than the new dance Gainsbourg had devised with its off-colour directives for the male to gyrate with his groin pressed against his partner's bottom and his hands over her breasts. Because it was by Serge Gainsbourg, 'La Décadanse' was not regarded by those who'd enjoyed *Melody Nelson* as the aural equivalent of some distasteful movie. It might even have been Art. Claude Berri thought it was, and seized it for his forthcoming *Sex Shop* comedy. Art or not, 'La Décadanse' was without question a flop – because only the truly rash would cavort to it – and disco fever as a commodity had yet to sashay to its John Travolta zenith.

The attempted pulling of another 'Je T'Aime…' stroke, however, was still sufficient at MIDEM for stick-mikes to be thrust towards Serge's mouth to maybe catch him putting his foot in it like he had at the Yves St Laurent event or for any zany merriment about whether he and Jane had named the day. They'd better get a move on, hadn't they?

Nothing had been decided by May 1971 when Jane, seven months into her confinement, was holidaying on the Isle of Wight with Serge and Kate. She remained in England to go into labour on 21 July in a private clinic in London as, in the days before fathers were encouraged to attend births, Serge with Uncle Andrew whiled away the waiting with a couple of drinks – and a couple more and a couple more after that…

A virus picked up by Jane in Yugoslavia necessitated the removal of her and her new daughter, Charlotte, to a better-equipped hospital in the suburban calm of Middlesex. A less pressing worry was that, according to British law, illegitimate children could not bear the father's surname. His pride stung Gainsbourg had assured the press that he and Jane were to marry in spring 1972 – adding, with a puckish grin, "six months after the birth of the baby", in case anyone couldn't count.

Lucien ("Lulu") and his twin
sister Liliane in 1928

Olia and Joseph Ginzburg in
1919, shortly after exile from
Russia to France

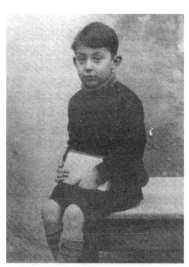

Lucien with his *croix d'honneur*
for attainment at school

A Jewish teenager at war: Lucien was
concealed in a woodshed during a
Gestapo descent on his secondary school

Serge with Brigitte Bardot, jackpot
of all lotharios, 1960

Serge and Beatrice shortly after their
marriage on 7 January, 1964

France Gall with the composer of her
Eurovision Song Contest winner,
Naples, 21 March, 1965

Gainsbourg's 1960s stage act was
inconsistent. When he was bad, he
was very, very bad

"Evelyne" (Jane Birkin) and her leading man get acquainted in *Slogan*, 1968

Juliette Greco Chante Serge Gainsbourg

John Barry, Jane's first husband, gets to grip with another "James Bond" soundtrack

Jane, Kate Barry and Serge in 1969

1971's *Histoire De Melody Nelson* was the first album to be attributed to Gainsbourg alone since *Percussions*

Charlotte Gainsbourg with Papa, summer 1971

En famille. L-r: Nana, Serge, Jane, Kate and Charlotte in Cannes

In the 1980s, Isabelle Adjani released an entire album of Gainsbourg items

Françoise Hardy's 'L'Anamour' was the first of many Gainsbourg titles she would record

The lyric of 'Je T'Aime...Moi Non Plus' was inspired, reportedly, by a one-liner from Salvador Dali

In the early 1960s, a commission to write for Zizi Jeanmaire was a considerable feather in Serge's cap

Joe Dalessandro, Warhol "superstar" and male lead in *Je T'Aime...Moi Non Plus*, Gainsbourg's first essay as film director

L-r: Jane, Charlotte, Serge and Kate at home, May 1978

The gangster and his moll on the *Top A Gainsbourg* TV spectacular, 4 May, 1974

Catherine Deneuve was a source of solace in the weeks after Jane left him

Now a mainstay of French "contemporary" rock's ruling class, Serge restored the years subtracted from his age long ago by a publicist

Serge and his old crony Coluche, shortly before the comedian's death in June 1986

Serge and Bambou, a new lady friend, share a joke

L-r: Kate, Charlotte, Jane and Serge together again in 1986 after the 'Lemon Incest' business

Virtuoso reggae exponents Sly Dunbar and Robbie Shakespeare were nicknamed "mes chimpanzees" by Gainsbourg during the *Aux Armes Et Caetera* sessions

Besotted with Bambou, Serge was initially blind – or indifferent – to her shortcomings

April 1989: Serge had been terrifying in his wrath following an attempt to kidnap Charlotte

November 1988: Serge and his two-year-old son with Bambou, the second Lucien "Lulu" Ginzburg

A pensive moment in April 1989

Serge in a setting similar to that outlined decades earlier in 'Defence D'Afficher', September 1988

Serge is enraptured by the nymphette allure of Vanessa Paradis at a *Victoire de la Musique* presentation, February 1990

chapter ten

Love For Sale

The anticipated crowds were too much for Jane who cried off on the day of a Paris wedding that had to be rescheduled and the new date kept secret from a nosy world. Only members of the immediate family attended a ceremony that they'd stopped talking about by the time the press got wind of it, and bride and groom were back at work; Serge in a film short, *La Dernière Violette*, directed by Just Jaeckin as a dry run for *Emmanuelle*, 1974's sequel-spawning movie, lauded by default as an erotic classic and, like the earlier (and more pretentious) *Last Tango In Paris*, believed to be so by those who never saw it.

Meanwhile, the new Mrs Gainsbourg and Brigitte Bardot were naked in bed together in Roger Vadim's *Don Juan 1973 Ou Si Don Juan Etait Une Femme*. Under the editorial lash, it must have occurred to many a muckraker that, with the same man in common, the situation contained potential ugliness; the worst case scenario being the scoring of catty points off each other culminating in quarrels you could hear all over the set, varnished fingernails raking faces before an ebbing away that left the combatants livid with hatred, glowering at each other from the opposite ends of a make-up room, and muttering conspiracy to respective sidekicks. Instead, there was less altercation than amusement and light banter from the girls who, required by Vadim to croon softly to each other, chose 'Je T'Aime...Moi Non Plus' – what else? – after rejecting Brigitte's suggestion of 'My Bonnie Lies Over the Ocean'.

'Je T'Aime...' was to enjoy a further few weeks in the UK hit parade when reissued in 1974 by Antik through the offices of the British singer Dave Dee who ran this Atlantic subsidiary. This second coming gave Gainsbourg's bank balance a welcome shot in the arm, but, gazing at the gold disc it had earned first time around, he wondered how much longer it would be before returns on even this, his greatest hit, diminished. Frank Sinatra would never cover 'Je T'Aime...' – or any more likely Gainsbourg compositions – like he had 'My Way', the song that had bought Claude François his mansion near Fontainbleau.

As a recording artist too, Serge was being overtaken domestically once again by contemporaries nearer his own age such as the irrepressible Dalida – back on top with an arrangement of an ancient Greek fisherman's song, 'Daria Diradada' – and in English-speaking territories by Charles Aznavour who was about to charge further ahead with two huge hits, 'The Old Fashioned Way' and, Barclay Records' most lucrative international earner, 'She', his theme for ITV's *Seven Ages Of Women*.

Sacha Distel's best-remembered moment outside France had come with 1970's ambulant 'Raindrops Keep Falling On My Head' from Oscar-winning *Butch Cassidy And The Sundance Kid*. While he was not to make much more than the mildest ripples afterwards, he retained his pulling power in cabaret throughout the globe – unlike Adamo who, though million-selling 'Petit Bonheur' confirmed his status as a national pop attraction, could not duplicate this feat to any large extent in other areas.

What did it make Serge Gainsbourg when Adamo at thirty was regarded as a pop Methuselah by teenagers? Yet that the likes of Adamo were still forever on TV screens, on sell-out barnstormers or blaring from radio and juke-box, only stressed the sense of impending hangover in Gallic pop. *The* hit song of 1974 in France was to be 'Sugar Baby Love' – shooby-doo-wahs, insane falsetto and spoken bridge passage – and its perpetrators, The Rubettes, touted in the media as "*les nouveaux* Beatles".

Just as these white-capped Londoners had shut down a translated cover, so other failed heists of British chartbusters were symptomatic of creative bankruptcy. By the mid-1970s, no less derivative talent surfaced that measured up to any of the older contenders who, like the aliens clogging up the charts, were – for all the "good" foreheads, chicken necks and belts loosened to the last holes – intriguing an adolescent market, envious of their unquiet pasts.

Serge and Jane's younger sub-divisions of kindred may have helped keep them abreast of the latest developments during this slow moment in pop's turbulent history. The Rubettes had been glam-rock latecomers, and, though punk rock precedents were being forged by The Ramones and their sort in New York's twilight zone, and The Sex Pistols' exploratory rehearsals in London, there was little of the hysteria and craziness that keeps pop alive in 1974 – unless you counted such desperate pastimes as headbanging and streaking.

Only the whoosh of an occasional aeroplane was needed to remind the Gainsbourgs of the squalid holocaust of pop over the hills in Paris, London, New York and Los Angeles during holidays with their extended families on the Isle of Wight, on Cap Camarat just outside St Tropez, and other places chosen for their distance from the rest of the world. Beneath such untroubled skies, the jubilations and ordeals of 'Je T'Aime...', *19 Djevojaka I Mornar et al* could be reduced to matters of unimportance.

Nevertheless, settling down to cheery lassitude in which nothing much was guaranteed to happen, year in, year out, was not to be the path for Serge Gainsbourg and Jane Birkin. Films alone took them three years into the future. Without exception, the ones they did together – like *Trop Jolie Pour Ete Honnetes*, *Les Diablesses* and 1975's Bunuel-esque *Serieux Comme Le Plaisir* – had husband subordinate to wife in the acting credits.

However, Serge did not resent being "Mr Birkin" as Sean Penn did to becoming "Mr Madonna". Neither had he minded when, in 1973, Jane starred in another film, *Projection Privée*, without him, and was singled out by Philips to make solo records, albeit with himself at their creative helm. As epitomised by the use of one of the rude *Lui* shots on the sleeve of *Lolita Goes Home*, her second solo album, this strategy had more to do with Jane's status as France's adopted sex siren than her singing.

Her debut in this capacity, *Di Doo Dah*, caught one of the currents of post-Woodstock pop in that it sailed the primarily acoustic waters of what was called "self-rock" if you liked it, and "drip-rock" if, like *Melody Maker*'s Allan Jones in a scathing article, you didn't. All you had to do was sit on a stool and ululate "beautiful" cheesecloth-and-denim ballads with lyrics that could make listeners embarrassed to be alive, not forgetting to emit a small, sad smile every now and then. The idea was to sound so bound up in yourself that every trivial occurrence or emotion was worth reporting in song to the entire planet.

Once more, European pop was taking its cue from the States and adjusting as best it could, not quite getting the point sometimes. As the Royal Couple of the US wing of the genre were James Taylor and his missus, Carly Simon, so the most serious applicants for the job in France were Serge and Jane. On the surface, *Di Doo Dah* had as low a dynamic and as yawnsome an ennui as Taylor's *Mud Slide Slim*, David Crosby's *If I Could Only Remember My Name, Four Sides Of Melanie* and like drip-rock classics.

If far less well-mannered and precious, *Di Doo Dah* was as self-obsessed too as many of its tracks – all penned by Gainsbourg with help from Jean-Claude Vannier – may be seen to address real or imagined aspects of the vocalist's personality and incidents in her life – her youth as a *garçon manqué* (tomboy) in the title song; inflating condoms – 'Les Capotes Anglaises' – and sending them soaring from a balcony, and getting chucked by a boyfriend via a postcard ('La Baigneuse De Brighton'). Elsewhere, there's the most un-Melanie-like suicidal hitch-hiker of 'Help Camionneur'; the lonely one of 'Leur Plaisir Sans Moi', desired only for her body; a comparison of differing methods of kissing in 'Mon Amour Baiser'; the girl on a 'Kawasaki' motorcycle, and the erotic dancer of 'La Cible Qui Bouge'.

Musically, the LP embraced lush melody on the 'C'Est Ca Vie Qui Veut Ca' finale; a raw guitar introit to 'Encore Lui' that hinted at The Troggs' gloriously dim 'Wild Thing', and dark 'Ode To Billy Joe' strings on the title song – but, overall, *Di Doo Dah* was glutinous with plodding "laid-back" tempos and the seemingly obligatory swirls of steel guitar that plagued every other album heard in university campuses in the early 1970s as the "twanging plank" disco bass would on records directed at the same market group a decade later.

Whilst jumping on this bandwagon, Gainsbourg could not help but impregnate it with a little individuality – a Mozart-like coda here, a tangle of jazzy electric piano there – and, with his customary patience, instigate minor tracking and miking experiments – such as the dual-tracked (rather than double-tracked) singing on 'Encore Lui' – and encourage the prizing of endearing imperfections as much as squeaky-clean meticulousness.

Within her limits, Jane too had functioned as effectively, even stretching herself to the top of her range in 'Banana Boat', just as Twiggy had refined her cockney squawk to something more euphonious when she too had been pushed in front of a studio microphone. Jane, however, needed no Professor Higgins. She was advantaged too by having a songwriter with her best interests at heart: "He was describing somebody he knew well. It was himself, another side of him. He couldn't sing [the songs he gave me] himself because that would be somehow *impudique*, so he gave me all the pain to sing – which was strange and difficult. He wrote in one of them, 'One day you'll know that I gave you the best of me' – and he did. He liked to sing provocative songs and he gave me the sad ones."

Whilst not refuting Jane's professional commitment to her records or her wherewithal to acquit herself admirably in the vocal isolation booth, she had climbed to so high a plateau as a film actress that Top Forty success was not as crucial to her as it was still for France Gall. Unable to get a hit to save her life by the mid-1970s, she'd turned once more to Gainsbourg who gave her 'Les Petits Ballons' and 'Frankenstein', numbers she'd disliked but needs must.

It was the end of a line too for Jean-Claude Vannier who, tired of his role as Gainsbourg's sidekick – and with an inner ear cocked to the far-off roar of the crowd, insinuated to his manager that it might do no harm if he struck out as a recording artist in his own right. Without rancour, Serge alone understood perfectly the frustrations of being in someone else's shadow – and Jean-Claude was pleased for his old partner (and a little flattered) that collaborators of the calibre of Jean-Pierre Sabard – Jacques Dutronc's arranger and conductor – Dutronc himself and the lyricist Philippe Labro were among those who would attend to functions that he, Vannier, could no longer fulfil for Gainsbourg.

One of the last Vannier-Gainsbourg compositions was 'L'Amour En Privé' for Françoise Hardy to sing in *Projection Privée*. She'd also been recipient of a congratulatory note from Serge on the birth of her son Thomas in May 1973 in the American Infirmary in Neuilly where Paris bleeds into the countryside.

The message had been sent from another ward where Gainsbourg was recuperating after a coronary brought on through a culmination of unusually high-spirited escapades dating from a fancy dress ball at the Union des Artists on 5 May where, in the arrow-patterned garb of a convict, he'd been persuaded, apparently, to perform a song whilst balanced on a tightrope. Ten nights after that, he'd reeled into Rue de Verneuil just as roaring drunk – and straight into a row with a wife exploding with anger and irritation at being jerked out of her dreams by his noise.

He awoke hours later in agonised bewilderment at a tightness across the rib-cage, and his entire body vibrating with shuddering gasps, every pore on his ashen complexion bestowed with a pinprick of sweat as his exhausted heart came to a near-standstill. To the agitated clang of an ambulance bell, he was hastened, breathing like a bellows, to hospital. Off the danger list by the following afternoon, his sticky eyes parted as if slit with a knife. There was a whisper of a smile as his hand tightened in Jane's. Neither a hypochondriac nor malingerer by nature, a rise from his half-death became more perceptible as he flirted with the nurses and joked with doctors who spoke to him as if he was a retard whilst gingerly prodding his body as if it were some dead sea mammal stranded on a beach. Gruesomely hilarious remarks hid the downcast and shaken man beneath to everyone but Jane for whom the old-young creature looking towards her with his arms out still had every appearance of being seriously unwell despite reassurances that he was on the mend.

After three days of visits by expected well-wishers, the patient wondered why the gentlefolk of the press weren't disgracing themselves in pursuit of some mean scoop concerning his condition. Where were the journalists disguised as staff or the snap-shotters perched diligently in trees, their long-distance lenses trained on what an educated guess said was his window? Where were the "SERGE'S VEGETABLE EXISTENCE IN ISOLATION WARD!!!" headlines or even just a stray paragraph born of alarmist conjecture? Why wasn't anyone interested in his brush with eternity?

Recovery sat ill with wounded pride, so *France Soir* was offered an exclusive bedside audience with the 'Je T'Aime...' superstar. The reporter who'd drawn the short straw scribbled quotable jocularities about how the interviewee had hovered between life and death, and what cardiopulmonary procedures had winkled out about the cause of his seizure: high blood pressure, organic deterioration and extensive arterial blockage. He'd been prescribed, he said, a course of drugs; the avoidance of stressful situations; a regime of bland food and – as far as he was able – abstention from booze, and, generally, the living of a boring life for a while.

The tallest order of all had been to cut back on and, eventually, give up tobacco. During a long convalescence with Jane in a villa she'd purchased in Brittany, he insulted her intelligence by persisting in denials that he was smoking in secret against all the evidence of yellow fingers, and the fag-end that had defied flushing, floating in the toilet bowl. Though it upset her, she stopped making an issue of it back at Rue de Verneuil when he stopped pretending and was inhaling, wheezing and spluttering quite openly and so often that anyone looking at a drawing of him by Charlotte would be drawn at first glance to the giant cigarette she'd put in his mouth.

Before she was out of nappies, Charlotte could not have helped but become aware of Papa's celebrity, even if he was no longer the chart assailant he used to be. The million-selling Calvary that was 'Je T'Aime...' seemed like a previous existence in 1974 when thirty thousand copies would be the best that his latest album, *Vu De L'Extérieur*, could shift. Even with punk on a distant horizon, shock tactics weren't what they were, what with the mid-1970s vogue for situation comedies fraught with innuendo about wogs, poofs and tits, and now that glam-rock had undermined sexual stereotyping so that cross-dressing and overtly camp mannerisms on the pop stage did not mean automatic uproar. Alice Cooper – glam-rock from the charnel house – had violated ultimate taboos in 'Dead Babies' and 1973's 'I Love The Dead', and Frank Zappa's albums were attracting, for better or worse, a wider audience in their drift from incisive aural junk-sculptures towards the lavatorial "humor" that informed *200 Motels* – his only major essay as a film director – and such masterpieces of song as 'Don't Eat The Yellow Snow' and 'Titties And Beer'.

As well as sharing Zappa's workaholism, Gainsbourg had a similar penchant for viewing eroticism as more of a fundamental expression of everyday life than the pseudo-courtly tweeness of drip-rock. Like Frank too, neither did he baulk at capsizing in song any assumptions that humans could only be gratified sexually by the plain-and-simple "missionary" position, without mechanical appliances and only with other humans.

Chimpanzees, orang-utans and other apes were more prominent than the artist on the photo-collage packaging of *Vu De L'Extérieur*, a collection that, however obliquely, opened a veritable Pandora's box of "kinky" predilections, dwelling on such as inflatable dolls, coprophagy, the carnal aspects of farting and, in the title track, anal sex and a couplet that ran: "You're beautiful seen from the exterior/It is a contrasting story for me, the one who penetrates to your interior." However, an outburst of female sobbing towards the end of 'Je Suis Venir Te Dire Que Je M'En Vais' – from a text by Verlaine – may be ascribed to emotional rather than physical pain as this heartbreak ballad with its twinkling piano arpeggios was innocuous enough for Gainsbourg to sing on prime-time television when playing "Le Prince" in *Le Lever De Rideau*, a drama screened in November 1973.

This plug prompted the song's release as a promotional single, a loss leader as a deceptive incentive to buy an album that a righteous, God-fearing brouser in a record shop couldn't handle without wishing he'd worn rubber gloves. Yet, if you were pining for a bit of smut, the general effect of *Vu De L'Extérieur* was disappointingly tedious – like being cornered at a party by the sort of pathetic fantasist who, with any given situation an avenue for grotesque unholier-than-thou verbal exhibitionism, fills each unforgiving minute with sixty seconds of drivelling toilet talk and lies about what he'd got up with girls who'd never give him a second glance. As the evening progresses, his voice gets shriller, the language coarser and face redder before he staggers off to vomit.

You could view this sordid slice-of-life as a metaphor for the remainder of Serge Gainsbourg's life and work. In the years left to him, the increasingly more outrageous content of his output – to the point of overkill – kept track with a physical decline that had accelerated after that first heart attack that had left him green about the gills for so long afterwards that not a note was to be commercially released under his own name throughout 1974. Furthermore, only two new compositions

– for a Jane Birkin forty-five – registered with SACEM other than 'Les Petits Lolos De Lola', unrecorded but featured in *Top A Gainsbourg*, a television spectacular transmitted on 4 May.

Serge's participation in national radio and TV broadcasts was still considered a feather in the cap of the most coolly professional programme planner (particularly if Jane Birkin was part of the deal). Moreover, his rebellious behaviour during a topsy-turvy career in mainstream pop had not been regarded by *Top A Gainsbourg*'s investors as a preparation for a graceful old age as a French showbusiness treasure, but as the whole point of Gainsbourg now that *Vu De L'Extérieur* had made the blood of transfixed adults run cold, even if their children considered him a has-been. Provocation was, like, Serge Gainsbourg's gimmick.

Thus he was was given *carte blanche* with respect to presentation and guest stars, but rather than raise eyebrows, he opted for scripted and non-controversial ad-libbing with Jacques Dutronc (jovial voice of experience to cheeky young shaver) and Jane to preface the three's crack at 'Les Petits Lolos De Lola' – while Jane and Françoise Hardy tackled 'Les Petits Papiers', the Régine A-side from 1965. A spot by comedian Guy Bedos was the icing on the cake of a rather routine extravaganza that lacked the diversity of *Le Bardot Show* of blessed memory.

As run-of-the-mill as *Top A Gainsbourg* after its fashion was *Les Diablesses*, after he'd passed the medical examination required by the insurers of a venture in which he sat in his usual backseat to Jane as an actor. Yet if rather attempting to restore the balance by supplicating for the job of penning the soundtrack, he occupied idle hours on location thinking about the overdue follow-up to *Vu De L'Extérieur*, calculating what form of wickedness to explore – and exploit – next.

Vu De L'Extérieur had been a mountain for Philips' press office, but 1975's *Rock Around The Bunker* was an entire range as big as the Alps. How did one go about petitioning a radio disc jockey to spin something called 'Nazi Rock', the opening track of an album in which old Serge had sunk his teeth into another attention-grabbing assortment of connected and purposely tasteless topics. More so than its predecessor, every number was potentially a branch on which to hang him – for he'd made a pop record of the ill-formulated doctrine that had changed Europe forever via the invasion of its countries, the genocidal atrocities of the Final Solution and an aftermath that had bisected the continent into east-west zones as contrasting as the Moon to the Earth.

Like a feminist comedienne might imagine that she could crack a sexist gag with impunity, so Gainsbourg's obligatory wearing of a yellow Star of David during the war gave him, he felt, the credential that justified *Rock Around The Bunker*. How were you supposed to take it? Is it on the level? Was a track like 'Est-Ce Est-Ce Si Bon' a hymn of praise to the SS or should it be appreciated in the same spirit as 'Springtime For Hitler' ("winter for Poland and France"), the overture to the play-within-a-play in Mel Brooks' black comedy, *The Producers*?

Just as Brooks had considered the Third Reich good for a laugh, so Serge had represented the SS in both 'Tata Teutonne' and 'Nazi Rock', as sodomites, respectively an unsavoury brute and dancing queens in make-up and black stockings. The intention, he said, was to aim sarcastic missiles at the SS and associated bullseyes, whether Hitler (in 'Eva' and the descriptive 'J'Entends Des Voix Off'); the exile starting at shadows in 'SS In Uruguay', or, less specifically, contemporary neo-Nazism absorbed by such as white youths with Prussian haircuts – called "skinheads" in Britain – attracted by a distorted patriotism that masked terminal racism.

Unhappily, wit was too easily lost on such people as illustrated a year later by David Bowie's outspoken – and ironic – public remarks about the Führer being "one of the first rock stars...and, yes, I believe very strongly in fascism" that many of his fans were to accept at face value.

Bowie's fellow English glam-rock colossus, Bryan Ferry – then linchpin of Roxy Music – had been on the radio all over Europe in 1974 with a reading of the Jerome Kern warhorse, 'Smoke Gets In Your Eyes' that dissolved outlines between quality and *kitsch*. One of Hitler's mistress, Eva Braun's eternal favourites (and one that drives Adolf to distraction in 'Eva'), it was brought into play by Gainsbourg a year later as a barbed instrument (and the first non-original in his recorded *oeuvre*) of *Rock Around The Bunker*'s thematic continuity.

Present with her brother at the sessions, Jane Birkin would recall Serge's working method as "the most exciting thing we'd heard, the way he wrote, the way of carrying one word on to the next line, a bit like Cole Porter, and the thing of double meanings". As always, his lyrics – like dadaist poems – were less evocative on paper than in delivery. The jazzer of yore peeping out, the emergency of the moment rather than premeditation induced astounding instances of, say, the dragging out of vowels; seizing upon the onomatopoeic *ratatatata*s of 'Tata Teutonne', say, or the *"ombe"*-sounding syllables in 'Rock Around The Bunker' itself, and sliding together sibilant "s" sounds on 'Est-Ce Est Ce Si Bon'.

Back in the studio later that year for Birkin's *Lolita Go Home*, Serge arrived in London with hardly anything prepared and hoping for the best. He'd hit a blind spot over lyrics, but was able to supply some rough ideas (such as that for 'French Graffiti', set in a public toilet) when delegating responsibility to Philippe Labro – who was to piece together a mosaic of words for the seven Gainsbourg melodies that mingled with Birkin revitalisations of oft-recorded standards such as Cole Porter's 'Love For Sale' and 'There's A Small Hotel' from Rodgers and Hart.

During this period, most of the favoured accompanists on Gainsbourg and Birkin records – and, incidentally, those of Charles Aznavour – were British. From a pool of regular helpmates, Serge called the shots most often to guitarist Alan Parker and keyboard player Alan Hawkshaw. Having learnt his trade as one of Emile Ford's Checkmates and in Tony Sheridan's post-Beatles backing group in Hamburg, Hawkshaw was one of the first dyed-in-the-wool rock 'n' rollers to emerge as a familiar figure on the London studio scene – while Parker had ministered to recent hits by Blue Mink, Family Dogg, CCS and Elton John.

This versatile pair had also been together in Rumplestiltskin, a failed "supergroup" drawn from session circles in 1969. Since then, serving comparative unknowns like Hungry Wolf, Laurie Styvers and Terry Durham had been a springboard to proudly augmenting the more prestigious likes of Donovan, Hank B Marvin of the disbanded Shadows, Alan Price, The Strawbs, the reformed Walker Brothers, Chris Spedding, John Williams – and Serge Gainsbourg who requested their presence to help with music pertinent to his debut as a film director.

The genesis of this development lay in a chance meeting in Cannes with Jacques-Eric Strauss, a movie producer of consequence who had seen and liked *Top A Gainsbourg*. "I got the impression that all the ideas came from you," was his correct assumption during an opening gambit that contained a sentence that had left Serge round-eyed with amused disbelief: "Anytime you want to make a film, get in touch with me." When convinced that Strauss had been completely serious,

Gainsbourg gave substance to a scenario he'd been toying with since 1969 by mapping out a detailed outline after consultation with screenwriters he knew.

Among these was Andrew Birkin, on the rebound from 1975's *Flame*, a vehicle for Slade, a glam-rock outfit who were Wolverhampton's as the Beatles were Liverpool's. "Andrew came on the road with us," recalled guitarist Dave Hill, "to get a feel of what we were like and see what went on – because we wanted something with real stories in it. There are some bits in *Flame* that are very true to life that embarrassed people in the music business as they exposed things they were trying to cover up." Pragmatism as much as *Flame*-like realism pervaded a proposal with the working title of *Je T'Aime...Moi Non Plus* that Gainsbourg submitted – initially as a comedy – to Jacques-Eric Strauss. Its bare bones were the adventures of two homosexual truckers on reaching a small town where a van selling burgers and soft drinks is manned by a free-spirited English girl (to be played by – you guessed it – Jane Birkin). Her nickname – "Johnny" – and face devoid of cosmetics causes the younger driver, Krass, to mistake her for a boy. A mutual attraction has him rubbing his hands metaphorically at the prospect of a tryst in a hotel room. Prior to the men driving away in the final reel, episodes include Krass's slighted male lover attempting to kill Johnny in a bath, and herself shrieking as she's subjected to unlubricated buggery.

Sounds hilarious, eh? Shortly after cameras began to roll, it had become clear that *Je T'Aime...Moi Non Plus* adhered no longer to its original light-hearted treatment, and that, though the odder sequences might provoke laughter, it had mutated into a taut drama that sought to leave an aftertaste of despair. That's as maybe, but while it might hold appeal for intellectuals who, via some complex inner debate, might have tuned into its frank low-life aesthetic, it belonged also to a public that patronised a celluloid sub-culture of seedy flicks with titles like *Whipcord Girls* and *Gay Boys In Bondage*.

Commercial pornography or meaningful socio-sexual comment, *Je T'Aime...Moi Non Plus* was, reckoned Donald Thomas in a 1992 biography of the Marquis de Sade, reflective of "a hero exalted elsewhere in Weiss's *Marat-Sade* or by a critique of fascism in Pasolini's *Salo Or The 120 Days Of Sodom*".*

* The Marquis De Sade *by D Thomas (Virgin Publishing, 1992). When the jokes got sick after Pasolini was murdered by a rent boy in 1976, some wag suggested that the Italian director himself had engineered it as a publicity stunt for* Salo Or The 120 Days Of Sodom

Nevertheless, though the latter example – Pasolini's latest (and final) movie – had been on general release in France when *Je T'Aime...Moi Non Plus* was on the drawing board, Gainsbourg had received more obvious stylistic wisdom from other doyens of extreme cinema such as Bunuel, Malle, Warhol, Jaeckin, Bertolucci – maker of *Last Tango In Paris* – and Jacques Rivette whose work was characterised by both a preoccupation with paranoia and despondency, and rigorous scissoring by the censor.

Though its defenders argued that Rivette's *La Religiouse* attacked godlessness, France had washed its hands of it altogether on grounds of blasphemy – and, while *Emmanuelle* had slipped the net, Britain had banned 1975's *The Story Of O*, Jaeckin's sado-masochistic fantasy in which a woman allows herself to be enslaved, whipped and branded. "A third of the films produced in France in the mid-1970s were mediocre soft-porn," concluded Domenique Hoff of London's Institut Français, "and *The Story Of O* was the culmination. It shows how far we were in terms of bad taste. The chance to treat sex in an interesting way disappeared because of films like this."

Beset with misgivings about *Je T'Aime...Moi Non Plus*, certain of Jane Birkin's payroll courtiers had hoped to talk her out of it. However, while loyalty to her husband might have been one factor that bound her, another may have been that *Je T'Aime...Moi Non Plus* was more challenging fare than the mostly cheeky but intrinsically non-confrontational – some might say insipid – roles that had been her lot since *Slogan*. "I got plenty of film parts," she agreed, "but it always felt like I was being given a head-start in a race because of my bad French. Nobody ever said, 'Oh Jane Birkin, she's a great actress.' It was more a case of 'Oh, she's so sweet' – and there came a time in my life when that was no longer enough."

One of few similarities between the majority of Jane's "safe" movies and *Je T'Aime...Moi Non Plus* was a good-looking leading man. Joe Dalessandro had been a "superstar" in Andy Warhol's interesting-but-boring *Flesh-Trash-Heat* trilogy: all hand-held cameras, extemporised dialogue and the sexual flexibility that was crucial for Dalessandro's type-casting as "Krass".

If Joe and Jane's simulation of sex in front of the cameras bothered Serge, it was not evident throughout the autumn shooting in the coastal district around Uzes in the south of France. Riding roughshod over any petty jealousies were trepidations about his hitherto untried skills as a director. Having loaded total responsibility upon himself, he had never been out on a longer limb. Yet the fledgling film-maker kept wobbling confidence in check, even in the teeth of criticism that his approach seemed as off-hand as it was in the recording studio – as if he was making it up as he went along.

There was, indeed, a degree of improvisation *à la* Warhol, and scenes that may have seemed like a good idea at the time. Nevertheless, production staff were often stunned by Gainsbourg's learned recommendations about rhythm and pacing, and, also deduced from comprehensive shadowing of Poitrenaud, Koralnik *et al*, his use of expressions like "field", "gate" and "aperture" as applied to a camera.

Instances of technological naivety were noted too, but gleaning what he could by trial-and-error, shape and outcome shone through with increasing clarity after he lay down the "cut!" megaphone, rose from the canvas-backed chair with his name printed on it, and repaired to a darkened room for post-production travail that meant weeks of daily scrutiny of each reel, frame by frame, during interminable re-runnings of each celluloid mile.

He had less reason to wring his hands over a chore with which he was vastly more conversant. The *Je T'Aime...Moi Non Plus* music blasted open memory banks in its exhumation of the old, old melody – for solo pipe-organ, as a reverberating Shadows-type exercise in metallic guitar picking, and, the circle unbroken, an arrangement that surpassed Sounds Nice in blandness – for Serge was enough of a soundtrack shellback to know that nothing must divert attention from the action.

Sung by Birkin, a haunting new composition, 'Ballade De Johnny Jane', released on forty-five as a taster for the soundtrack LP, was known to a smaller faction within the audience at the premiere in central Paris on 10 March 1976. As popping flashbulbs floodlit his and Jane's entrance to the cinema, Gainsbourg cut an impressive "movie mogul" figure, but once inside, he was barely able to contain a tension unrelieved by the almost palpable wave of goodwill that washed over him as he took his seat and the lights dimmed.

chapter eleven

The Oldest Teenager In The Business

Most of the morning papers found much to praise in *Je T'Aime...Moi Non Plus*, and in Paris alone, nearly 200,000 attended showings. Yet no deluge of further directorial contracts for the silver screen thumped immediately onto the Gainsbourg doormat, but it was flattery of a kind that, correlated with the film, the first offer arrived for him to appear in a TV commercial.

While the cash proffered was a powerful factor in his acceptance, the notion of endorsing biros, consommé – and lemonade for gawd's sake on the small screen appealed to his sense of the absurd as maybe an apotheosis of Pop Art nihilism via its paradox of earnest fascination with the brashest of trash culture. Warhol's soup cans were the conspicuous tip of an iceberg of mannered revelling in hard-sell advertisements, Top Forty radio, soap opera, lurid escapist cinema, comics, glossy magazines – indeed, any modern artefact dismissed generally as silly, vulgar and fake.

Gainsbourg had been there already with *Hercules Unchained*, the Eurovision Song Contest, *Charlie Brown*, you name it. Why not go the whole hog like the poet Gordon Comstock capitulating to a "proper job" in Orwell's *Keep The Aspidistra Flying* – or, for that matter, Andy Warhol ending up as a bland media personality with an interesting past? Perhaps that was nearly the point.

Apart from anything else, the process turned out to be quite fun: the sloganising, the gimmicks, the hype, the cramming of everything a merchandiser wanted said about a product into even less space than a two-minute single. Assisted by longtime collaborator Babeth Si Ramdane, he began directing commercials as a sort of hobby – or, more pragmatically, whenever there was a worrying tax demand – like there would be in 1981.

Four years earlier, a single, 'My Lady Heroine', had sprung from a commission for Vogue, but the zenith – if that is the word – of Serge's entanglement in advertising was donning the smartest of suits and clearing his face of stubble to peer enormously from hoardings plastered all over France next to a caption translating as "A suit can change a man, can't it, Monsieur Gainsbourg?". That his name was invoked likewise to sell a cheap make of razor was an ironic comment on a fully-fledged public image – not entirely assumed – of an almost wantonly unshaven and open-necked scruffiness.

Far harder to capture in a photograph was the aura of sexual malpractice that some insisted they could sense effusing from Gainsbourg as others might the "evil" from child murderer Myra Hindley's eyes. It was something he and everyone else to whom notoriety had accorded charisma had come to identify when, in this bistro or that bar, strangers on distant tables spoke in low voices and glanced towards him, and the most familiar hail-fellow-well-met conversationalists on adjacent stools would fall suddenly silent and stare for a steady split-second, wondering if he was real.

Since *Vu De L'Extérieur*, Serge had not discouraged such moments when he, say, presented himself as a sex maniac on the telephone to Jane Birkin in 'Raccrochez C'Est Une Horreur', B-side of 'Ballade De Johnny-Jane'. As the Sonny and Cher of eroticism, the couple were leading, said Birkin, an "exhibitionist and rather jolly life" then. Nonetheless, though a tabloid editor might sacrifice his soul in exchange for a fly-on-the-wall perspective of, say, the Gainsbourg-Birkins *en famille*, this may have proved too disappointingly normal – or at least too much like how the most susceptible fan might have imagined. Onsets of tickling, pillow-fighting high spirits when putting Charlotte to bed, and Serge giving his florid vocabulary its head in her presence were often the most alarming blips on the daily test-card. With Papa granting her far more attention than he had his children by Béatrice, Charlotte's infancy, if as privileged as her mother's, had been as undramatic and as free of major traumas as the restrictions of her parents' celebrity would permit. It was a period that Serge was to recognise as the nearest he ever came to contentment. For balance, there was the occasional hiccough such as the early and unexpectedly upsetting death of the family's bull terrier, Nana – named after Zola's fictional courtesan – in May 1976, and the advancing infirmity of Ginzburg *grand-maman*, now touching ninety. Though she was crotchety and prone to dispensing unasked-for advice, her Lucien was an exemplar of filial affection during her final years, visiting as often as he was able, bringing gifts and sometimes distinguished friends to pay respects, among them Marcello Mastroianni, an elderly matinee idol of an actor, once favoured as a romantic lead by Fellini, and much admired by Olia. Perhaps that's how the Serge Gainsbourg story should have finished – like an Edwardian operetta with the villains bested, the inheritance claimed, and the hero pondering a golden future with a girl at his side and a song in his heart.

During this less hectic phase of his career, songs that had less to do with Gainsbourg's heart than his wallet were demonstrative of his uncanny ability to duplicate any known musical style. A Brassens-type *chanson* for Pierre Louki? Give me till tomorrow afternoon. Something to suit Nana Mouskouri? I'm not really in the mood for Nana this minute, but if there's no hurry, I can get it biked over by Tuesday. Zizi Jeanmaire wants an album's worth of numbers for another in-concert recording? I'm fresh out, but there should be some in soon – as long as she doesn't mind sharing 'Tic Tac Toe' with Régine and doing a re-write of 'Stormy Weather' (as 'Ciel De Plomp'). If Françoise Hardy rings, tell her that her order's in the post...

Planning a next offensive of his own on the record-buying public, Serge had been investigating reggae, a marriage of rock and various shades of the West Indian pop – ska, mento, calypso, bluebeat etc – that had provisioned Desmond Dekker, Prince Buster, Max Romeo and similar upmarket practitioners with isolated hits in the later 1960s. Though a few Caucasian pastiches had been attempted – notably by The Beatles in 'Ob-La-Di Ob-La-Da' plus, more recently, Cat Stevens with 'Can't Keep It In' and, also in 1972, Paul Simon with his 'Mother And Child Reunion' – reggae had been despised by most of the so-called intelligentsia as "skinhead music" until the mid-1970s when Bob Marley and his Wailers, Burnin' Spear and Sly And The Revolutionaries were chief among those who persuaded the white collegian to swallow their neater reggae medicine.

Outflanking even blues as the new "twisted voice of the underdog" and students union disco accessory, it captured Gainsbourg's imagination just as brand-leader Marley took the form from the campus to the proletariat by placing 1976's *Rastaman Vibration* in European Top Twenties. Yet 'Marilou Reggae' on Serge's new *L'Homme A Tête De Chou* – more erudite a concept album than *Rock Around The Bunker* – did not overshadow companion tracks that veered towards other ante-punk idioms.

Given a head start over 'Marilou Reggae' with regard to exposure on the saturated December wavelengths of northern Europe, the sample A-side, 'Marilou Dans Le Neige', was countrified drip-rock: Charles Aznavour-as-James Taylor with jingle-jangle guitar, jazzier vocal phrasing and a melody not unlike Tim Hardin's 'Lady Came From Baltimore'. On the flip, the LP's title song was riven with one of these new-fangled synthesizers, 'L'Année Erotique' organ towards the fade and dirty heavy-metal fretboard picking low in a mix dominated by the spoken lyrics that were to be more and more characteristic of Gainsbourg as the years passed.

The title of "L'Homme A Tête De Chou" – and an image sustained by Gainsbourg throughout the album – had been lifted from that of a sculpture by a Claude Lalanne, purchased by Gainsbourg in 1976. Not quite the thing for Average Joe to have on a plinth in the front room, it triggered an intellectual rather than aesthetic sensation, being literally a model of a man with a cabbage head.

With Alan Hawkshaw central to its musical direction, the *L'Homme A Tête De Chou* LP had smouldered into form in London and had been issued in January 1977 to critical acclaim. Nevertheless, while it had had all the attributes of a smash on paper – and was plugged scrupulously on television – the man-in-the-street in Alençon or Avignon was not prepared to blow his Christmas record token on an LP about a chappy driven so insane by the pain of love that he imagines that his head is, indeed, metamorphosing into a vegetable, the first symptoms – as delineated in 'Premiers Symptômes' – being cauliflower ears.

Matters take an even more serious turn when he uses a fire

extinguisher to batter to death (and cover with snow-white foam) the object of his desire, Marilou who is the shampoo assistant at Max's, the local hairdresser. She is the titular subject of most of the tracks including 'Variation Sur Marilou', a seven-and-a-half minute prelude to masturbation – with a lot of funny business about Levi jeans, Lewis Carroll, "Alice" (presumably In Wonderland), "Baby Doll" and various English-language pop idols on her record-player.

Conflicting emotions beset Serge about this non-starter of an album and Jane Birkin's pidgin-English hit that spring with 'Yesterday Yes A Day' from Just Jaeckin's *Madame Claude*. This film musical, however, was swallowed up commercially by Just's *Emmanuelle* – whose unforeseen success had had Gainsbourg kicking himself as hard for rejecting a chance to compose its soundtrack as perhaps the English drummer Clem Cattini, a colleague of Alan Hawkshaw, had for preferring the security of studio work to joining million-selling Led Zeppelin. Therefore, Serge was not going to spit out another potentially *Emmanuelle*-sized bite of the cherry by refusing *Madame Claude* too. Neither did he duck out of a title song – that he sang himself – for the barrel-scraping *Goodbye Emmanuelle*.

Also promising more than it delivered financially was Gainsbourg attempting to work commercial magic on Alain Chamfort, a lean and handsomely hatchet-faced Breton who, following a three year showbiz apprenticeship as Jacques Dutronc's keyboard player, had struck out on his own in 1969 as a soul shouter of Wilson Pickett and Otis Redding's gritty stamp. While he could go down a storm on the boards, his discs didn't sell well, and with his latest record label, CBS's patience snapping, Alain pressed the bell at Rue de Verneuil. Looking him up and down, Jane decided that it might be worth her husband's while taking trouble over Alain. If nothing else, it might enable Serge by affinity to reach past the hard core who'd forever ensure that he'd get at least within hailing distance of the album list's lower rungs. The younger market that Chamfort could attract might have been intrigued by *L'Homme A Tête De Chou* had they ever heard it.

'Baby Lou', Alain's debut under Gainsbourg's aegis, left a high enough tide mark in the charts to hold on hoping – especially as it was to spawn two or three covers (including one by Chamfort's girlfriend, Lio) – but when the associated album, *Rock 'N' Rose*, failed to live up to this encouraging beginning, its composer lost heart. All the same, if wondering privately whether he'd another Dominique Walter on his hands, Serge was to continue contributing songs to Chamfort's portfolio, despite the greater fiscal import of a project more finely tuned to prevailing trends.

Gainsbourg had been invited to participate in the session booked for the taping of a revival of 'Les Papillons Noirs', the number he'd penned for Michèle Arnaud back in 1966, by Bijou, a guitar-bass-drums "power trio" in transition between heavy metal sound portraits of Genghis Khan carnage and the two-minute bursts of aural debris that were becoming common now that the punk rock thunderclap had resounded. Yet, for all punk's affected disrespect towards pop's Grand Old Men, all three of Bijou had paid assiduous attention to their guest's music from earliest youth – or so he'd been led to believe. Serge would never know for certain whether they liked 'Les Papillons Noirs' in absolute terms or for reasons connected with a feigned unawareness of the camp humour in dredging up such an old chestnut – like Bryan Ferry's xerox of Lesley Gore's 'It's My Party' (with no lyrical revision) or Marc Almond's amused 1989 remake of 'Something's Gotten Hold Of My Heart' as a duet with its neatly-coiffeured, besuited originator, Gene Pitney.

Whatever Bijou's motives, Gainsbourg approved of an arrangement enlivened by an implanted riff. He agreed furthermore not only to sing along, but also to write 'Betty Jane Rose' for the group's consideration as a future A-side. Above all, he thought them such strong musicians in their field that he was to call on their assistance in the studio* until their sundering in 1982, and help get singing bass guitarist Philippe Dauga's solo career off the ground.

Of more significance was Bijou being the catalysts of Serge Gainsbourg's first stage performance since 1965 when he'd been a poorly-received support act to Barbara. The venue was an auditorium in Epernay, seventy miles east of Paris. Ostensibly along for the ride, he had only just sat down in the dressing room when the group united in roundabout persuasion and then naked pleas for him to come on for a couple of numbers. Polite refusal, hesitation and final assent chased across his visage, but there was no guarantee that the jumpy guest vocalist wouldn't bolt at the last second.

* In the first instance for another remake of 'Les Papillons Noirs'

In the wings, Serge steeled himself to face facts, but he needn't have worried. A moment of silent disbelief greeted his nervous advance towards stage centre before a tidal wave of whistling, cheering and stamping unfurled, and Bijou blasted out the opening bars that launched 'Les Papillons Noir'. Next, the drummer counted in 'Des Vents Du Pets Des Poums' from *Vu De L'Extérieur*. A hostage to the beat, Serge savoured every moment as, like some venerable luvvie actor in a stage musical, he talked more than sang the words over thrillingly slipshod accompaniment that enhanced an impression that everything could fall to bits at the drop of a hat.

Gainsbourg's return to the footlights might not have been of the magnitude of equally long-gone Bob Dylan's at 1969's Isle of Wight Festival, but it was a triumph because the teenage audience wanted it to be. With a glimmer of how much Serge had on his plate, they loved him for wanting to please them. Who'd have imagined that the old boy still had it in him? Home and dry, he was beside himself with excitement and relief. "I don't believe it," he kept exclaiming, "I just don't believe it!"

The Gainsbourg experience was new and disquieting for the most bigoted punk rocker there on that night-of-nights. However, not a week would go by in 1977 without another fresh *cause célèbre* ringing some changes. It was usually in the form of a bunch of regional oiks making a horrible racket and being rewarded with Niagaras of appreciative spittle and a fawning write-up by a fairweather hack freelancing for a pop music journal that had sniffed the wind of change. Somehow most such outfits looked and sounded just like The Sex Pistols: ripped clothes, safety-pin earrings, slim-jim ties and guitars thrashed at speed to machine-gun drumming behind a ranting johnny-one-note who'd given himself a self-reviling name like Kenny Rubbish or, if French, maybe Gaga Merde.

From The Sex Pistols' London, the movement had slopped over the rest of Europe. France had put forward challengers in the shape of acts like Stinky Toys (formed after catching the Pistols at a Paris club in September 1976) and roly-poly Little Bob Story, whilst over in Brussels, spike-headed Plastic Bertrand – once Roger Jovret, department store salesman – was added to a meagre list of world-famous Belgians via a global chartbuster, 'Ca Plane Pour Moi'.

Less a pin-up than a favourite if rather batty uncle, Serge was one of few older artists held in any respect by the Blank Generation. As such, he inhabited an area bordered by disparate punk founding fathers like Lou Reed – former creative pivot of The Velvet Underground – Marc Bolan of T Rex, Alice Cooper – all namechecked in 'Variations Sur Marilou' – David Bowie, Screaming Lord Sutch, Iggy Pop, Bryan Ferry – and Ian Dury, an olde-tyme rock 'n' roller at heart (like *Petit* Bob *Histoire*), but described with vague accuracy in a British tabloid as "a sort of dirty old man of punk" as he sputtered in "Oi! Oi! Cockney" his explicit perspectives on London's low-life.

More Gainsbourg's opposite number in the UK than Jonathan King had been in the mid-1960s, Dury had just vanquished Patrick Duvet and his Sweet Perversions' Frankish version of his 'Sex And Drugs And Rock And Roll' when news of the death of Elvis Presley, bloated and addled, in his bathroom drew malicious cheers in a basement club frequented by Parisian punks – just as Jacques Brel's passing a year later would have a person or persons unknown risking prosecution by spraying "BREL IS DEAD. HURRAH!" along a railway cutting between Liege and Brussels.

It was a harrowing season for Grand Old Men. Marc Bolan had perished in a car crash, and the Grim Reaper would come for Keith Moon of The Who in September 1978. A few months earlier, Claude François had never been off the airwaves after the domestic accident involving high voltage that had snuffed him out on 11 March. His life – marred by divorce and maladies such as chronic insomnia – was laid bare during a media field day as "Clo-Clo" was mourned in microcosm as passionately as Elvis had been.

The years had caught up with Johnny Hallyday when a hip operation kindled dispiriting headlines discussing whether he was a has-been, but at least people were still writing about him. Where were the likes of Richard Anthony, Les Chats Sauvages and the Singing Nun these days? Nearly all the old heroes were either in the legion of the lost or sagging on the ropes now.

Exceptions that proved the rule were Dalida – reinvented as a forty-something disco diva via France's first native genre hit, 'J'Attendrai' in 1976 – and Serge Gainsbourg. The sly old rascal was to leave the 1970s on an upswing after the Epernay bash had catapulted him back on the concert bulletin, initially by affecting a Grand Entrance, admittedly after an overture of facetious comments about his age and sex life, as "featured singer", to all intents and purposes, with Bijou. The band held the stage for the first part of the set before Cecil B de Mille-sized crowds at, for example, a sports stadium in Lyons and the open-air "French Rock Mania" summer festival in Paris on a huge stage framed by sky-clawing scaffolding, giant video screens and lighting gantries like oil derricks.

Not only had he never been seen so well, but with such innovations as graphic equalizers, programmable desks and even synthesized drums winning easy victories over adverse acoustics, the notion of touring again on a regular basis was almost alluring enough to erase flashbacks of how dreadful it had been in the distorted 1960s.

While Papa was growing old disgracefully as frog prince of the punks, Charlotte was running parallel with the hormonal disturbances of early adolescence, and her mother was away in Egypt for the Agatha Christie whodunnit, *Death On The Nile*, her first British film in a donkey's age, acting alongside such celluloid legends as Peter Ustinov, Bette Davis and David Niven.

Jane and Serge's respective workloads kept them on different schedules. Frequently, they only saw each other when the edges of these overlapped. They may have had less dewy-eyed lust for each other as they entered their seventh year of marriage, but there was no trouble in paradise as yet. With his wife in mind for a major role, Serge had plugged a gap in his itinerary to draft a screenplay, *Black-Out*, for what he hoped would be his next movie as a director. This time, it'd be two women and one man benighted in a Californian town house illuminated only by car headlights owing to the power cut that would last for most of the running time.

Asked for his opinion during a weekend at Jane's place in the country, Claude Berri saw *Black-Out* as, he said, a "cinematic poem" that dwelt on characters and situation at the expense of plot – like *Last Tango In Paris*. Warming to his theme, Berri agreed that naturally his hostess should take one of the female leads. The fireside palaver continued with theoretical decision-making about the other main parts. Alain Delon would be ideal as the bloke, and, as a barometer of Birkin's status as one of the country's foremost screen queens, the role of the other girl boiled down to Isabel Adjani, now spoken of as a black-haired Bardot after she'd acquitted herself ably as the lover of a squirming alien in the psychodrama, *Possession*.

To Gainsbourg's chagrin, *Black-Out* didn't progress much further than talk (including him ruminating on it on *Les Rendez-Vous Du Dimanche*, a TV arts magazine, on 17 September 1978). Delon turned his nose up at it, and so would all the "angels" wooed for finance. Adding insult to injury, it was discovered that a Hollywood flick of the same title was well into the final stages of production.

He channelled some of his frustration into Birkin's *Ex-Fan Des Sixties* which, like the two that came before, was an ersatz Gainsbourg album by any other name. The Franglais cuteness of the title track's recurrent *"comme tu dansais bien le rock 'n' roll"* line was clouded slightly by rueful salaams to disbanded groups like The Shadows, Beatles, Animals, Doors and Moody Blues as well as mention in the last verse of the decade's pop fatalities such as Buddy Holly (*sic*), Eddie Cochran, Brian Jones, Otis Redding, Jim Morrison, "T Rex" (*sic*) and Elvis (*sic*) in a manner bereft of the sparkling conceit of The Righteous Brothers 'Rock 'N' Roll Heaven' (where "they got one hell of a band") four years earlier. Despite its name, the album was not devoted to nostalgia for the 1960s as, say, The Mothers Of Invention's *Cruising With Ruben And The Jets* had been to the 1950s. There was no lyrical interlocking *à la L'Homme A Tête De Chou* except very dubiously in Gainsbourg's now trademark focus on phonetics in 'Exercise En Forme De Z', 'Classée X' and the clever juxtaposing of 'tu', 'vous', 'tout' and 'tus' in the succinct opening verse to 'Vie Mort Et Résurrection D'Un Amour-Passion'. Otherwise, *Ex-Fan Des Sixties* flits fitfully from relationships gone sour – so sour in 'Nicotine' that there is doubt whether a lover who has popped out to buy cigarettes will ever return – virgins rising up from an ocean of blood (!) ('Le Velours Des Vierges'); the private memory provoked by 'Mélodie Interdite'; 'Dépressive' wondering if being slapped around a bit might make her pull herself together; the 'Classée X' model posing for a camera; much ado about nothing in 'Mélo Mélo', and what seems to be a lot of why-oh-why what's-the-point? mithering in a number first offered to Françoise Hardy, 'L'Aquoiboniste' (ie one who doesn't give a damn). Serge wouldn't have been Serge if there hadn't been a shovelful of sexual innuendo somewhere in *Ex-Fan Des Sixties*, most blatantly in 'Classée X'. Sparing Jane the bother, he'd come right out with it himself on his two new items for the *Les Bronzés* soundtrack. As well as orgasmic gurgling from the girlie chorus, 'Sea Sex And Sun' had a French man (who "don't speak very well English") enraptured by a sunbathing English rose with baby-blue eyes who looks sixteen "but your smile twenty-two". Drooling with lechery, he goes for the direct approach: "I would like to make love with you." It is not known how far it got him.

Young sex was more of an obsession with *Les Bronzés*' cold-hearted 'Mister Iceberg' who "likes his leedle girls in socks". Some kind of "Lolita" character had cropped up repeatedly throughout Gainsbourg's professional life – from 1958's 'Mes Petites Odalisques' onwards – and that it was he who had been chosen to read an excerpt from Nabokov's novel on the television book programme *Tiens Y'A De La Lumière* on 19 July 1975 was symptomatic of the widely-held – and undenied – supposition that compositions like 'Mister Iceberg' and 'Sex Sea And Sun' were reflective of the composer's erotic Achilles' heel.

These latest manifestations were arranged by Alan Hawkshaw. Absent from a few sessions for this, *Ex-Fan Des Sixties* and *L'Homme A Tête De Chou*, Alan Parker had been busy on two albums for Georgie Fame who, in the decade after he'd made his most prominent commercial mark, had indulged himself on subsequent records in a patchwork of different styles. 1980, for example, began with Fame's all-reggae *Closing The Gap*. That same year, a more recent British chart entrant, Steve Gibbons put out *Street Parade* which, though taped in Suffolk, had also been influenced by West Indian sounds.

Under the same spell, but with greater resources, Joe Cocker had gone as far as block-booking a studio in Kingston for 1976's *Stingray*, and both Bob Dylan and Mick Jagger were to make use of virtuoso native drummer Sly Dunbar – (the "Sly" in Sly And The Revolutionaries) and his partner, bass guitarist Robbie Shakespeare. That faintly sickening word "funky" was used to describe the economic "tightness" of this Jamaican rhythm section that – if James Brown, a bandleader of some discernment, reckoned they had no idea – were an automatic choice for other non-Caribbean pop stars wanting to dabble in reggae.

In 1978, Steve Winwood had brushed up his reggae by pitching in with Sly and Robbie on Ijahman's *Haile I Hymn*, released by Island, the record label founded by Chris Blackwell, an Anglo-Jamaican whose sheltered boyhood in Kingston's Waterloo Road had been worlds removed from the Jamaican capital's poorest suburb, Trench Town with its dirt-poor shanties and reeking squatters' camps rife with disease and swarming with undernourished children descended from black slaves. However, it had been brash Rude Boy music – notably by Bob Marley And The Wailers – from these ghettos that had been the making of Blackwell after Island declared its independence of its parent company, Philips, in 1967.

Yet Philips remained responsible for Island's distribution in France – and this was how Serge Gainsbourg and his latest console messiah, Philippe Lerichomme, were able to charge Peter Tosh, Marley's musical lieutenant until 1975, with fixing them up with a session team in Jamaica to play on the next Gainsbourg album. Percussionist Sticky Thompson and other recruits were guitarist Tosh's own sidemen while the female backing trio was none other than The I-Threes – led by Marley's wife Rita – who augmented The Wailers on the boards and on disc. Through Chris Blackwell, Serge and Philippe were introduced to Dunbar and Shakespeare, who took no offence when Gainsbourg – the first Frenchmen to employ them – christened them "*mes chimpanzees*" during the five days set aside for recording the album to be named after 'Aux Armes Et Caetera', the track selected as its first single.

With a chopping reggae afterbeat to the fore; Robbie's lithely contrapuntal bass as much a vehicle of melody as rhythm, and a lead vocal rendered almost *sotto voce* in a complex "dub" mix, it was not instantly obvious that 'Aux Armes Et Caetera' was actually 'La Marseillaise'. Written by artillery officer Rouget de Lisle as 'Chant De Guerre De L'Armée Du Rhin', it had become France's national hymn in 1792 when adapted by the new republic after pro-Revolution volunteers from Marseilles had marched into Paris to this strident rabble-rouser that had the same rat-a-tat-tatting power as 'Lillibulero', whistled and sung by the Prince of Orange's forces as they dethroned Britain's James II just over a century earlier.

The strains of 'La Marseillaise' were to be perceivable in

Schumann's song, *The Two Grenadiers*, and in Tchaikovsky's *Festival Overture* (the "1812") – while its introduction would be lifted wholesale in 1967 by The Beatles for their flower-power anthem, 'All You Need Is Love'. Gainsbourg, however, had been inspired by a facet more oblique: the phrase *"aux armes et caetera"* in Rouget's hand to signify choruses on the original manuscript (which Gainsbourg was to acquire in 1981). Of lesser antiquity – and lending itself more readily to reggae – 'You Rascal You' was an opus from the 1930s that Gainsbourg had rediscovered probably in 1978 when Dennis Potter's *Pennies From Heaven* was first broadcast. 'You Rascal You' was amongst other breezy 1930s dance tunes that commented on the action in this widely-networked television series. Appealing to Serge were its odder propinquities such as 'Whistling In The Dark' while anti-hero Arthur stands trial for the murder of a blind girl; 'I Like To Go Back In The Evening' in the condemned cell – and 'You Rascal You' when Arthur's wife dances on his grave and consigns him to imaginary hellfire.

From Gainsbourg's own catalogue came eye-stretching revivals of 'Le Javanaise' and the 'Marilou' theme (as 'Marilou Reggae Dub'), and new material, much of it completed during an overnight flight from Paris to Kingston where he landed with a stockpile of compositions, whether detailed demo tapes or nebulous ideas computed in his brain, that was too immense for one album.

Remaindered items would include 'Nagusa Nagast', a glance in the direction of Haile Selassie, lately deposed emperor of Ethiopia, known as "The Lion of Judah" and worshipped as a living god by dreadlocked Rastafarians, a religious sect given to Bible readings, dope-smoking and back-to-Africa sermons. It didn't do to provoke this, Jamaica's most feared sub-culture, so Gainsbourg was urged to amend a reference to Selassie as "a dark idiot" to "a dark idol". Nevertheless, as he was less ignorant about humble "Lola Rastaquouère Rasta", her tale of selling her body for immoral purposes was untouched in any of the spoken verses or sung hooklines.

Lyrically, the rest of *Aux Armes Et Caetera* was the expected mixture of sleaziness – hotel rooms let by the hour with the body smells of others still lingering in the sheets in 'Les Locataires' – sickening imagery – urination and breaking wind in 'Eau Et Gaz A

Tous Les Etages' – and fixation on particular syllables – *"ool"* in 'Relax Baby Be Cool' – and words – *"des laids"* (the ugly ones) and *delai* (delay) in 'Des Laids Des Laids'. One man's view of his immediate world, it alluded also to coming up for a breath of marijuana-tinted air in 'Brigade Des Stups' and close acquaintance with the parochial lasses immortalised in 'Daisy Temple' and, of course, 'Lola Rastaquouère Rasta'.

The accompaniment to the latter piece typified the *Aux Armes Et Caetera* music. Reggae's light and space rather than its jerky intensity was the watchword. Yet passages of double-time neo-military cross-rhythms stirred up mixed visions of tribal ceremonials and the output of London's Adam And The Ants, who were about to dominate European charts on injecting the most palatable aspects of punk with a massive shot of West African chanting and percussion as mooted by The Sex Pistols' former svengali Malcolm McLaren. During a self-imposed exile in Paris in 1979, he had been collating blue movie soundtracks from public domain archives that contained the spell-binding abundance of Third World sounds that, after he washed his hands of pop management, was to inform his initial promotion of none other than himself as a recording artist.

This had been on the agenda when Gainsbourg, back from the West Indies, joined McLaren for a restaurant dinner. While this rendezvous unharnessed a common sense of humour, it did not presage what might have been an interesting collaboration. Life was too short. Serge had said as much in 'Pas Long Feu', the song selected as *Aux Armes Et Caetera*'s penultimate track. It stated too that when his time came, he'd be glad to go.

chapter twelve

Gainsbourgmania

In the shops by April 1979, Gainsbourg's LP earned a platinum disc within six months. The premeditated reconstruction of 'La Javanaise' gave off a peculiar afterglow – especially if the song had nostalgic significance for those ageing Swinging Sixties adolescents who'd been lovestruck and irresponsible when first they heard the dusty old 1963 EP. Yet it was as if this consumer group had willed *Aux Armes Et Caetera* to soar high in the album list as concrete proof that you didn't have to be under twenty-five to be cool.

While absorbing sufficient of current fads not to turn off older fans, to those young enough not to have fully grasped who he was, Serge was seen as neither a dotard old enough to be their grandfather nor the-oldest-swinger-in-town, but another hitmaker with hip names listed on his album sleeve, old-young looks, trendy "designer" stubble, a vulpine smile, hair flecked then with only a little grey, and a waistline not yet noticeably marred by middle-age spread.

Moreover, like crippled Ian Dury and rotten Johnny of The Sex Pistols, Serge was emitting much of the still-fashionable aura of fascinating depravity. "Ugliness is superior to beauty because it endures" was an homily attributed to a man who, like Oliver Cromwell, forbade the camouflaging of his physical blemishes in portraiture. There was no air-brushing out of a scab on the bridge of his nose in a couple of deadpanned publicity photos; the nerdy spectacles that irritated it into being in others, nor the particularly twisted vortex of his belly-button in one as conspicuous for the symbolism of the clock he held in his right hand – maybe an allusion to *"le temps qui passe"* of the late Brel's 'Le Mort' or "the countdown" in his lesser-known 'L'Agé Idiot' – for Gainsbourg chose also to restore the years subtracted from his age long ago by a Philips publicist.

He may have retold anecdotes from the old, old story on *Midi Première*, a noon chat show, but the items he chose to perform were both from the new album that his interviewer may or may not have heard. As Dick Dale, moth-eaten "King of the Surf Guitar", became a name to drop in grunge-rock circles after a 1993 album span incessantly on "alternative" radio across the USA, so *Aux Armes Et Caetera* lifted Serge Gainsbourg's head above the waters of mere nostalgia. He was the toast of both professors who'd bought *No 2, Juliette Gréco Chante Serge Gainsbourg et al* when students themselves, and today's freshmen who, as eight-or nine-year-olds had watched him sing 'A Boy Named Charlie Brown' on *Samedi Soir* or, in 1971 too, 'Comic Strip' with Jane on *Petit Dessin Pour Grandes Personnes* – just as their British counterparts had Gary Glitter on *Top Of The Pops*.

After some heart-searching hours with his calculator, Glitter, the fallen overlord of glam-rock had figured out too that his infant fans were now young adults on degree courses, and had staged a spectacular comeback as the *kitsch* king of the campus crowd with a set that contained virtually nothing that hadn't been a smash for him when his regained audience had been knee-high to a platform heel. Gainsbourg, however, had been resurrected on a strength of interest in his latest output that had less to do with its musical worth than how much the title song, issued as a single, annoyed staider parents.

Foreign precedents included Jimi Hendrix's instrumental disembowelling of 'The Star-Spangled Banner' that, screaming from a lone guitar at Woodstock, had been interpreted generally as a vote of no confidence in the Nixon administration. In Britain, there'd been PJ Proby's little-known arrangement of the National Anthem as a bossa-nova, but, infinitely more harrowingly us-versus-them was The Sex Pistols' 1977 original, 'God Save The Queen' – a withering blast at the royal family that almost topped the charts at the height of the sovereign's Silver Jubilee celebrations. No disc since 'Je T'Aime...Moi Non Plus' had caused so much upset in the kingdom, sparking off as it did widespread airplay bans and an advisedly "secret" UK tour by a group already subject to eleventh hour nixing of scheduled concerts by municipal burghers. As early as 1976, The Sex Pistols had been barred from appearing at the "First European Punk Rock Festival" in Mont de Marsan for "going too far". Four years on, though France was over the cultural incursion that they had spearheaded (and its grubbing music industry had stolen punk's most viable ideas), it was hardly surprising that, even if Gainsbourg's 'Aux Armes Et Caetera' forty-five was more Proby than Pistols musically, senior civil servants, retired admirals and their ilk took a dim view. Voicing their complaints, a leading *Le Figaro* columnist laid into Gainsbourg in the June 1979 edition, thus increasing the volume of the outcry and counter-argument. Suddenly, his 'Aux Armes Et Caetera' was everywhere, encroaching on public consciousness to the degree that it was fodder for comedians' gags, and its most vehement critics would be vexed at hearing themselves humming it.

Catching it on the wireless or on *Midi Première, Les Rendez-Vous Du Dimanche* and other TV spots by Gainsbourg, indignant listeners – mostly war veterans – telephoned their protests, stinging receptionists' ears with words like "desecration", "unpatriotic", "disgrace" and "repugnant". What more did Serge need to do to be the toast of teenage France? He was now its Mirabeau, Robespierre and Napoleon rolled into one now that it seemed that punk, if superficially riveting, had been doomed always to be ineffectual, to not change a damn thing. Nevertheless, masquerading as lions of justice, striking a blow for decent entertainment for decent folk, some roughnecks had tried to re-sculpt Johnny Rotten's face with a razor during the 'God Save The Queen' episode. Back in the 1950s, Nat "King" Cole had been beaten up by segregationalist fanatics midway through his act in front of a mixed-race audience in North America's so-called "Bible Belt" – and, following media sensationalisation of John Lennon "boasting" that his outfit was more popular than Christ, The Beatles' tour of the States in 1966 had broken box office records below the Mason-Dixon line, despite – or because of – public bonfires of their records there, picketing of shows by Ku Klux Klansmen and the possibility of an in-concert slaughter of one or all of the group by divine wrath (or someone acting at the Almighty's behest). Closer to home, Jacques

Brel had invited similar trouble in 1959 after fellow Belgians had been offended by his, 'Les Flamandes', a *chanson* that could be seen to represent them as ignorant and servile.

When the viper in France's bosom took *Aux Armes Et Caetera* on the road with his Jamaican musicians, initial reaction was unnervingly subdued. Apart from isolated catcalls and tongue-tied autograph-hunters panting up to the likes of Rudolf Nureyev, Françoise Hardy and other luminaries slipping unobtrusively into the night afterwards, ten days at the same Paris venue, Le Palace, passed without incident: no frustrated strategies by nasty pieces of work who wanted to make everything else nasty too.

That this run* had sold out in advance boded well for ventures into injun territory next month when the furthest-flung provincial leg of the tour took in Strasbourg, the key Rhine valley port in Alsace-Lorraine where the European Parliament meets and, more relevant to this discussion, where de Lisle had been stationed when he wrote what became 'La Marseillaise'. Before that, there was Marseilles itself – where the most murmurous section of the crowd were so determined to hate the main event that the show was called off. Then it was like that clichéd movie sequence of dates being ripped off a calendar to a backgroup of clips taking chronological liberties and mixing enthusiasm and venom...a standing ovation in Lyons...police intervention here...a bomb threat in a Holiday Inn there...a matinee added in Brussels to cater for demand...and a slow dazzle prefacing Strasbourg!

A certain Colonel Jacques Romain-Desfosse, president of the Union Nationale Des Anciens Parachutistes (Section Alsace), shuddered to think of the consequences if the city's mayor didn't order the cancellation of the performance on 4 January forthwith. Attempted peltings of the singer of this 'Aux Armes Et Caetera' nonsense with decayed fruit and more odious projectiles might be the least of it. His Worship compromised with a burly phalanx of stewards beneath the lip of the stage in case the latent energy of the masses erupted into something as ugly as the Nat "King" Cole fracas or the murder that climaxed The Rolling Stones disastrous free concert at Altamont in 1969.

Anxious in the press compound, Jane Birkin – for once, less of a focal point than her husband – was to recall that Serge – with sound

* *Where a double-album,* Enregistrement Public Au Théâtre Le Palace – *and a spin-off single – reworkings of 'Harley Davidson' and 'Docteur Jekyll Et Monsieur Hyde' from the Bardot period – were taped*

reason – "thought the extreme right were going to kill him. They were waiting for him – and so were the Paras too. It was so frightening that he told the Rastas to stay in the bus, and he went on stage alone. He sang 'The Marseillaise' in the original version, no changes. The Paras were in the front row, and they just didn't know what to do. Some of them were standing up and saluting. They wanted to get him, but they couldn't. When he finished, he made a sign – up yours! – and walked off. He was a national hero overnight."*

That's entertainment. On the face of it, such bravado would have been tantamount to commercial hara-kiri once upon a time, but who could have resisted sticking in a pin while the enemy's hands were tied? Within minutes of his stage-crafted wind-up, the dressing room was as deserted as the Marie Celeste because, flanked by retainers, Gainsbourg had dashed pell-mell to a ticking-over limousine that would be speeding him out of Strasbourg even as the buzzing tribes shuffled out of the auditorium, having participated, however passively, in the proverbial "something to tell your grandchildren about".

The dust was still settling when Serge went to MIDEM a fortnight later, overwhelmed but revelling in a media blitz that had magnified his antics in Strasbourg like a fisherman's tall tale. Outlaw chic aside, it was almost as beneficial to trade as his 'Poupée De Cire Poupée De Son' triumph had been in 1965. First in the queue, Sacha Distel bought a novelty song for his forthcoming extravaganza at the Olympia. Among other lucrative contracts would be lyrics for Julien Clerc, both sides of a single by Les Toubins – a combo of Bijou bent – and a near-hit in Martin Circus's 'USSR/USA'.

The *Aux Armes Et Caetera* LP was coming home to roost too, Whatever the likes of Colonel Romain-Desfosse may have felt, one million Serge Gainsbourg fans couldn't be wrong, and he was to be presented with the commensurate platinum disc on the occasion of the unveiling of his wax likeness – a *poupée de cire* indeed! – in the Musée Grevin – Paris's Madame Tussauds – as a ring of press fell down on their knees with their cameras and flooded him in light.

Hot on the heels of this eerie experience was the writing of his only published book. A slim volume entitled *Evguénie Sokolov*, it was a yarn about a sick boy in hospital, whose surroundings fill him with melancholy reflections. Occupational therapy includes artwork at

---

* *To a lesser extent, so would be Yannick Noah, flamboyant and dreadlocked ex-captain of France's Davis Cup tennis team, who, with his group Urban Tribu, was to cause uproar with a politically correct rap version of 'La Marseillaise' – as 'La Reve' – in autumn 1997*

which he proves to be surprisingly accomplished – so accomplished that, on recovery, his paintings make him rich and renowned. Unhappily, this renown rests on the touch he had when infirm, and he has to recreate the same disorientated conditions for the sake of his art. Like many first-time novelists, Serge inserted an element of autobiography in the hero's Russian name and, perhaps, in drawing from his memories of a respiratory ailment serious enough to require his immediate removal to a children's hospital.

Along with the wax effigy, Gainsbourg's entry into literature crowned his return to pop prominence after the stock "wilderness years". Yet, in many ways, 'Aux Armes Et Caetera' was the final Serge Gainsbourg moment, never to return – for subsequent output and behaviour was less akin to cuddly Gary Glitter hanging on for all he was worth than a cultural equivalent of the Ancient Roman general Caius Marius who, back from growing old in exile, was elected consul by a popular party, and thus given leave to vent a remorselessly bloody rage tinged with insanity upon the Eternal City that precipitated his professional and spiritual decline.

Now a fully integrated mainstay and wanted party guest of "contemporary" rock's ruling class in France, Gainsbourg started playing up to it, dominating *soirées* with the Brooding Intensity, "penetrating" stares at whoever was addressing him; passing judgement on whatever was said in intricately-chiselled one-liners, and swinging into rambling – and sometimes contradictory – monologues full of categorical imperatives about his life, his soul and a despair that, for all his fame and wealth, was for real.

Much of the time, it was the drink talking. Jane – a handy peg on which to hang his frustrations – held no steadying sway over him any more as he began bobbing on a shoreless sea. Whatever the tipple of choice, it was but a temporary analgesic, an alleviation of the pangs of an unexplainable depression gathering in intensity. Perhaps a quarrel that may have frothed and fumed at Rue de Verneuil might brim over into fist-shaking ravings as he clambered into a taxi, and the loitering newshound on the scoop would see no reason why the episode could not be presented as a common occurrence. A more specific story went the rounds that during another row, Jane – a non-swimmer – had taken a highly-strung running jump into the Seine, and had to be rescued by the fire brigade. Therefore, while neatly sidestepping libel via conciliatory statements, the shabbiest showbiz gossip rags were able to amass sufficient ammunition to hint at sojourns in clinics to sweat out Serge's blue devils, and, less erroneously, that the Gainsbourg-Birkin fairy-tale was going wrong.

The mist of resigned despondency shrouding the couple so thickened that one muckraker's persistence squeezed from Serge, eyes bloodshot with alcoholic and emotional fatigue, a waylaid denial that he and Birkin were on the verge of separation, even as he observed covertly that the situation was draining her of her former vivacity. While the haplessness of her own gloom cut Jane ever more deeply as she listened to him fulminate and bluster home truths, he appeared to take it for granted that he was the only one allowed to flare up, have neuroses, be unreasonable – and that there'd always be another dismal morning after on which to bridge the widening abyss between himself and his wife.

By summer 1980, the gap had become too wide for either to negotiate, a situation to be summarised in song eventually in 'Le Mal Intérieur', a kind of Gainsbourg 'You've Lost That Lovin' Feelin''. As if vaguely amused by the memory, Jane would recount that "Serge told everybody I left him because he was insupportable, so drunk and so difficult, which was true. It was true that when he came home at four o'clock one morning, and he couldn't even get his key into the lock, I was so irritated that I couldn't resist giving him a little tap on the back of the head that opened up his eyebrow on the rather excessive mouldings that he had round the door. I wiped up the blood and patched him up with Scotch tape. The next day, he saw the black eye, but didn't know what had happened. 'You fell over,' I said. 'That's strange,' he said, 'people who are drunk don't usually hurt themselves when they fall down.' How true, I thought, unless some evil-minded person is standing behind you and giving you a shove. *Ce n'est pas le fairplay*, I know."

On a more even level with Birkin now that his celebrity had been upgraded, while he might drop the urbane public mask for domineering hauteur at home, he could turn on the old sweetness-and-light whereby an aeon of mutual character assassination would conclude with tearful reconciliation. In a fool's paradise, he imagined that this would be the means of winning Jane back, of re-establishing the old routine as if nothing had happened. "One day, he wrote me a song," she said. "It was a little bit sexy, a little bit sweet, but it didn't ring true. When I told him I was depressed, he said, 'Why? You have everything. You have this house. You have the children.' I said, 'I don't know why' – but it was one of those times when the inside didn't correspond to the outside.

"I suppose somebody comes along and you think you've been discovered. It's said to be a fatal age, thirty-four or whatever it was. I thought suddenly I'd been understood by somebody who realised how unhappy you were." The "somebody" was Jacques Doillon, a film director who'd headhunted her for the title role of La Fille Prodigue, a part that corresponded in many particulars with her doleful uncertainty. When Jacques offered more than a shoulder to cry on, Birkin and her daughters fled Rue de Verneuil. In a grand gesture of moral and material generosity, Serge pursued her to the hotel suite she was occupying with Doillon, pardoning what he saw as a mere fling, and bringing her a brand-new Porsche Cabriolet.

Knowing that he knew she wasn't qualified to take the wheel of a car – and with memories of the strain of life with him still fresh – it crossed Jane's mind fleetingly that the sub-text of his graciousness was a hope that, throwing caution to the wind, her delighted and careless test-drive round the zooming, funnelling traffic lanes of central Paris would terminate with squealing brakes, mangled chrome and gore-streaked tarmac.

"In fact, he never wished me harm," she'd realise after the door closed, but not brutally. While the marriage itself was irreparable, there remained a laconic affection that manifested itself in laughter at each other's fantasies, the shared recollections, the impulsive embraces, the harmless verbal reviling of each other the way old intimates do. Then there was Charlotte to consider. Whether inserting the lullaby 'Shush Shush Charlotte' on his next album or pestering Muhammed Ali, a fellow passenger on a flight to Nassau, for his autograph on her behalf, Serge was not to push his daughter into the background of his life as he had his offspring with Béatrice – who, hearing of the break-up, suggested that they meet for a chat over coffee.

While this did not bring about the reconciliation that Béatrice may have longed for, he began seeing more of Vania and Natacha, now so much of a young adult that hoi-polloi noticing her and Papa together in public may have assumed that she was Serge Gainsbourg's new girlfriend. Another candidate was Catherine Deneuve, perhaps the most crucial source of solace during those care-worn weeks when he needed to hear sympathetic noises while he flooded his mind with booze in what amounted to a wake for his marriage, feeling his anguish all the more sharply for realising how much of a void his estranged spouse had left as an adjunct personality.

Tolerating his bouts of woozy boorishness, Catherine was simultaneously an attentive audience to his disjointed mopings, a mother confessor and a massager of his aching ego. Through her too, Rue de Verneuil became less of a home-help's nightmare of leftover food, unwashed utensils, empty bottles of liquor and overflowing ashtrays. "She made sure he slept and ate," agreed Birkin, "and stopped him from walking too close to windows."

Furthermore, with Deneuve as prompt, the years without Jane began professionally with Serge trying to memorise his lines and write the music as well as additional scenes for *Je Vous Aime*, a film that coalesced elements of his own character – with director Claude Berri going so far as basing the set design on the Gainsbourg home – and Catherine's headlining role as a woman of forty looking back at the men to whom she'd once been manacled, just as Mae West had done two years earlier in her final movie, 1978's *Sextette*.

Catherine's men were played by a *ménàge* that included Gainsbourg and a young turk of French cinema, Gérard Depardieu, heard singing on a soundtrack LP that also embraced 'Dieu Fumer De Havannes' and 'La Fautive', duets by Serge and Catherine. The most popular of Gainsbourg's latter-day flicks, *Je Vous Aime* had been given an extra boost via television plugs such as a pairing of a sedate Deneuve and a Gainsbourg rather the worse for liquor.

Despite this, Catherine went shrewdly ahead with plans for her first album with Gainsbourg in charge. He couldn't prevent a little off-hand breast-beating in lush 'Overseas Telegram', sent to the very "*Post Office anglais*" as the one that had declared his love for Jane in 1969. Unfairly castigated as an ersatz Birkin LP by one reviewer, *Souviens-Toi De*

M'Oublier had strong melodies, clever if largely by-the-book lyrics and Deneuve's singing as adept as it had ever been. In short, it – like certain past Gainsbourg-associated commodities – satisfied all the requirements of a best-seller, but none that actually grabbed the public at large.

While Catherine was instrumental to Serge's domestic and artistic rehabilitation, there was no tang of impropriety – other than trivial conclusions the scum press could draw. However, after a short pause over the typewriter keys, there came printed whispers of a new lady friend in Serge's life. A young-looking twenty-one-year-old, she was named as "Bambou", a stage alias adopted at the onset of a quest for pop stardom. Vulnerable at the best of times when girls such as she gave him a second look, Serge had swung rapidly from dejection to devil-may-care jauntiness on breathing the musky air near this shapely, beautiful brunette nearly a quarter of a century his junior. As completely infatuated as aged Henry VIII had been with young and indiscreet Catherine Howard, he was in the first instance blind – or indifferent – to her shortcomings. Purportedly, she had not been immune, for example, from the temptations of stimulants more sinister than spirits and those substances that had been swallowed rather than injected in the bohemian cliques Serge had been around since the 1950s.

Arsenic rather than heroin was the poison mentioned in 'Suicide', a Gainsbourg number for Canadian vocalist Diane Dufresne in a TV thriller series. Preoccupied as he was with his new-found love, he had been lackadaisical about other overdue items. Julien Clerc was piqued at postponing record dates because of the non-arrival of the librettos commissioned at MIDEM. Finally, he bullied Gainsbourg into bringing in the unfinished items, and, with the studio staff on stand-by, stood over the errant composer until 'Belinda' and 'Mangos' took workable shape. Later, a desperate Clerc – not the world's greatest wordsmith – wrung what he could from overhearing Serge's half of a telephone conversation with Bambou, but Julien's producer felt it might be prudent to sanitise the resulting 'Amour Consolation'* before any middle-of-the-road Mister Wonderful tried it.

As if making amends for his heavy patience, Clerc was to invite Serge to join him for 'Mangos' and 'Belinda' at a concert in Paris in autumn 1980. This was a welcome break during sessions for Jacques Dutronc's new album, *Guerre Et Pets*, in an atmosphere solid with

* *Though it was to be revised five years later by Gainsbourg*

nicotine – as a trait that Dutronc shared with Gainsbourg was that he was an eternal smoker too. Another was that each could no longer take chart entries for granted.

At least they'd had them. One who'd never been there in the first place was Gainsbourg's nephew, Alain Zacman who was to suffer a flop forty-five 'Discométèque' under the *nom de théâtre* "Alain Ravaillac". It was produced by Uncle Serge – whose training as an artist was put to use too in the design of its picture sleeve. Two other Alains also featured in Gainsbourg's professional undertakings in the early 1980s. Still inseparable from Bambou, Serge was all for him and Alain Chamfort taking their respective paramours along for the ride to Los Angeles, thus mixing business and pleasure in the making of *Amour Année Zero*, Chamfort's next LP, with a crack US session crew equally at ease reading dots for Frank Sinatra as Frank Zappa. The land of opportunity had beckoned other French artists too. Several degrees from obvious bandwagon-jumping, Johnny Hallyday was thriving still on a hip sensibility demonstrated by his hiring of fashionable studios in North America, employment of resident musicians and teaming up with such as country-rock *chanteuse* Emmylou Harris with whom he was to record a bi-lingual 'If I Were A Carpenter' in Nashville in 1985. Among familiar faces that popped by when Chamfort and Gainsbourg were in California was Michel Polnareff, French pop icon since the mid-1960s, then contemplating a permanent move to the States.

Whether hirelings or visitors to the studio, few found Serge the easiest person to rub along with, concerned as he was that the time spent on Chamfort was eating into that set aside for his follow-up to *Aux Armes Et Caetera*, delayed for so long that the issue of in-concert *Enregistrement Public Au Théâtre Le Palace* had been a necessary ploy to stop marginal Gainsbourg enthusiasts drifting away to fresh entrapments. Nevertheless, another obligation prior to attending directly to his own career was the penning of *Play Blessure*, a collection for Alain Bashung, a waning star who had theorised that, in view of what 'Baby Lou' had done for Chamfort, Gainsbourg was just what he needed – and, in a manner of speaking, history repeated itself with a flush of success that was not sustainable.

Neither did Serge's own *Mauvaise Nouvelles Des Etoiles* prove to be more than a holding operation to its predecessor, even inducing accusations of artistic laziness from oracular *Rock Et Folk*, France's leading pop periodical. It has to be said that its appeal was to the sort of consumer for whom information that a preferred entertainer's latest disc is like the one before is praise indeed. While his crack at 'Overseas Telegram' might not have been out of place in the repertoire of a Las Vegas balladeer, reggae remained the dominating style, thanks to the re-enlistment of Sly, Robbie and Co, with whom it had been polished off in Nassau's Compass Point complex.

The West Indies had been assimilated lyrically too. An aural tableau of the overthrow of Haile Selassie as seen through the ganja haze of one of his Jamaican devotees, 'Negusa Nagast' had sprung from Serge running around with parochial Rastafarians during the *Aux Armes Et Caetera* sessions. However, other *Mauvaise Nouvelles Des Etoiles* tracks journeyed deeper into matters that stunned listeners with their lingering intimacy. Baby-talking 'Mickey Maousse' was a paeon to its composer's penis and the "mousse" that spurted from it...I cannot go on...but, no, as a biographer, I mustn't shun the seamier aspects of the job in hand – even the toilet paper in 'Toi Mourir'; his daughter soiling her underwear in 'Shush Shush Charlotte'; the detailing of the fleecier characteristics of women he had 'known' in 'Strike', and the more cerebrally self-centred 'Ecce Homo' – in which he likens himself to Jesus at Golgotha – and 'Juif Et Dieu' – an apparent speculation that God might be a Russian Jew like himself.

Self-obsession may have contributed to *Mauvaise Nouvelles Des Etoiles*'s self-destruction. Its commercial foundering during 1981's Yuletide sell-in coincided with the release of *Le Physique Et Le Figure*, a five-minute cinema short extolling the virtues of a brand of cosmetic, directed by Gainsbourg with assistance as usual from Babeth Si Ramdane.

More equivocal a project – or, if you prefer, more exquisite an Art Statement – was *Bambou Et Les Poupées*, a publication centred on his photographic images of Bambou. Snapped in a single eight-hour sitting, it was a pictorial essay that revelled in cold artificial colour – mainly electric blue and the faded red of plaster roses – and simulated sexual congress so surreal that it was frequently hard to distinguish where Bambou ended and her mannequin partners began.

It was, I suppose, a self-administered and more convoluted reprise of the *Lui* chapter with Jane Birkin. The stock of shock tactics was running out, and Serge was thinking aloud to anyone listening about twirling off the merry-go-round of pop and, while still able, leading a full life that wasn't dependent upon staying in the public eye and being compelled to churn out product on a regular basis. Whereas Brel had escaped to the high seas in a yacht, the most attractive option for Serge was a return to painting.

On the evidence of below-par *Mauvaise Nouvelles Des Etoiles* and that physically he was none too hale, some were speaking of him almost as if he was an old nag soon to be put out to grass. *Rock Et Folk* supported a rumour about a mysterious album he was preparing in which he would sing of the aethereal phantoms engulfing him and his own imminent demise; hearsay that he himself had fuelled through accosting death in 'Toi Mourir', 'Shush Shush Charlotte' – echoing the "you know your daddy is bound to die" sentiment of quasi-traditional 'All My Trials ' – 'Bana Basadi Balalo' from the same LP, and, with the ink still damp, 'Norma Jean Baker' – about Marilyn Monroe's gathering of final thoughts prior to ending it all. In *Libé* ("Liberation") magazine in 1982, he chose to give a cheerless interview from the imagined perspective of a suicide already in the grave. "To want to survive is a monstrous arrogance," he maintained. "The only reason for survival is to procreate like dogs do."

The majority of the terminally sick are not in bed. Like Brel in what he understood to be his final years, Serge, when he was old, seemed very much a man in a hurry – and not just because of the backlog that was piling up in his metaphorical in-tray. If as uncertain of tomorrow as the subject of Aznavour's 1971 'Yesterday When I Was Young' – the deploring of a wasted youth – Gainsbourg still shared vulgar jokes and grinned askance at the futilities of life, but now and then seemed faraway. A shadow of unspeakable misery would cross a woebegone countenance, and those in closest contact became as uneasily aware as he was that there might be as little as five, maybe ten years left before his body's final rebellion after a lifetime of unstoppable violation.

Yet still permitting himself the luxury of hope, he embarked on *Equateur*, his second movie as a director and screenwriter, in summer 1982 after drumming up a low budget from a government fund and his own coffers, and a cast from familiars such as Francis Huster, Joe

Dalessandro's stunt double in *Je T'Aime...Moi Non Plus*. Concentrated on a villainous young hero – if you get my drift – his dominatrix lover, a double murder and a hotel with all the tell-tale signs of having known better days, it stemmed from *Le Coup De Lune*, a Georges Simenon novel set in Africa, but wandered so far away from the plot that Gainsbourg was to be considered by French law to be its co-author.

Perhaps Simenon's ghostly annoyance at this mangling of his work put a jinx on *Equateur*. One leading actor, Patrick Dewaere, killed himself just before filming. During the day-to-day shooting on location in Wonga-Wonga – chosen because Serge was amused by the name – nearly everyone from the lowliest make-up girl to Serge himself was overcome to varying degrees by the feverish heat and tropical infections – notably an eye complaint – that always lurked behind the beauty of the blue lagoons, rich jungle and pearly mountains of the Congo.

That Serge was able to even bring to birth his celluloid baby was an achievement in itself, but at its official première at the Cannes film festival in May 1983, jaded and inattentive pundits could only judge what was actually set before them. A patent sitting duck for their sniping, the rubbishing of *Equateur* – admittedly, rarely very suspenseful during a slow-moving hour-and-a-half – condemned it to swift withdrawal from general circulation.

Upset but able to shrug off *Equateur* as the fortunes of war, Serge coped as he always had by drowning his sorrows and burying himself in work. On the immediate horizon was writing a sketch – a mock-up of an imagined scene from the 1930s gangster movie, *Scarface* – for the television show, *Ciné Parade*. An obvious moll to his Capone-like racketeer was Jane Birkin.

Far from facing this assignment like a dog would a bath, he found his ex-wife pleasant company. Moreover, they dealt with each other as amicably when it made as perfect sense for him to cross to London with a folder full of songs and, with Alan Hawkshaw at his elbow, assist on her new album, *Baby Alone In Babylone*, a pot-pourri of recent songs for other artists; a title narrative about a newcomer to Hollywood looking for screen stardom but confronted ultimately with the silver star of a federal police officer; the seedier 'Les Dessous Chic', and a huge residuum of new items too anodyne and "girly" for

Gainsbourg's own needs. In blue mood, Serge-via-Jane tells of lost love ('Partie Perdu'); laughing to hold tears of regret at bay ('En Rire De Peur D'Être Obligée D'En Pleurer'); a farewell message in lipstick on a mirror ('Rupture Au Mirror'), and the end of an affair that is 'Con C'est Con Ces Conséquences'. As phonetically contrived as the latter was 'Haine Pour Aime', but the bitter-sweet 'Fuir Le Bonheur De Peur Qu'Il Ne Se Sauve' spilt the guts of both composer and Birkin about the sadness of romantic happiness.

Knowledge of Serge and Jane's marital upheavals makes you wonder how they found the emotional detachment to tackle songs so close to the bone, but, like the gangland slayings in *The Godfather*, it was connected to business – good business too for *Baby Alone In Babylone* garnered a "Disque D'Or" at 1984's *Grand Prix De L'Academie Charles-Cros* ceremonies. At this French "answer" to the Brit Awards, Gainsbourg alone collected the prize and made a not over-modest speech.

He was up on the podium again that evening to receive another accolade, this time with Isabelle Adjani who had kept Gainsbourg to his half-promise made on *Les Rendez-Vous Du Dimanche* in 1975 to write her a song. As if it had accumulated interest, he dug out an entire album's worth of compositions – including 'Le Mal Interieur', arranged almost like a Viennese waltz – and cut their backing tracks in England for Isabelle to invest with her breathy lead vocals in Paris for release in the same month as *Baby Alone In Babylone*.

A recording session is not a spectator sport, but British observers who infiltrated those for the Adjani and Birkin albums were to drop into dining table tittle-tattle the snippet that the 'Je T'Aime...Moi Non Plus' cove seemed incapable of working well unless he'd got on the outside of the few drinks that rendered him neither drunk nor sober. Back in France, readers of newspapers over breakfast had seen a photo of him sporting the black eye he insisted was the legacy of a scuffle with an intrusive paparazzi lensman – though, in truth, he had no recollection whatsoever of how it had happened.

Much more morbidly spell-binding was an ostensibly routine appearance on *7 Sur 7*, an evening chat show, on 11 March 1984. In the past, he'd often knocked back more than he should to steel himself for such programmes, but had got a grip on himself somehow as soon as the autocue rolled. He'd never been as far gone like he was now as he exaggerated his usual mannerisms, and alternated between raising his voice almost to a shout and dropping it to near-inaudibility before rounding off the interview with his party trick of applying a cigarette lighter to a banknote.

His proudly unconcerned incineration of 500 francs touched a raw nerve even in households that didn't run on perpetual mental arithmetic to eke out the week's wage that this amount represented. The perplexed host eyed him and then the monitor uneasily and debated whether to storm off, effervescent with real or pretend righteous indignation. Meanwhile, up in the control room where his producer was barking excited instructions to the camera operators, it was fantastic television.

chapter thirteen

Gain-Gain

Before he died, there'd been negotiations to make Jacques Brel something more in North America via a collection of duets with Barbra Streisand. In 1989, Juliette Gréco was to give her first UK concert at London's Barbican Centre, and, as the 1990s slid out of neutral, Johnny Hallyday would be hammering on foreign doors yet with an all-English album and an intended debut at the Royal Albert Hall.

Nearly everyone else of the same vintage had all but given up. Whilst allowing that a 'Je T'Aime...Moi Non Plus'-sized smash wasn't entirely out of the question, Serge Gainsbourg was concentrating on the possible by attempting to recover ground lost in France since the market decline signalled by disappointing dividends from *Mauvaises Nouvelles Des Etoiles*. He was, it seemed, flogging a dead horse with reggae, and thus, in April 1984, he and Philippe Lerichomme traced the same scent as The Bee Gees – musical paladins of *Saturday Night Fever* – David Bowie*, Steve Winwood, Malcolm McLaren, even Petula Clark before them, to New York to conduct a field survey of the Manhattan disco scene. In cosmopolitan clubs like the 3,500-capacity Fun House, the electro-funk of Grace Jones – one of Chris Blackwell's West Indian protégés – Rufus And Chaka Khan, and Chic – whose Nile Rodgers had produced Bowie's recent US Number One, 'Let's Dance' – bounced off the walls. Madonna – another Rodgers client – had been just one more disco vocalist until 1982's 'Everybody' had been a turntable hit there.

More "street", however, were pioneering probes into the brutish

---

* *Namechecked by Gainsbourg in 'Beau Oui Comme Bowie' on the Isabelle Adjani LP*

braggadocio of rap , and break-dancing to the "scratching" hip-hop of disc-jockeying Grandmasters Flash and Melle Mel, and the World's Famous Supreme Team – with whom McLaren had had a smash in 1982 with a desecration of the traditional 'Buffalo Girls' hoe-down. If a victim of a different artistic passion, Winwood had enthused that New York was "a fantastic place to work. There's a lot of energy, a lot of music there, a lot of great players. There's a great drive to get things done which I find very attractive." Putting his money where his mouth was, he'd laid out a six-figure sum to hire the then-unfashionable Unique Recording Studio off Times Square in which to record the bulk of his Grammy-winning *Back In The High Life*.

His imagination captured likewise, so began Serge Gainsbourg's "American" period, twenty years after its premonition in 'New York USA' from *Percussions*. His Nile Rodgers was to be Billy Rush, guitarist and songwriter with New Jersey R&B combo, Southside Johnny And The Asbury Jukes who had enjoyed the patronage of "Little" Steven Van Zandt – leader of the twelve-piece Disciples Of Soul – and, crucially, Bruce Springsteen, a local lad of global renown for his Yogi Bear vibrato, animated stage act and some critics declaring him the "new Dylan". He himself had the nerve to imagine that he had all it took to usurp Elvis Presley's throne as King of Rock.

With Springsteen in the midst of his fattest years commercially Rush's connections and *curriculum vitae* were sufficiently impressive for Gainsbourg, a supplicant once again, to arrange an exploratory meeting. Billy, however, wasn't as keen on working with Serge – merely some French pop singer – but, after a few pina coladas, it was surprising how much more intriguing the idea of working together sounded. Fastening a pensive seat-belt prior to take-off from Newark airport, Gainsbourg was visualising already being back where he belonged, set up as a chart gladiator for another maybe three years after turning yet another reversal of fortune on its head.

Nevertheless, he was unable to go beyond fantasy for the two months needed for Rush to clear professional decks and book a studio just over the New Jersey state line for taping the raw material, and the Power Station in the Big Apple itself for mixing. He'd also scurried off to pick and choose suitable musicians such as saxophonist Stan Harrison of The Asbury Jukes, backing vocalists from The Simms

Brothers Band, and Peter Gabriel's US keyboard player, Larry Fast.

Aware of the dollar sign over each note, the principal artist paced his in-session drinking to its most creatively effective capacity, redeeming himself in Billy's eyes by constructive if jargon-ridden suggestions through the talkback, and a brisk finesse that had a basic album in the can within a week. State-of-the-art gadgetry intruded upon the grit, but essentially Gainsbourg had a more immediately saleable proposition than *Mauvaises Nouvelles Des Etoiles*.

Taking responsibility but not blame for a lover's suicide, the "beautiful sadness" of 'Sorry Angel' also encompassed one of the most forlornly catchy hooklines in pop as well as the syntactic pattern that typified the remaining *Love On The Beat* vocals of quasi-rapping spoken verses – often rigidly configurated, notably in 'Harley David Son Of A Bitch', 'No Comment' and 'Hmm Hmm Hmm' – and, sung by persons other than Gainsbourg, choruses that were usually either wordless or in English (*à la* Michel Polnaroff's 'Love Me Please Love Me').

While flurries of woodwind and an Eric Clapton-esque "woman tone" guitar – with a *soupçon* of phasing – flowed through 'No Comment', the tracks – particularly the takes used on its three singles – were peculiar for not so much instrumental soloing and obligatos as over-stretched codas gorged with a generous helping of synthesized strings that glanced backwards at the moderato soul style – smoother than Stax or Motown – that had ceased wafting from Philadelphia after the likes of The Three Degrees and The Stylistics had neared their sell-by date.

An extended fade matched the main vocalist's increasing prospects of imminent sexual intercourse in 'No Comment' as a bass throbbed lewdly beneath 'Lemon Incest', an opus that could be interpreted easily by the-man-in-the-pub as an unfunny serenade to sexual assault on children or as "darkly humorous" by a rock scribe trying to be cool, now that molestation of minors had been covered already in 'Pretty Paedophiles', a two-minute waste of time by some forgotten punk group. If you liked, it could also be a pre-emption of author Blake Morrison's owning-up in 1996 to getting an erection – the same as any red-blooded dad, he'd imply – when his own little girl sits on his lap.

To the 'Lemon Incest' composer, it was part of his "search for the truth by injection of perversity. I am only looking for the purity of my childhood." Flying this flag for all to see, he apportioned lines such as "the love we make (never together) is the most beautiful, the most violent, the most pure, the most intoxicating..." between himself and daughter Charlotte, cooing like a cross between her mother and the mutant fairy in David Lynch's cult movie, *Eraserhead*. As arcane a pleasure was the sado-masochism of the title track, but rather more routine a subject for song these days was the overt homosexuality of 'Kiss Me Hardy'.

The travesties of legitimate love within were promised in a *Love On The Beat* sleeve concept that had Gainsbourg beautified beyond belief via processed hair, a cosmetic miracle and skilful photography. It had all been been done before as far back as the early 1970s by David Bowie in an unambiguous dress and toying feyly with his hair on *The Man Who Sold The World*, and Edgar Winter, dolled-up like a lady on *They Only Come Out At Night*. In his send-up of glam-rock ten years too late, Serge came on like a 1930s vamp from the kiss-curl and tomato-red lipstick to fingers with varnished, talon-like nails, gripping a cigarette in up-ended holder.

Just as 'Aux Armes Et Caetera' had been the selling point of the album of the same name, so the saturation publicity campaign that accompanied *Love On The Beat* clotted round the expensive 'Lemon Incest' video. This did not adhere to a straightforward synchronisation with a musical performance but, centred on a bed scene with Charlotte, it projected a dramatic situation in which she proved as able as her Papa – who now saw no reason why there shouldn't be another entertainer in the family, although – as it was with Julian Lennon's maiden chart strike that same year – a famous surname could often furnish offspring with both the best and worst start to a showbusiness career.

Yet preconceived notions about Charlotte's ability were not confounded. If a late developer as a pianist, she was making headway as a film actress. Following *L'Effrontée* with Claude Miller, she was to star in *Charlotte Forever*, conceived and directed by Serge after a skeletal treatment was considered sufficient for producer Bertrand Blier to authorise financial support; his only condition being that Serge himself took the male lead. Determined that Charlotte – a little out of her depth anyway – should not serve as mere witness to upstaging by his character, Gainsbourg back-pedalled by pruning down his involvement as an actor to ten lines in as many pages. He was also quite ruthless in wringing the best possible performance from his daughter, cast as a personable, lively fourteen-year-old, the very antithesis of his "Stan", a scriptwriter whose thoughts of suicide are reined by his affection for Charlotte, the only light in a miserable existence.

This plot was mirrored too accurately in private life. The only emotional constant to which he could cling appeared, in actuality, to be Charlotte now that he and Bambou had entered a phase blighted by deafening explosions of temper – muttered trepidation building to Hitlerian screech – and the more insidious drip-drip of hovering aggravations. One of the most recurrent bones of contention was the continued ubiquity of syringes and other drug paraphernalia around the house. "If you don't stop, I'll smash your face" was the promise he was driven to make as Bambou's first pregnancy progressed into its middle months.

On top of worry about the well-being of an unborn child was that concerning one whose time was running out. On 16 March 1985, Olia slumped into a coma in her armchair. At the hospital, the falling away of her burden of infirmity was not gruesome or even unexpected, just a smooth slipping over the edge and away from a world of pain and discomfort. His mother's death was not so terrible, but with it came the ringing headaches, the cold sweats, the panic attacks, the knotted stomach, the restlessness and further tell-tale symptoms of Serge's next – and, so far, worst – bout of depression that gave force to the thought that, "The idea of happiness is foreign to me. I can't define it, so I don't look for it."

Hyperactivity would defer to sitting alone and unapproachable, lost in melancholy and paranoia. Nevertheless, to those who knew him only by what they read in the newspapers, saw on television or heard in his frequently hilarious lyrics, even during what they apprehended as the darkest hours, he could never be a sad sack like Dalida, now a grandmother and in the middle of what was to be a lauded Egyptian movie, *Le Sixième Jour*. "Yes, I have always longed for celebrity," she'd agree as the hammers beat increasingly harder on her brain, "but it has not made me happy. Yes, I have succeeded in life, but my life, it has not been very successful."

If teetering on a similar precipice as Dalida, Serge Gainsbourg did not lose himself as deeply in interminable contemplations of this mortal coil. Indeed, he was all smiles on the 7 July 1985 edition of something called *Jeu De La Venty*, making a finger-fluttering entrance to a prolonged spattering of goodwill from the studio audience. Perhaps out of respect to his mother, he had been on the wagon for a week to compose himself for this TV show, rehearsing anecdotes and jocular ripostes for any question fired at him.

As if on tenterhooks to conjurer Tommy Cooper's comic nervous procrastinations prior to a complicated trick, viewers experienced a "Will he? Won't he?" suspense whenever a chance appeared for a strangely restrained Gainsbourg to light touchpaper of switchboard-jamming outrage. He would not, however, bite any such bait. Taken to task over the business of the incinerated 500 franc note, yes, he had to confess to appalling behaviour, one way or another, over the past few years. There and then, in front of the cameras, he signed a cheque for 200 times that amount as a donation to the *Medicins Sans Frontières* charity.

Most accepted this as an atonement, and that here was a reformed character, albeit like a promiscuous schoolgirl playing virgin. While the bohemian minority may been dismayed by this display of bourgeois liberalism, Gainsbourg's dissipating of the lumpen proletariat's hostility was to be reflected in the social composition of ticket-buyers – of all ages – for autumn concerts that began on 19 September at the Casino de Paris when the curtains parted on a combo exemplified in proficiency and style by Gary Georgett, impassive and technically dazzling before a bank of patched-in polysynthesizers, and Tony "Thunder" Smith, a drummer whose explorations of "fusion" music had included stints with Jan Hammer and Jeff Beck, one of very few rock guitarists capable of playing jazz-rock convincingly.

As they were just what he needed, Smith and his colleagues' newest employer hadn't quibbled about their high wages – nor was he an enforcer of order like, say, John Mayall, avant-garde jazzer Annette Peacock and like abstemious bandleaders who wouldn't tolerate drunkenness – and God help you if they caught you with drugs. No such killjoy, Gainsbourg didn't mind what his musicians got up to off-duty as long as they were as punctual and tidy on the boards as he intended to be, despite well-founded stories that he was back on the booze again.

No sooner did this occur to anyone waiting for the singer they'd paid to see at the Casino de Paris, than the thought was, seemingly, acknowledged. The spotlight homed in on a familiar-looking figure so sozzled that, with the spooky deliberation of a dream's slow motion, he reeled from behind a curtain, reaching stage centre by the last cadence of 'Love On The Beat' in overture, only to fall flat on his face. To stupefied onlookers, this wasn't television or a pie-eyed photograph: before he'd sung a crotchet of the opening number, Serge Gainsbourg had been so overcome with drink that he'd collapsed in front of them – or had he?

No, he hadn't. It was a lookalike, one of Serge's little jokes. Though as immobile before the microphone as he'd ever been, a patriarchal joviality pervaded a performance immortalised on the in-concert *Live* album. Whilst leaning most of all on the newer releases – ranging from the notorious 'Lemon Incest' to obscurer 'Dépression Au-Dessus Du Jardin' (which sneaked up on *Anna*'s 'Sous Le Soleil Exactement') from Deneuve's *Souviens-Toi De M'Oublier* – it spanned earlier trackways of his professional career too. With repackaging factories in full production by then – and with clearance for the remixed issue of the Bardot 'Je T'Aime...Moi Non Plus' in 1986 – it made as much sense to plug 'Harley Davidson' as 'Harley David Son Of A Bitch'. However, even the most credulous teenager present could not have pretended that this was what it must have been like even as recently as the Epernay bash with Bijou in 1977.

Everything was different. Everything was the same. Coca-Cola in the imprisoned luxury of a hotel in Bruges tasted just like a Coca-Cola in one in Bordeaux as this tour and those that came after had him traversing a French-speaking world less and less interesting. For idle hours in this characterless dressing room or on that cramped aircraft seat, he'd be a bad loser in chess tournaments with Billy Rush. For more solitary diversion, he might've taken a challenging book by Rimbaud, Artaud or someone else ending in an "*au*" sound that he'd mentioned in 'Hmm Hmm Hmm'. However, in drained moments of self-loathing, it would occur to him that he'd scarcely peeked at it the entire trip.

A common journeyman musician's memory is glowering from a window of a Trust House, Ramada or Crest and realising that the highlight of the day wasn't the concert with its lethargy of songs predictable to the diphthong, but the building-up in a theatre's green-room and the winding-down in the motel lounge where Serge would switch from champagne to tequila as dawn drew nearer. Contrary to myth, Gainsbourg holding court was more likely to engender the French equivalent of what's-the-best-pint-you've-ever-had ennui than anything resembling *Satyricon* or a BBC mock-up of an imagined drugs-and-sex orgy with pushers, groupies and loud-mouthed showbusiness periphery almost smothering the noise of an interminable four-chord turnaround on an improvised stage.

Let's tarry for a while on the tour coach with its tired driver. Serge is suffering from a headache, an eye-crossing cough and a certain queasiness after that last plateful of overpriced lard-and-chips, hours of torpid warmth ago in a nameless service station on a Belgian autobahn. Now he is on a chartered flight to a soundcheck somewhere in Switzerland. Eyes glazed, brain numb, he could soundcheck forever.

While the star turn is often in a protective bubble away from the shabbier aspects of life on the road, he'd pace in wearied despair as shiftless equipment changeovers keep the second house in Toulouse waiting. The stagehands loaf about, eating sandwiches and smoking. Isolated in the midst of it, what was there left to enjoy about such a debasing job in which, like them, you couldn't wait until knocking-off time.

Yet sufficient pride and concern about the delivery of the show lingered to add to his residual problems. There was no let up in his depression even if the show went the distance without keening feedback bleeps, one of the sound crew blundering on to replace a dead microphone, a saxophonist lurching into a riff a semitone flat, audience interruptions or anything else that wasn't either in the script or the way he wished it to be. When he finally got to bed, the "whirling pits" of alcohol fought stress-related tension in his muscles and bones, and had him lying as rigid as a Knight-Templar on a tomb.

The monk in Gainsbourg might have fizzled out gladly as a recording artist; sloughed off whatever attention was still directed at him as a has-been, and reclaimed his niche as a backroom boy of the music industry. What he couldn't confess even to himself was that he had developed a taste for being in the limelight, a focal point of eyes grateful to him for merely existing. How would he have felt if polite clapping rather than foot-stomping ovation had followed the valedictory 'La Javanaise' to bring him back for an encore?

The beloved entertainer – now conferred with the diminutive nickname "Gain-Gain" as Claude François had been "Clo-Clo" – would wave good-humouredly, effectuate a "champion" handclasp, and even utter a few syllables of thanks before plunging into a reprise of 'Love On The Beat'. When Mick Jagger reached his fifties too, time would unwind and he'd prove as capable of whipping up pandemonium as he'd always been, but Serge was not so lean and fit, never had been even thirty years earlier when still realising his potential. It was as if he'd always been old. He'd put on a good show most nights, but he'd come over as less a hip-shakin' pop demigod than a professor who'd lived all his adult life in an atmosphere of books, armchaired tutorials and dialectic gymnastics.

Indeed, while it might have kindled a derisive snigger among those who remembered 'Poupée De Cire Poupée De Son', Serge was proud, perhaps boastful, after the French ministry of culture awarded him the highest grade of *la croix d'officier de l'ordre des Arts et des Lettres*, just as Bob Dylan had been in 1970 when inaugurated as an *ex officio* don of Princeton University, and Van Morrison in tasselled cap and the approved gown would be when receiving an honorary doctorate at the University of Ulster. Not far ahead lay less cerebral milestones of pop's road to respectability in knighthoods for Cliff Richard, Paul McCartney and Elton John.

Loaded with honours he'd accepted with a becoming if false modesty, the gateway to Gain-Gain's old age was arched with good works and, to outsiders, a pain-free lifestyle. Who could begrudge him his joy when, on 5 January 1986, Bambou presented him with a son. Perhaps as a hopeful harbinger of his father's personal rejuvenation, the boy was launched into the world as "Lucien Ginzburg". Naturally, Serge wrote a song about this "*enfant de l'amour*" that he couldn't stop himself calling by his own cradle enunciation of "Lucien".

Fittingly, 'Lulu' was Bambou's first single, but bringing more money into the house was Gainsbourg's fee for the music to another film, Bertrand Blier's *Tenue De Soirée*, praised as exuberantly at Cannes as

Le Sixième Jour with Dalida – and more so than the rushed *Charlotte Forever*. Serge blamed 'Lemon Incest' and his own reluctant role as "Stan" for lending the movie – received indifferently at the box-office too – an antagonising implication of off-colour (and off-camera) doings.

Not helping either was a title like 'Oh Daddy Oh' on the associated soundtrack. Using the *Love On The Beat* hirelings and Alan Hawkshaw, what was, to all intents and purposes, Charlotte Gainsbourg's debut album was almost as much an outlet for Serge's gentler musical sensitivities as Jane Birkin's *Di Doo Dah* had been in the drip-rock 1970s. Most of its texts, however, drank from the same cloudy pool as 'Lemon Incest'.

Somehow *Charlotte Forever*, film and album, both belied and bolstered its composer's fully-fledged public image as a composite of Oliver Reed, footballer *manqué* George Best, PJ Proby, Ringo Starr and every other professional drinker who made a clown of himself before screen-watching millions in the late 1980s. On *The John Davidson Show* in the United States, Starr's fuddled demeanour – repeating the questions as well as his own answers whilst fiddling with a Polaroid – had caused Davidson to storm off and, recounted a contrite Ringo, "They had to convince him to come back – but I was in the dressing room, having a few more cognacs." Less publicised had been the antics of Proby who, incoherently outstaying his welcome on a magazine on UK provincial television, had staggered from the Plymouth studio to busk on a carelessly-strummed guitar in the foyer of the nearby Drake Cinema.

Serge's turn had come on *7 Sur 7* in 1984, and, judging by his appeasingly non-controversial slot on *Jeu De La Venty*, it had been thought that he had learned his lesson. However, he'd demonstrate that this had been a tactical retreat during a sofaing beneath sweaty arc-lights on *Champs Elysées* in April 1986 that was to thrust him back fleetingly to the forefront of national notoriety. The other guest on this prime-time chat show was Whitney Houston, a cousin of Dionne Warwick, who had sung backing vocals for Chaka Khan before 1985's 'Saving All My Love For You' became the first of her seven US Number Ones. Hailed as a "female Michael Jackson", her repertoire was divided – like the sides of her maiden solo single, 'Greatest Love Of All'/'You Give Good Love' – between the romantic and the explicit. On *Champs*

Elysées, she performed an item from the latter canon.

It was feasible that former gospel chorister Whitney's notion of what she was singing about conflicted with that of the incorrigible and calculating Gainsbourg – who could not let it go without comment. After platitudes to Michel Drucker, a Gallic Terry Wogan, about how beautiful Houston was and blah blah blah, he added a stentorian sentence in English in deference to the lady – or to leave no doubt about the hypocrisy he perceived in her and her song. It contained an expression that even viewers who couldn't follow the language recognised as highly offensive, just as any UK school child given to looking up dirty words in a French dictionary might "con" or "merde".

A split-second of stunned silence was broken by a shriek of "What did he say?!" from La Houston, and a "Maman, change de chaine" ("Mummy, change channels") from Drucker, his knuckles whitening but trying to make out that it was all a laugh. Attempting further damage limitation, the host bit back on his anger with a light-hearted, "Pay no attention. He's always like that. It was his way of saying that he wanted to offer you a bouquet of flowers."

"No, no, no," interrupted a baleful Gainsbourg. "You don't translate for me. I said that I would like to *fuck* her."

How could she resist? Michel did not pardon this correction, an articulation of what a lot of adult males tuning in had been thinking. None of them stoved in the screen of their sets as a lorry-driving father had when The Sex Pistols cursed likewise on early evening television ten years earlier in London. Though the foreseeable outcry about Serge's naughtiness – like the explosions in cordite-riddled Ypres in the Great War – was heard across the Channel, readers of stray newspaper paragraphs in Britain and other English-speaking regions the next day were mildly amused by the incident, and those among them with but the merest interest in pop would recall Serge as the 'Je T'Aime...' fellow like they would Chuck Berry only for his biggest chart strike, 1972's *double entendre* 'My Ding-A-Ling'.

L'affaire Whitney Houston, such as it was, didn't, however, work up sufficient interest for many overseas consumers to buy or so much as listen to *Love On The Beat* or 'Lemon Incest'. Even in France, Serge's outburst was a nine-day-wonder – like John Lennon's *Self-*

Portrait, a post-*Two Virgins* short starring his willy, or Chuck Berry's eighty-minute *Sweet Little Sexteen* video featuring himself in manifold sexual activities. All were akin in macrocosm to the pranks of a boringly attention-seeking classroom nuisance: pay no attention – he's always like that.

The backfiring of this latest attempt to jump back on his 'Je T'Aime...' perch – and the realisation that his *guignol* (fool) act had worn itself out – combined with the widely-held suspicion that the standard of Gainsbourg's compositions had long fallen. If he was aware of this himself, he couldn't get used to the idea. After all, his creative volcano may have been encrusted with petrified lava, but it could still stir without warning and vomit up a 'Dépression Au-Dessus Du Jardin' or a 'Sorry Angel'.

Latching onto the belief that he had not deteriorated as a songwriter, but become simply an old one, Serge booked tentative sessions for an LP that, so he assured anyone listening, could be his last before retirement from what he – like Brel – regarded as no more or less of a craft than bricklaying or carpentry. "I have had enough of music," he'd tell you. "If I make another album, it will be to prove that I am the best, writing in words of fire in what is a minor art form. I don't wish to pass to posterity after my death. Fuck posterity."

chapter fourteen

Requiem 91

L *e vieillard terrible* was soon past caring about surpassing any previous standards as, shuttered in a subterranean studio throughout autumn 1987, his headphoned ears felt like mildly braised chops, his vocal cords became increasingly more tattered, and his skull split with neuralgia. More and more often nowadays, he was turning up nauseous and out-of-sorts, and it didn't improve his constitution to be kept hanging about during some boring mechanical process at the console or a constant retake of some minor percussion overdub – or to chance raising his pulse count by plunging into the heart of those occasional contretemps about, say, degree of echo on a guitar track.

Yet he drove Philippe Lerichomme, Billy Rush and the musicians – all the usual shower – like slaves, working himself sometimes into a foot-stamping state, like a child who can't get his own way. Allied to a discernible sense of urgency, hurried meticulousness vied with premeditated carelessness to lend transcendental edge to *You're Under Arrest*, an album that walks a line between artistic *faux pas* and worthy epitaph, with many Gainsbourg fans regarding it like Debussy did Wagner's *Das Rheingold* – as a "glorious sunset mistaken for a dawn". Musically, it was a consolidation rather than development of *Love On The Beat* in that Serge's vocals wavered mostly between talking and breaking into vague melody. To tempo announcements in English, the cats laid down a mid- to late-1980s groove of programmed drumming in perfect time here, trebly neo-*chukka-wukka* guitar scratching away there, twanging-plank bass on this track and stabbing block chords on keyboards on that one. On the title song – and first single off-cut – underlying interjections in the verses rose to the surface in the tension-breaking rap chorus by a black American of "You're under arrest because you're the best/G-G-G-G-Gainsbourg" as it explored the old *Lolita* pothole, this time with a scent of jailbait and buying off the cops when held for questioning about the babysnatching of thirteen-year-old ankle-socked Samantha, a black Marilou from the Bronx.

Once again, a Gainsbourg narrative posed the tacit but eternal question: was the lyricist projecting himself into a situation or did it really happen? If it did, was it embellished in the retelling like a fisherman's tall tale? Either way, thank God his poor mother wasn't around to hear about it.

Trying as hard to spell out how much life there was still in the old dog – and borrowing from David Bowie's 'Cracked Actor' of 1973 – Serge implores "Suck, baby, suck/To the CD of Chuck Berry Chuck" in another serenade to real or fictitious Samantha. Then he breaks up with her (not the other way round) in 'Baille Baille Samantha' and goes on about her pubic hairs in 'Dispatch Box' and his enormous erection in 'Five Easy Pisseuses' – though the effect of being a wonderful-for-his-age hipster is rather spoiled when he wags a Dutch uncle's finger in funereal and s-s-sibilant 'Aux Enfants De La Chance' – reminiscent of Brel, and the album's longest track at just over four minutes – which castigates Samantha and her pals for drug-taking during what ought to be their richest and most rewarding years.

Moreover, mention of Thelonious Monk, Berry, Bill Haley, Bob Dylan's 'Lay Lady Lay' and even Donald Duck would dredge up only dim recollections for Samantha's parents, let alone Samantha herself. Nevertheless, he also namedrops Bronski Beat, a collision of disco, homosexual activism and the Glaswegian falsetto of Jimmy Somerville, whose awareness of pop's deeper legacy was almost as acute as the older Serge's – as demonstrated in the outfit's various revivals of Berlin, Gershwin and Porter, very much in the air then. Just as 'Need A Man Blues' had been trilled by Somerville – a known Gainsbourg admirer – in 1984 with no lyrical revision, so another standard, 'Lover Man (Where Can You Be)', was by Udo Lindenberg, a kind of German

Bowie, to expose what he called his "flexible" sexuality.
More crassly homo-erotic in 'Kiss Me Hardy' from *Love On The Beat*, Serge had also fished out an old chestnut ('You Rascal You') for *Aux Armes Et Caetera*, and Julie London's 'Cry Me A River' may have been an inspirational current beneath the depths of 'J'Ai Pleure De Yang-Tse', a number he'd just written for Bambou. Lest we forget too, *You're Under Arrest* framed an exhumation of 'Gloomy Sunday', penned in 1939. Perhaps the saddest song of the past fifty years, it dealt with a jilted lover's impending suicide, and was so depressing that a few listeners in Hungary, its country of origin, found the after-life solace espoused in its libretto irresistible. If nicknamed 'The Budapest Suicide Song', none were attributed to 1940's swing version by Artie Shaw and his Orchestra or that of Chicago beat group, The Apocryphals in 1965. Notable among more recent arrangements are those of Sinead O'Connor – and Serge Gainsbourg.

Psychological turbulence as well as a profound physical weariness that he sought to hide were sub-flavours of an album with which the common herd were not immediately enchanted. You needed to have studied the books, viewed the exhibitions or seen the films as an essential aid to get beneath the shallow crudity of a number like 'Five Easy Pisseuses', its title a pun on the 1970 movie *Five Easy Pieces* and Picasso's 'La Pisseuse', and its lyrics smirking with references to the writings of the slightly older abstract painter Francis Picabia, and Catullus, erotic bard to the Caesars.

Too erudite to appeal to the younger siblings of those who'd wasted student grant money on *Aux Armes Et Caetera*, only Gainsbourg's actual – as opposed to artistic – death would revive his flagging recording career as it would that of Dalida when, after her overdose of barbituates in 1987, merchandisers moved in slowly but surely with Dalida biographies, glossy Dalida coffee table books celebrating her sartorial style, Dalida white boots, Dalida silver sequinned gowns, limited-edition Dalida bronze statues and the downloading of Dalida's farewell note onto an Internet site. Even while the cadaver was still warm, record industry moguls had been forced to meet demand kindled by tragedy by rush-releasing product such as the compilation album that topped the national chart for weeks, and a package of twelve compact discs of old material, some of it subjected to reprocessing and superimposition of sequencers so that it could be pumped out at triple-*forte* in specialist French discos.

That was what the future seemed to hold for Serge Gainsbourg too as he slipped beyond that point in life where time is marked by the first funerals of members of one's own over-the-hill generation. The previous June, old crony Coluche had been taken in a motorcycle mishap. This loss cut Serge the sharper for the frequency that his and the comedian's professional as well as personal lives had intertwined since that 1959 tour with Brel; Coluche, for example, writing lyrics for Serge's 'La Chanson Du Chevalier Blanc' for 1977's *Vous N'Aurez Pas L'Alsace Et La Lorraine* film, and both friends appearing on the same list of recipients of the *croix d'officier de l'ordre des Arts et des Lettres*.

An even more intimate tragedy was averted when police apprehended a gang who'd been plotting to kidnap Charlotte Gainsbourg for a ransom based on a supposition that her Papa's wealth was beyond calculation. Sensitive at the best of times, Serge was terrifying in his paroxysms of weeping hatred for the three dastards involved, and pressed for a punishment as harsh as the law would permit. Likewise, a young squatter who'd made himself at home in Rue de Verneuil during a brief absence by its owner was surprised when, showing not the least inclination to listen to what he had to say, Serge Gainsbourg, venerated symbol of cool, summoned the *gendarmes* without further ado; his fright turning to rage in the swift minutes prior to their arrival.

Perhaps the intruder might have guessed what the attitude of the creator of 'Aux Enfants De La Chance' would be. It was the same as that of the responsible step-father who had so taken to heart Jane Birkin's concern about the late hours that an adolescently wilful Kate Barry had been keeping that he used his influence to have her barred from certain discothèques and clubs. Kate outwitted bouncers by using disguise, but turned out to be a "good kid" at heart, guiding herself back to the straight-and-narrow by making a go of clothes design in Parisian fashion houses as another noted musician's daughter, Stella McCartney, was to do years later.

Serge had been quick to offer his professional services to his ex-wife too when Philips was agitating for another Jane Birkin album – *Lost Song*, issued in 1987 – and when he presided over the filming of her appearance at an early summer music festival in Bourges. It must have been a strange sensation for him to be merely some bloke blocking the view for an audience that began voicing its displeasure. He was also ordered to get out of the way for Ray Charles and then Jerry Lee Lewis – who were interviewed by him afterwards for the subsequent – and poorly-received – televisual documentary.

Facing each other, Lewis and Gainsbourg compared notes about similarly crowded lives on opposite sides of the Atlantic. If anything, Jerry Lee's was the more riven with mercurial whims of fate. As self-obsessed as a genius could be, "The Killer" had survived high living, destitution, oceans of booze, last-minute tour cancellations, police arrests, his shooting of a bass guitarist, the accidental deaths of two sons and a wife, and more marriages than Henry VIII – including one to a fourteen-year-old cousin that had got him hounded from British shores decades before a near-fatal stomach operation in 1981 that his doctors warned would recur unless he changed his ways.

Heroin, tranquillisers, whiskey, beer – whatever the drug of choice – were hastening other celebrities nearer to that bourne from which no traveller returns. Ringo Starr, Wayne Fontana, Alice Cooper, PJ Proby, Keith Richards and Elizabeth Taylor – pictured portly and plastered on the dust-cover of Kenneth Anger's *Hollywood Babylon* exposé – were a handful that mastered inner chaos and pulled back from the brink, but not so lucky were the likes of Keith Moon, Harry Nilsson, Beach Boy Dennis Wilson – drowned when his judgement was impaired by too much vodka – and a shockingly aged Serge Gainsbourg.

While yet denying that his alcoholism was critical, he'd be noticed sitting alone at a club's most secluded table, a pathetic isolate prone to hallucinations, uncontrollable trembling, severe heartburn and dizziness even when sober. What company he kept was of others united by a taste for liquor, who were as fearful as he of going anywhere that meant not being able to have a drink.

His easy access to alcohol, even when *en route* from A to B, was an an amenity provided on a laser-lit tour that commenced in March 1988 with seven evenings at the Zénith in Paris and a resulting in-concert double LP, *Le Zénith De Gainsbourg*. In addition to the good old good ones and other previously-issued items captured on tape was a poignant new number, 'Hey Man Amen'. This loosely-arranged *You're Under Arrest* afterthought was a remorsefully affectionate address to the infant Lulu from the perspective of a deceased father gazing down from a meritocratic heaven where he shares a cloud with Schumann and Stravinsky. Jumbling up past participles, he vacillates between urging his son to forget him and hoping that a few nettles will be planted on the grave when "little one, you have read all about me [and] you will know how many Lolitas I have had in my bed".

For those who like collating macabre allusions on record, chilling lines from 'Hey Man Amen' and other Gainsbourg librettos were to provide hours of enjoyable time-wasting with the benefit of hindsight. However, at the Zénith, he was as belligerently alive to the riff-raff as to Jean-Paul Belmondo, Johnny Hallyday, Catherine Deneuve and an assortment of new pop starlets allowed past security to a wisecracking, bear-hugging backstage area where the champagne flowed.

An agenda of thirty dates across France and Belgium was followed by an eagerly-awaited trip to Japan. A fan base, twitchy with anticipation for any new Gainsbourg release, was sufficient to fill five thousand seats at concerts in Osaka – and Tokyo's Nippon Budokan Hall, exactly ten years after the wordier Bob Dylan, another pop singing *keto* polluting this temple of martial arts, had likewise swept along an audience with emotional rather than linguistic communication.

To the Japanese disciple, a show by a living legend like Gainsbourg was on a par with Muhammed Ali's last hurrah in Las Vegas, and only a miracle could have rescued it from anti-climax, even for those so intent on digging him that they agonised when he flagged, glowed when he got second wind, and gave vent to a bedlam of clapping, whistling, cheering and stamping as he waved into the blackness and vanished from their sight forever.

Minus the rose-tinted spectacles, the set was no better or worse than any other he and his band had dished out that year for ticket-holders in the provinces at home where he'd come and gone by night. When asked what such-and-such a town had been like, he was damned if he could find it on a map.

Furthermore, regardless of the presentation's quality and diversion, an ever-present danger of a constant diet of tour-album-tour sandwiches was of attendances falling off as the artist became as too familiar as he'd been in the Parisian clubs, circa 1955. Like a Metro train, if you missed one Gainsbourg recital, there'd be another along if you waited.

Yet those in the know had ascertained – at least subconsciously – that there might be no more freshly-minted commodities to promote. An appraisal of Gainsbourg – headlined "Marquis de Sadness" – by Nick "Momus" Currie in the *New Musical Express* in 1989 – the French Republic's bicentennial year – read almost like an obituary, and, while "Gainsbourg is not waiting for death to be immortal" was to be the party line in attendant publicity, *De Gainsbourg A Gainsbarre*, a nine-CD retrospective – more than 200 tracks – was in preparation as the last word on Serge for devotees who had to own everything on which he ever breathed.

There'd be no time left for their idol to listen to it in its entirety. The sands were running out, and he was also engrossed in tying up loose ends such as lyrics for 'Amour Puissance Six' by a certain Viktor Lazlo. An exercise in rhymes and suspected negative symbolism, it presaged some of the same on *Made In China*, a 1988 album for Bambou, backed mainly by personnel warmed up by the Japanese expedition.

This was an illustration as good as any of what might be a rather sweeping generalisation about Gainsbourg-associated output since the late 1970s: as playing and production got better, creative values fell in favour of the blinded-by-science sound at any given interval. The difficulty was that, long before *Made In China*, Serge Gainsbourg had lost me. Somehow, his music had become too pat, too dovetailed, too American – but that's the feeling of a regressive who prefers The Troggs, Gary Glitter, The Spice Girls – anyone to Bruce Springsteen, Elton John, Phil Collins and other purveyors of cultured "contemporary" pop that forty-somethings like me are supposed to enjoy.

I suppose *Made In China* was all right if you do enjoy it, but to ask my opinion of it is like asking me about railway lines or donkeys' false teeth – because I can't say anything objective about them either. Like Bambou's album – or, for that matter, *Lost Song* and *You're Under Arrest* – they're just there. Nonetheless, I must add the raw information that when the first *Made In China* single, 'Nuits De Chine', was a miss, Serge sprang to his lady's defence by blaming the massacre of hundreds of civilians by armed forces in Tienanmen Square in central Beijing on 4 June 1989 for killing off airplay.

Though responsible for only its music, it was beyond him to confess to the public that 'Nuits De Chine' wasn't that brilliant a song anyway – or that his inventive reserves were ebbing. However, an admission of artistic weariness and disillusion with himself might be construed from his doleful "Somewhere along the line, success has destroyed me, destroyed my soul, my conscience, my sub-conscience".

The rest of him was in a bad way too. Respiratory and digestive problems had him in and out of hospital four times in January 1989 alone. Even in the distance from car to clinic for out-patient appointments, a doddering Gain-Gain would be helped along by Fulbert, a burly manservant taken on after the incident with the squatter. On 11 April, he was under the scalpel for a major operation on his abused liver to remove damaged and scar tissue in a bid to isolate the believed source of his diverse maladies so that the rest of his body would respond better to treatment.

As soon as Serge was able to pace the corridors of the hospital, he discharged himself, and booked a suite in the Hotel Raphael where he ordered Fulbert to direct staff not to serve him alcohol. Though his smoking continued unabated, the new guest was impressive too in his imbibing of mineral water at the bar while all around him were knocking back harder stuff. A rounder face, tauter skin and further outward signs of seemingly miraculous remission were correlated with a renewal of professional activity.

Before he checked out, he'd been ensconced in his room for hours at a stretch, drafting a scenario for a televisual short, *Stan The Flasher*, a title that said it all. Some of the dialogue was a feast of remembrance, including as it did both direct excerpts from his songs, and lines that wouldn't have been out of place in them.

Like Alfred Hitchcock, he had written himself a minor tableau, but Claude Berri, he decided, was ideal for the raincoat-clad title role. Busier these days with work behind the cameras, Berri wasn't particularly keen, but tipping the balance was the persistence of his old pal, a five week "window" in his schedule, and a sufficiently powerful financial incentive taken from a budget supplied by the ex-manager of Telephone (a French rock combo) and the Canal television channel. However, when the faithful Babeth Si Ramdane was given a free hand to expand the basic idea, it evolved into an entity that, slightly too long for Canal's faint-hearted programme planners, was deemed more exploitable in the cinema – where, in 1990, it proved a hit with both pundits and public, and remained in circulation until the latter end of the decade.

This was most gratifying, but a return to hospital for two days' observation, and a subsequent prescription for a bathroom cabinet's worth of medications for a debilitating condition that was losing him a race against death was not the firmest foundation for Serge to make long-term plans. Nevertheless, with less than a year to go, he was game enough for one more Birkin album, *Amours Des Feintes* – certainly more game than Jane herself.

While she remained a huge concert attraction, Birkin was blooming once more as an actress. Nowadays, a parallel career in the theatre might have her in the flesh in *Quelque Part Dans Cette Vie* at the Bouffes-Parisien while ten times larger than life on the screen in a provincial fleapit in *Daddy Nostalgie* with Dirk Bogarde. Yet if hot contemporary property in France – to the degree of having a new make of handbag named after her – she was a curio from the recent past to most of her fellow Britons. On a level of 1960s pop culture above Twinkle but below Marianne Faithfull, she rematerialised, a little nervy but otherwise very well-preserved, on *The Trouble With The Sixties*, a BBC television nostalgia romp with Dave Berry, Donovan, The Troggs, *Romance Of A Horse Thief* co-star Oliver Tobias and other of the era's celebrity survivors.

Back in her adopted country, she had gone beyond the mere glamour of *Blow Up* and the flimsiness of *Romance Of A Horse Thief* to more challenging, even *grande dame*, parts – especially on the legitimate stage where she had mouthed confident Old French without affectation in Marivaux's eighteenth century *Le Faisse Suivante*, and directed her own blacker comedy, *Pardon Tu Dormais!*.

When in a translation of Israel Horowitz's *Park Your Car* in the Harvard Yard, "I'd ring Serge every night on my way to the theatre. I wanted him to come and see the play, and in the end he did. He sat in the front row, drinking and smoking cigarettes, and making a lot of noise. He laughed and cried more than anybody else."

Jane's assessment of her relationship with her former husband in his decline is worth quoting at length: "We'd become...well, friends is hardly the word. He wouldn't be pleased to hear that anything that had been so passionate and strange and rare could have a name like that. In fact, I had become his mother in a funny sort of way. He was quite pleased by that. I used to go and look after him and see that he didn't fall over things. I didn't push him in the back anymore. I saw to it that he got his key in the lock. When it got too cold for him to sleep at the house at Rue de Verneuil, I'd take him home with me.

"Some people love you so much that they have the capacity of never wanting to get out of your life – and, perhaps in the end, I can say that Serge made a success of our separation. He made us both into something untouchable. Serge and I had a place in each other's lives – and, funnily enough, it took up more and more of a place. This meant that towards the end Serge used to say, 'I don't think that there are enough photographs of me on your staircase.' I'd say, 'Perhaps you're right.' I'd tell Jacques [Doillon], who'd say, 'I think there are quite enough.' It's terribly hard on the other person."

Hearing an occasional spin of 'Je T'Aime...Moi Non Plus' on the radio was a fact of life, but Jacques was to reverse his car precisely over a flower basket, a gift to Jane from Gainsbourg, as an expression of annoyance about his wife's apparent unwillingness to lay the ghost of her previous marriage as completely as he would have liked, and her continuing dependence as a recording artist on horrible old Serge – who, not stopping at simply composing the songs, had designed the *Amours Des Feintes* jacket.

There'd been an uneasy atmosphere, verging on the surreal, about the sessions as Gainsbourg hectored engineers with histrionic fastidiousness before subsiding suddenly into a blithe, jesting fatalism. "The pain had dulled," said Jane, "and become something else."

He was confronting finally the plain truth that all he had to look forward to was the past, whether in listening to segments of *De Gainsbourg A Gainsbarre* or in companionable chats with Jane when delivering Charlotte back to her custody. Still he felt the familiar stirrings which assailed him at the sight of a pretty girl, but, if plagued by temptations that he was no longer as capable of succumbing, he sublimated them with cerebral largesse such as 'White And Black Blues' for the pulchritudinous Joelle Ursull's entry in 1990's Eurovision Song Contest. This opus almost repeated his triumph of that dear, dead springtime a quarter of a century ago. Could anyone not empathise with Serge's mortification when only Italy's topical 'Insieme 1992' blocked its passage to victory, even if a Eurovision win wasn't the automatic licence to print money that it once was.

Young Joelle may have fascinated him, but not as much as Vanessa Paradis, who, as a fourteen-year-old in 1988, had both secured a trans-European smash – Britain too – with 'Joe Le Taxi' and been introduced to a charmed Gainsbourg. When they met again two years later on a television show, he noticed that while retaining her nymphette allure, she'd filled out most becomingly. Picking up the signals, she pinned him down with a sleight of verbal judo in wondering aloud why he kept his recording – as opposed to just composing – projects in the family these days, ie only bothering with a hands-on approach with regard to Jane, Charlotte and Bambou.

The following day her producer was on the phone to Serge. Surely he remembered saying that he'd like to write and oversee the taping of a new single for Vanessa. Convinced that he had, Gainsbourg received the two of them at Rue de Verneuil where both parties small-talked shyly, but parted with a promise of one song from the host. This became five and then an entire album, *Variations Sur Le Même T'Aime*.

It was time and effort that he could ill-afford, and, after recording the Paradis album and Birkin's *Amours Des Feintes* virtually back-to-back, Serge took a long holiday for the first time since God knows when. Maturing from young man to dotard in the hothouse of pop's endless adolescence, he'd been treated like a food pigeonhole in a self-service cafeteria. Now that he was not so sure of his tomorrows, it could no longer be taken for granted that Serge Gainsbourg existed just to vend entertainment with a side-serving of cheap insight.

He was, so it appeared, priming himself for the quiet life he considered he deserved, but, rather than, say, take up golf, he would retreat to a bolt-hole where his fans and the press would be unlikely to find him immediately. False names, decoy tactics and secret destinations were, he felt, as essential as spare underwear for an entertainer of his stature. Without these precautions, yesterday's retreat might become today's media circus. Therefore, with its facilities less important than the space between it and the nearest neighbours, he chose somewhere half-hidden by woodland, and set amidst rolling pastures and rustic calm within the tributary pull of the Yonne, some 100 miles south-west of Paris. So it was that the olde-worlde Hotel De L'Esperance around Saint-Père-sous-Vezelay sheltered Gainsbourg for what remained of summer and into the gold of autumn.

While conscious that his presence there was as profoundly disturbing an experience for some of the other guests as standing behind President Mitterrand in a supermarket check-out queue, it was a relatively undisturbed stay, and pleasant enough as the landscape melted into another endless summer day with not a leaf stirring, a touch of mist on the sunset horizon and a bird chirruping somewhere. When the season began to change, the harvest moon would shine as bright as day over the vastness of the story-book countryside, and the half-a-tree blazing in the fireplace would subside to glowing cinders that threw soft light on the stained glass, crossed swords and exposed rafters.

Alien to a mediaeval baron, however, were the swimming pool, snooker den – and the grand piano at which Serge sat for hours to ward off ennui when rural tranquillity lost its ivy-clung lustre. He was also more welcoming to visitors like Kate Barry, even when she burst in on him preening himself in a mirror. He smiled his old smile, and, before she left, agreed to put his celebrity and talent at her disposal for a forthcoming catwalk parade.

He also marshalled enough energy to touch base in Paris in order to play the eighty-eights for Kate's mum on some TV spectacular. Otherwise, he was sighted less frequently than the Loch Ness Monster by the general public. It was now rather than posthumously that the legend began to take root, and far-fetched rumours abounded about what was happening with Serge. Mention of him brought out odd and contradictory accounts of what people claimed to have seen or heard, but no-one could cite an exact fount of information. There were even cynics who theorised that his "condition" had been a pretext for him to seek refuge from fame – like Bob Dylan's "motorcycle accident" had been in 1966.

Dylan's broken neck – if he'd had one – had mended and he'd re-emerged with *John Wesley Harding*, an austere, understated new morning. Blowing on duller embers, Gainsbourg pencilled in April 1991 to record the follow-up to *You're Under Arrest* in New Orleans with the cream of that jazz city's musicians – as death seemed to be sparing him to purchase from his plight a few months – possibly years – of respite.

However, when they heard of him likening his heart to "a hand-grenade that might go off at any moment", long-standing friends began looking him up to talk of when the Earth was young. It seemed so far away now: Milord L'Arsoille, 'Le Poinconneur Des Lilacs', *Hercules Unchained*, Elek Bacsik, France Gall, *Anna*, *Le Bardot Show*...

Retired from films, Brigitte had found a more selfless occupation as perhaps Europe's most conspicuous champion of animal rights. Now that he was on his last legs, a soft spot for her former lover awoke in BB an impulse to break telephone silence in 1990. "For the last few months of his life, they called each other and just talked," recounted Jane Birkin. "That meant a lot to Serge. He was alone and very lonely and just by talking to him on the phone, I think he rediscovered a genuine friendship."

Much left unresolved from his marriage to Jane came home to roost too, and she would cherish a pen-and-ink likeness of her sketched from his bed after the months had shrunk to weeks, and Bambou became even more hospital orderly than passionate inamorata. Yet, while he passed many a lethargic hour dozing in front of the television, Serge was able to organise a fireworks display for Lucien on New Year's Eve, and, with Charlotte at his side, even fly to Barbados for another vacation – but, though there physically, his mind was generally elsewhere, and he could rarely be coaxed from his bed before noon for the day's sightseeing and sunbathing.

He shuffled through passport control in Paris in time to celebrate Bambou's birthday on Friday, 1 March. Perhaps he had too much fun – for that night, he suffered a cardiac arrest in his sleep. An ambulance arrived, but there was nothing the paramedics could do – and, just in time for the evening news bulletins, Serge Gainsbourg was pronounced dead.

Before twilight thickened, the black carnival was well underway. It was to culminate on the Thursday with a send-off at the necropolis at Montparnasse, complete with celebrity eulogies and readings, but mass grief had surrounded the house instantly like it had Claude François's mansion on that creepy day in 1979. When the fans' vigil for Gainsbourg was over, there'd remained residual tons of votive offerings: mostly flowers, but also cartons of cigarettes and bottles of booze – as if the coffin lid was to be prised open and a dram poured down the corpse's throat, and a Gitane inserted between his lips.

Record store windows bloomed with his splendour, and an element of morbid inquisitiveness pervaded as customers stampeded in as if Gainsbourg discs and cassettes were being given away. To that moon-faced girl at a bus stop with a newly-purchased *Le Zénith De Gainsbourg* under her arm, the whole business beggared belief. While those who knew Serge personally were not totally surprised by his passing, some humble folk clung to the fantasy that he'd been simply spirited away somewhere – for, however muddled they become, all ingredients of survival myths represent a profoundly human instinct – not peculiar to pop – that holds facts too grievous to be borne at arm's length.

When it was clear that Serge Gainsbourg was not going to recover from being dead, panegyric statements from Mitterrand, Bardot *et al* emphasised the nation's official pride in him, just as the naming of a square in Montmartre after Dalida had been for her. Flags waved at half-mast and Gallic radio stations broadcast his music continuously in place of listed programmes, giving another lease of chart life to 1968's 'Requiem Pour Un Con', remixed as 'Requiem 91'. Estate agents wondered who was doing the probate assessments; publishers liaised with biographers, and sick jokes circulated among journalists shoving together hurried obituaries for the morning tabloids, quite rightly allowing that Gain-Gain's was a greater loss to popular culture than that of Clo-Clo, but distorting the old stories even more.

Versions

The patchy quality of his creative escapades since 1978 had the public at large wiser to Serge Gainsbourg's shortcomings. A more glorious past was a near-impossible yardstick for him to overcome – as impossible as Muhammed Ali regaining his heavyweight title in 1975 – but, while nothing of unreserved brilliance on *Love On The Beat*, *You're Under Arrest* and the rest had leapt out of the speakers, however much die-hard fans might have willed it, death impeded objective criticism, just as the tragedy of John Lennon's slaying in 1980 had given his and Yoko Ono's *Double Fantasy* album an undeserved piquancy.

London musician Bob Stanley* happened to be in France when Gainsbourg's funeral was pending – "and it was extraordinary. The entire country went into mourning." Jane Birkin might have capped this with "The French know all the songs by heart. He's that famous, and his lyrics are that well known. There were children of twelve and men of seventy waiting to follow him to the graveyard, but here [Britain], nobody knew his name."

It wasn't quite everybody. In the UK – and other Anglo-Saxon areas – Gainsbourg had been the exclusive property of undergraduates flirting with bohemia before becoming teachers. The 'Je T'Aime...Moi Non Plus' windfall apart, he was unnoticed by everyman for years until the likes of Malcolm McLaren, Jimmy Somerville, Suede's Brett Anderson – who was to record a duet with Jane Birkin – Black Grape and, especially, Momus and Mick Harvey (of The Bad Seeds) –

---

* *Known expert on European pop, and mainstay of St Etienne, London* nouveau vague *hitmakers, named after a French soccer team*

respectively, from Scotland and Australia – confessed his influence. This precipitated the issue of expedient compilations like 1991's *De Gainsbourg A Gainsbarre* – a whittled-down edition of the huge French collection.

Most of these products attracted as many people who'd read reviews in *The Guardian* as those who'd scanned the *New Musical Express*, and, come the mid-1990s, Gainsbourg was very much alive and well in gauche *après*-punk romanticism. In 1997, some arty quartet from Maidenhead named themselves 'Lemon Incest' (and thus barred themselves from most local venues). Their formation had been preceded by Jimmy Somerville's hit revamp in 1989 of Gainsbourg-via-Françoise Hardy's 'Comment Te Dire Adieu', and Hardy herself had joined others of her vintage on 1994's *Paris* by Malcolm McLaren whose dirty talk was suspended over disco accompaniment.

More open an acknowledgement of artistic debt were Momus's dedication of 1991's *Hippopotamus* to Gainsbourg, and Mick Harvey's tribute albums, *The Intoxicated Man* and 1997's *Pink Elephants*. "A French friend of mine gave me a compilation of around forty songs," he explained, "and I became intrigued by the strange qualities to his music. In terms of subject matter, everything was fair game, from the Torrey Canyon disaster to Bonnie and Clyde."

Though Harvey kept the faith, the most evangelical carrier of the Olympic torch of Gainsbourg was Jane Birkin. Doing whatever willingness and energy would do to further his cause, she launched a 1997 season of his films at London's L'Institut Français, and toured his compositions round France, its colonies and beyond to Germany, Japan – and the Royal Festival Hall on 15 April 1997 where, in keeping with the friendly, almost downhome ambience of the proceedings, she mounted the stage via the audience. Casually clad in white top and hip-hugging black jeans, Jane had hung onto her good looks and slim physique. Sometimes, a gesture or a facial expression would make the years would fall away altogether, and those buffs *au fait* with her movies might glimpse the profile of, perhaps, the "hippy chick" she'd been in *Les Chemins De Katmandou*.

This wasn't bad going for one who'd long been a grandparent, courtesy of the teenage son of Kate Barry. Moreover, there was also the first child of Charlotte Gainsbourg, whose acting career –

embracing *The Cement Garden*, directed by her Uncle Andrew, and Zeffirelli's *Jane Eyre* – would be put on hold in summer 1997 for the birth.

Back in the land that bore her, Charlotte's mother had granted interviews to "quality" periodicals as the Royal Festival Hall show loomed. She'd also appeared on Channel Five's *Jack Docherty Show* both in person and in a video clip of her new single, a chirpy revival of 'La Gadoue', penned by Serge for Petula Clark in 1964 – but was it a hit? No, but I wanted it to be as a verification of the lost value of someone singing a song as opposed to producing a production.

Serge's latter-day efforts as a recording artist had leant mainly on a production criterion rather than intrinsic musical strength, and to some fans, it was his misfortune to live on after he'd dumped the bulk of an artistic load that prompted belated and frequently empty revaluation by critics outside the French-speaking forum for which, principally, it was intended.

After a previous all-Gainsbourg British concert by Birkin in 1994, the papers were kind: "My mother faxed me all the newspaper reviews, and they all said, 'We walked by a genius and we didn't know.' It was too late for him to see it, but then I thought some painters and writers and poets aren't even known in their own lifetime. Something strange has happened since then: curiosity about Serge's career and about me and my songs has grown. There are cult records like *The Man With The Cabbage Head* and *Melody Nelson*."

Jane had cried real tears during one *lieder* by her second husband when taping a concert album at the Casino de Paris. Coming within a week of her father's death, Serge's heart attack had darkened further the shadow that he'd cast over her marriage to Jacques Doillon. "The balance went," she admitted. "Jacques once said to me, 'Do you hate me for not being dead?' I don't think I did, but perhaps that's how it came over."

It was since the subsequent divorce and the advent of a new man in her life, Olivier Rolin – once the anarchist "Antoine", but now a foreign correspondent for *Le Monde* – that Jane became, as one close acquaintance had it, "a living mausoleum" for Gainsbourg, devoting albums like 1996's *Versions* solely to items that he had either recorded himself or given to others, and stark remakes of such as 'Physique Et

Sans Issue' from *Lost Song*. Re-arrangements were broad enough to incorporate a solitary harp backing her on 'Dépression Au-Dessus Du Jardin'; Paris's good-time Les Negresses Verts on 'La Gadoue', and the strings on 'Ce Petits Riens' owing something to a *largo* interlude from Stravinsky's *Rite Of Spring*. Elsewhere, a jazz trio, African drummers, a blues guitarist and a Serbian brass band elaborated on and, in most instances, improved upon the originals.

Chronology

1895 Birth of Olia Ginzburg (mother)
1896 Birth of Joseph Ginzburg (father)
1918 Marriage of Joseph and Olia Ginzburg
1919 Ginzburgs leave Russia for France
1926 Birth of Jacqueline Ginzburg (sister)
1928 2 April: birth of Liliane (twin sister) and Lucien (Serge
           Gainsbourg) Ginzburg in Paris
1934 Birth of Brigitte Bardot
1940 Lucien commences studies at Lycée Condorcet
           Germany invades France
1944 France liberated by the Allies
1946 Birth of Jane Birkin
1949 Lucien begins national service
1950 Lucien completes national service
1951 Lucien's marriage to Elisabeth Levitsky
1954 Lucien passes SACEM entrance examination and files six
           compositions
1956 Lucien begins residency at Milord L'Arsoille, and adopts the
           stage alias "Serge Gainsbourg"
1958 Release of debut album, *Du Chant De L'Une!*, winner of *Le
           Grand Prix De L'Academie*
           Opus 109 tour
1959 Debut as movie actor in *Voulez-Vous Danser Avec Moi?*
           Release of *Juliette Gréco Chante Serge Gainsbourg*

1960	Birth of Bambou
1963	Marriage to Françoise Pancrazzi ("Béatrice")
1964	Birth of Natacha Ginzburg (daughter)
	Release of *Gainsbourg Percussions*
1965	'Poupée De Cire Poupée De Son' wins Eurovision Song Contest
	Retires from stage performances
1966	*Anna* musical on national television
1967	Broadcast of *Le Bardot Show*
	Birth of Vania Gainsbourg (son)
1969	Release of 'Je T'Aime...Moi Non Plus' by Jane Birkin and Serge Gainsbourg
1971	Death of Joseph Ginzburg
	Birth of Charlotte Ginzburg (daughter)
	Release of *Histoire De Melody Nelson*
1972	Marriage to Jane Birkin
1973	Release of *Vu De L'Extérieur*
	Suffers first heart attack
1974	Release of *Rock Around The Bunker*
1976	Debut as movie director in *Je T'Aime...Moi Non Plus*
1977	Resumes stage performances
1979	Publication of *Evguénie Sokolov*
	Release of *Aux Armes Et Caetera*
1984	Release of *Love On The Beat*
1985	Death of Olia Ginzburg
1986	Receives *la croix de l'ordre des Arts et des Lettres*
	Birth of Lucien Ginzburg (son)
1987	Release of *You're Under Arrest*
1990	'White And Black Blues' second in Eurovision Song Contest
1991	2 March: death of Serge Gainsbourg in Paris

Compositions

1954   Les Amours Perdues
1955-7   Le Poinçonneur Des Lilas/La Chanson Du Diable/La Cigale Et La Fourmi/La Purée/Ronsard 58
1958   Douze Belles Dans La Peau/La Recette De L'Amour Fou/Ce Mortel Ennui/La Femme Des Uns Sous Le Corps Des Autres/L'Alcool/Du Jazz Dans Le Ravin/Le Charleston Des Déménageurs De Pianos
1959   Le Claqueur De Doigts/La Nuit D'Octobre/Jeunes Femmes Et Vieux Messieurs/L'Amour A La Papa/Mambo Miam Miam/Adieu Créature/ L'Anthracite/Indifférente/Judith (instrumental)/L'Eau A La Bouche*/ Angoisse*/Black March*
* From the film *L'Eau A La Bouche*
1960   Cha Cha Cha Du Loup (instrumental)*/Générique*/Fugue*/ Les Loups Dans La Bergèrie*/Sois Elle Et Tais-Toi/Laissez-Moi Tranquille
* From the film *Les Loups Dans La Bergèrie*
1961   Chanson De Prévert/Les Femmes C'Est Du Chinois/En Relisant Ta Lettre/Les Oubliettes/Viva Villa/Personne/Le Rock De Nerval/Chanson De Maglia/Le Sonnet D'Arvers
1962   Black Trombone/Les Goémons/Intoxicated Man/Quand Tu T'Y Mets/Ce Grand Méchant Vous/Baudelaire/Requiem Pour Un Twister/Les Cigarillos
1963   La Javanaise/Un Violon Un Jambon/L'Appareil A Sous/Vilaine Fille Mauvais Garcon/Strip Tease*/Some Small Chance*/Wake Me At Five*/ Safari*/Chez Les Yé Yé/Elaeudanla Teiteia/Scenic Railway/Le Temps Des Yoyos
* From the film *Strip Tease*

1964   Sait On Jamais Où Va Une Femme Quand Elle Vous Quitte/
Le Talkie-Walkie/La Fille Au Rasoir/La Saison De Pluies/Amour Sans Amour/
No No Thanks No/Maxim's/Negative Blues/Comment Trouvez-Vous Ma
Soeur*/Eroticotico!/No Love For Daddy*/Rocking Horse*/Marshmallow
Man*/Joanna/Là-Bas C'Est Naturel/Pauvre Lola/Quand Mon 6.35 Me Fait Les
Yeux Doux/Machins Choses/Les Sambassadeurs/New York USA/Couleur
Café/Marabout/Ces Petits Riens/Tatoué Jérémie/Coco And Co
* From the film *Comment Trouvez-Vous Ma Soeur*
1966   Docteur Jekyll Et Monsieur Hyde/Qui Est In Qui Est Out/Shu
Ba Du Ba Loo Ba*/Vidocq* /Marilu*
* From the TV series *Vidocq*
1967   Chanson Du Forçat*/Chanson Du Forçat II*/Complainte De
Vidocq*/Comic Strip/Chatterton/Torrey Canyon/Hold Up/Wouaou+/Goering
Connais Pas+/ Siffleur Et Son One Two Two+/Woom Woom Woom+/
Caressante+/Elisa#/Friedman#/Les Americains#/La Brasserie Du Dimanche
#/Le Village A L'Aube#/L'Horizon#/Harley Davidson/Bonnie And Clyde
* From the TV series *Vidocq*; + From the film *Toutes Folles De Lui*; # From
the film *L'Horizon*
1968   L'Herbe Tendre*/L'Herbe Tendre (instrumental)*/Ce Sacré
Grandpère*/Manon+/New Delire+/Requiem#/Psychasténie#
* From the film *Ce Sacré Grandpère*; + From the film *Manon*; # From the
film *La Pacha*
1969   Evelyne (from the film *Slogan*)
1970   Cannabis (instrumental)*/Cannabis*/Le Deuxième Homme/
Danger*/Chanvre Indien*/Arabique*/I Want To Feel Crazy*/Jane Dans Le
Nuit*/Avant De Mourir*/Dernière Blessure*/Piège*/Cannabis-Bis*/Charlie
Brown+/Charlie Brown (instrumental)+/A Boy Named Charlie Brown+
* From the film *Cannabis*; + From the film *Charlie Brown*
1971   Valse De Melody/Melody/Ballade De Melody Nelson/Ah
Melody/L'Hôtel Particulier/Cargo Culte/En Melody/La Noyée/La Décadanse/
Les Langues De Chat
1972   Sex-Shop*/Quand Le Sex Te Chope*/Moogy Woogy+/Close
Combat+/Elle Est Si
* From the film *Sex-Shop*; + From the film *Trop Jolies Pour Etre Honnetes*
1973   Je Suis Venu Te Dire Que Me M'En Vais/Vu De
L'Extérieur/Titicaca/Panpan Cucul/Par Hasard Et Pas Rase/Des Vents Des
Pets Des Poums/Pamela Popo/La Poupée Qui

Fait/L'Hippopodame/Sensuelle Et Sans Suite
1975   Nazi Rock/Tata Teutonne/J'Entends Des Voix Off/Eva/Zig Zig
Avec Toi/Est-Ce Est-Ce Si Bon/Yellow Star/Rock Around The Bunker/SS In
Uruguay/L'Ami Caouette/Le Cadavre Exquis
1976   Ballade De Johnny Jane*/Le Camion Jaune*/Banjo Au Bord Du
Styx*/Rock 'N' Roll Autour De Johnny*/L'Abominable Strip-Tease*/Joe
Banjo*/Je T'Aime...Moi Non Plus Au Lac Vert*/Je T'Aime Mois Non Plus Plus
Au Motel*/Ballade De Johnny Jane (reprise)*/L'Homme A Tête De Chou/
Chez Max Coiffeur Pour Hommes/Marilou Reggae/Transit A Marilou/Flash
Forward/Aéroplanes/Premiers Symptômes/Ma Lou Marilou/Variations De
Marilou/Meurtre A L'Extincteur/Marilou Sous La Neige/Lunatic Asylum
* From the film *Je T'Aime...Moi Non Plus*
1977   Diapositivisme*/Discophotèque*/Mi Corasong*/Ketchup In
The Night*/Fish-Eye Blue*/Téléobjectivisme*/Putain Que Ma Joie
Demeure*/Burnt Island*/First Class Ticket*/Long Focal Rock*/
Arabysance*/Passage A Tobacco*/Yesterday On Fender*/Goodbye
Emmanuelle+/Emmanuelle And The Sea+/My Lady Heroine/Trois Millions
De Joconde/La Chanson Du Chevalier Blanc (from the film *Vous N'Aurez
Pas L'Alsace Et La Lorraine*)
* From the film *Madame Claude*; + From the film *Goodbye Emmanuelle*
1978   Sex Sea And Sun*/Sex Sea And Sun (in English)*/Mister
Iceberg*/Mister Iceberg (in English)*
* From the film *Les Bronzés*
1979   Javanaise Remake/Aux Armes Et Caetera/Les Locataires/ Des
Laids Des Laids/Brigade Des Stups/Vielle Canaille/Lola Rastaquouère/Relax
Baby Be Cool/Daisy Temple/Eau Et Gaz A Sous Les Etages/Pas Long Feu/
Marilou Reggae Dub
1980   Pas Long Feu/La Fautive*/Je Vous Salue Marie*/La P'tite
Agathe*/Dieu Fumeur De Havanes*/La Fautive (reprise)*/Dieu Fumeur De
Havanes (reprise)*/Papa Nono*/Je Pense Queue*/La Fautive (instrumental)*
* From the film *Je Vous Aime*
1981   Le Physique Et Le Figuré (from the film of the same name)/
Overseas Telegram/Ecce Homo/Juif Et Dieu/Mickey Maousse/Shush Shush
Charlotte/Toi Mourir/La Nostalgie Camerade/Bana Basadi Balado/Evguénie
Sokolov/Negusa Nagast/Strike/Bad News From The Stars
1984   Love On The Beat/Sorry Angel/Hmm Hmm Hmm/No Comment/
Kiss Me Hardy/I'm The Boy/Harley David Son Of A Bitch/Lemon Incest

1985   Dépression Au-Dessus Du Jardin
1986   Travelling*/Traviolta One*/Traviolta Two*/Travaux*/ Travelure*/
Entrave*/Travers*/Travelo*/Traverse*/Travelinge*/Traveste*/Trave*/Travelling
(reprise)*
* From the film *Tenue De Soirée*
1987   You're Under Arrest/Five Easy Pisseuses/Suck Baby Suck/Baille
Baille Samantha/Aux Enfants De La Chance/Shotgun/Glass Securit/Dispatch
Box/Mon Légionnaire
1989   Hey Man Amen/You You You But Not You/Seigneur Et
Saigneur/Les Dissous Chics
1991   La Horse (from the film of the same name)/Mélancolie Baby
(from the film *Melancholy Baby*)/Generique/Break Down (from the film *Si
J'Etais Un Espion: Break Down*)

**Gainsbourg, Anna Karina and Jean-Claude Brialy were the
principals in the 1967 musical *Anna* which featured the following
compositions:**
C'Est La Cristallisation Comme Dit Stendhal/Sous Le Soleil Exactement
(instrumental)/Sous Le Soleil Exactement/J'Etais Fait Pour Les Sympathies/
Rien Rien Je Disais Ca Comme Ca/Un Jour Comme Un Autre/Boomerang/
Un Poison Violent C'Est L'Amour/Roller Girl/Ne Dis Rien/Pistolet Joe/GI Joe/
Je N'Avais Qu'Un Seul Mot A Lui Dire/Pas Mal Pas Mal Du Tout/Photographie
Et Religieuses/De Plus En Plus De Moins En Moins

Gainsbourg released the following duets with Brigitte Bardot:
Bonnie And Clyde/Bubble Gum/Comic Strip/Pauvre Lola/L'Eau A La
Bouche/La Javanaise/Intoxicated Man/Baudelaire/Docteur Jekyll Et
Monsieur Hyde/Initials BB/Bloody Jack/Torrey Canyon/Shu Ba Du Ba Loo
Ba/Ford Mustang/Black And White/Qui Est In Qui Est Out/Hold
Up/Marilu/Je T'Aime...Moi Non Plus

With Jane Birkin, Gainsbourg released the following duets:
'Je T'Aime...Moi Non Plus' * (from the film *Slogan*)/Jane B/L'Anamour/
Orang-Outan/Sous Le Soleil Exactement/18-39/Soixante Neuf Année
Erotique/Elisa/La Canari Est Sur Le Balcon/Les Sucettes/Manon
* Also known as 'Le Chanson De *Slogan*'

Gainsbourg released a duet of 'Vielle Canaille' with Eddy Mitchell in 1986.

With his daughter Charlotte, Gainsbourg released the following duets:
Charlotte Forever/Plus Doux Avec Moi

The pieces below were written before 1957 and were not issued on disc by Gainsbourg or any other artist:
Fait Divers/Ca N'Vaut Pas La Peine D'En Parler/Promenade Au Bois/Trois Boleros/Nul Ne La Saura Jamais/Pour Si Peur D'Amour/ Abomey/La Ballade De La Vertu/Les Mots Inutiles/Zita La Panthère/ Panthère Blues (instrumental)/Arthur/Circus/Pourquoi/Charlie/ Locura Negra/Meximambo/ Mambo De Puebla(instrumental)/Tragique Cinq A Sept/Jonglerie Chinoise/ Le Trapéziste/La Danseuse De Corde/La Haltérophile/J'Ai Le Corps Damné L'Amour/Quand Je Me Lève/Je Broyais Du Noir/La Caravane Dans Le Désert/ L'Homme De Ma Vie/J'Ai Gôute A Tes Lèvres/Dalouncia/J'Ai Perdu Colombine/La Chanson De L'Ecureuil/On Me Siffle Dans La Rue

These songs (in chronological order of composition) were recorded by the artists in brackets but were not released by Gainsbourg:

Défense D'Afficher (Pia Colombo, Juliette Gréco)/Mes Petites Odalisques (Hugues Aufray et son Skiffle Group)/Il Etait Une Oie (Juliette Gréco)/ Friedland (Juliette Gréco)/La Jambe De Bois (Juliette Gréco)/Chanson Pour Téziquer (Philippe Clay)/Lily Taches De Rousseur (Philippe Clay)/ Accordéon (Juliette Gréco)/L'Assassinat De Franz Lehár (Catherine Sauvage)/Je Me Donne A Qui Me Plait (Brigitte Bardot)/Les Yeux Pour Pleurer (Nana Mouskouri)/OO Sheriff (Marie-Françoise, Petula Clark)/Il N'Y A Plus D'Abonné Au Numero Que Vous Avez Demandé (Isabelle Aubret)/ N'Ecoute Pas Les Idoles (France Gall)/Laisse Tomber Les Filles (France Gall)/Attends Ou Va-T'En (France Gall)/Les Incorruptibles (Petula Clark)/La Gadoue (Petula Clark)/Quand J'Aurai Du Vent Dans Mon Crane (Serge Reggiani)/Bubble Gum (Brigitte Bardot)/Les Omnibus (Brigitte Bardot)/Les Petits Papiers (Régine)/Il S'Appelle Reviens (Régine)/Poupée De Cire Poupée De Son (France Gall, Claude France, Janie Jurka, Sonia Christie, Oberkampf)/La Guérilla (Valérie Lagrange)/Baby Pop (France Gall)/Les

Sucettes (France Gall)/No Man's Land (Isabelle Aubret)/Pour Aimer Il Faut
Etre Trois (Isabelle Aubret)/Non A Tous Les Garçons (Michèle
Torr)/Mamadou (Sacha Distel)/Ballade Des Oiseaux De Croix (Michèle
Arnaud)/Les Papillons Noir (Michèle Arnaud, Bijou, Marielle Darc)/Qui Lira
Ces Mots (Dominique Walter)/Hier Ou Demain (Marianne Faithfull) (from
the *Anna* musical, but not selected for the soundtrack album)/Boum
Badaboum (Minouche Barelli)/Hip Hip Hip Hourrah (Claude
François)/Buffalo Bill (Stone)/Au Risque De Te Déplaire (Marie-Blanche
Vergne)/Nefertiti (France Gall)/Nous Ne Sommes Pas Des Anges (France
Gall)/Teenie Weenie Boppie (France Gall)/Contact (Brigitte Bardot)/Rêves
Et Caravelles (Michèle Arnaud)/Je Suis Capable De N'Importe Quoi
(Domenique Walter)/Ouvre La Bouche Fermez Les Yeux (Régine)/Capone
Et Sa Petit Phyllis (Régine)/Comment Te Dire Adieu (Françoise Hardy)/It
Hurts To Say Goodbye (Françoise Hardy)/L'Anamour (Françoise Hardy)/La
Cavaleuse (Marielle Darc)/Hélicoptère (Marielle Darc)/L'Oiseau De Paradis
(Zizi Jeanmaire)/Desesperado (Dario Mareno)/La Fille Qui Fait Tchic Toi
Tchic (Michèle Mercier)/Turlututu Capot Pointu (Michel Colombier)/Mallo
Mallory (Régine)/Laiss's-En Un Peu Pour Les Autres (Régine)/Frankenstein
(France Gall)/Les Petits Ballons (France Gall)/Le Sixième Sens (Juliette
Gréco)/Di Doo Dah (Jane Birkin)/Mon Amour Baiser (Jane Birkin)/Bébé
Gai (Jane Birkin)/La Fille Aux Claquettes (Jane Birkin)/Rien Pour Rien (Jane
Birkin)/Lolita Go Home (Jane Birkin)/L'Amour Prison (Jacques Dutronc)/La
Main Du Masseur (Pierre Louki)/Slip Please (Pierre Louki)/La Petite Rose
(Nana Mouskouri)/Yesterday Yes A Day+ (Jane Birkin)/Dusty Road+ (Jane
Birkin)(+ both from the film *Madame Claude)*/Disc-Jockey (Alain
Chamfort)/Ex-Fan Des Sixties (Jane Birkin)/Nicotine (Jane Birkin)/Les
Femmes Ca Fait Pede (Régine)/Betty Jane Rose (Bijou)/Chavirer La France
(Shake)/Belinda (Julien Clerc)/Mangos (Julien Clerc)/On N'Est Pas Des
Grenoilles (Sacha Distel)/Cuti-Reaction (Les Toubibs)/Le Vieux Rocker (Les
Toubibs)/USSR USA (Martin Circus)/Ballade Comestible (Jacques
Dutronc)/Jet Society (Alain Chamfort)/Baby Boum (Alain Chamfort)/C'Est
Comment Qu'On Friene (Alain Bashung)/Lavabo (Alain Bashung)/Digital
Delay (Catherine Deneuve)/Alice Hélas (Catherine Deneuve)/Overseas
Telegram (Catherine Deneuve, Jane Birkin)/Suicide (Diane Dufrene)/Adieu
Bijou (Phillipe Dauga)/J'En Ai Autant Pout Toi (Phillipe Dauga)/Norma Jean
Baker (Jane Birkin)/Baby Alone In Babylone (Jane Birkin)/Ohio (Isabelle
Adjani)/Pull Marine (Isabelle Adjani)/Quoi (Jane Birkin)/Amour Consolation

(Julien Clerc)/Mon Père Un Catholique (Elisabeth Anais)/Pour Ce Que Tu
N'Etais Pas (Charlotte Gainsbourg)/Oh Daddy Oh (Charlotte Gainsbourg)/
Elastique (Charlotte Gainsbourg)/Don't Forget To Forget Me (Charlotte
Gainsbourg)/L'Amour De Moi (Jane Birkin)/Lost Song (Jane Birkin)/Le Moi
Et Le Je (Jane Birkin)/Amour Puissance Six (Viktor Lazlo)/Made In China
(Bambou)/How Much For Your Love Baby (Bambou)/White And Black
Blues (Joelle Ursull)/La Vague A Lames (Vanessa Paradis)/Tandem (Vanessa
Paradis)/Ardoise (Vanessa Paradis)/Un Amour Peut En Cacher Un Autre
(Jane Birkin)/Des Ils Et Des Elles (Jane Birkin)/Love Fifteen (Jane Birkin)

**Many other Gainsbourg pieces were included in the stage and
recorded canons of France Gall, Brigitte Bardot, Petula Clark,
Domenique Walter, Zizi Jeanmaire, Jane Birkin, Françoise Hardy,
Jacques Dutronc, Alain Chamfort, Alain Bashung, Catherine
Deneuve, Julien Clerc, Isabelle Adjani, Charlotte Gainsbourg,
Bambou and Vanessa Paradis.**

A translation of 'Poupée De Cire Poupée De Son' was released in Britain by
Twinkle in 1966 (as 'A Lonely Singing Doll') – as was 'Comic Strip' by
Brigitte Bardot.

Unissued arrangements of 'Desesperado' and 'Nous Ne Sommes Pas
Des Anges' were recorded, respectively, by Marielle Mathieu and Barbara.

A version of 'Je T'Aime...Moi Non Plus' was released by Jacqueline
Maillan and Bourvil under the title 'Ca', Sounds Nice (as 'Love At First
Sight) and Judge Dread – as well as a 1969 spoof by Frankie Howerd and
June Whitfield (as 'Up Je T'Aime'). Its ostinato was quoted in the main title
theme of the 1995 film *The Perv Parlour*.

Six themes and items of incidental music to the 1969 film *Mister
Freedom* were co-written by Gainsbourg.

Lyrics to the following songs were published in *Dernières Nouvelles
Des Etoiles* by Serge Gainsbourg (Librarie Plon, 1994):
La Belle Et Le Blues/La Bise Aux Hippies.

Sleeve notes for Jean-Claude Vannier's 1972 album, *L'Enfant Assassin
Des Mouches* were written by Gainsbourg.

In defiance of every known copyright law, bootlegs of Gainsbourg
studio recordings have been circulating for years – as well as in-concert
items and others taped (with the expected variable sound quality) from

television and radio performances.

The following albums are available in the UK from Discovery Records, or from Polygram worldwide:

L'Histoire De Melody Nelson	1971	5320732
Vu De L'Extérieur	1973	5320752
Rock Around The Bunker	1975	5320742
L'Homme A Tête De Chou	1977	5320762
Aux Armes Et Caetera	1979	5320772
Mauvais Nouvelles Des Etoiles	1981	5320782
Love On The Beat	1984	8228492
You're Under Arrest	1987	8340342
Au Theatre Le Palace 80	1980	8305992
Le Zenith De Gainsbourg	1989	8381622

Compilations:

De Gainsbourg A Gainsbarre 2CD	5322212
De Serge Gainsbourg A Gainsbarre 3CD	5321302
Du Jazz Dans Le Ravin	5226292
Comic Strip	5289512
Couleur Café	5289492
De Gainsbourg A Gainsbarre 11 CD	5223352

(containing, but individually available:)

Le Poinconnneur Des Lilas	8383872
La Javanaise	8383882
Couleur Café	8383892
Initials BB	8383902
Je T'Aime Moi Non Plus	8383912
Je Suis Venu Te Dire Que Je M'en Vais	8383922
L'Homme A Tête De Chou	8383932
Aux Armes Et Caetera	8383942
Anna	8383952
Love On The Beat	8228492
You're Under Arrest	8340342

Charlotte Gainsbourg

Lemon Incest	8484832

Index

Adjani, Isabelle 171, 173, 211-212
Alt, Paul 34
Anka, Paul 36, 85, 96, 118
Anthony, Richard 58, 65, 74, 85, 97, 150
Arnaud, Michèle 31, 36, 38, 40-41, 46, 77, 80, 84, 148, 210-211
Aufray, Hugues 40, 53, 75, 88, 210
Aznavour, Charles 16, 32, 35, 52, 86, 101, 130, 139

Bacon, Francis 122
Bacsik, Elek 68-69, 196
Bambou 166-168, 177, 181, 187, 191, 195, 197, 204, 212
Barbara 79, 148, 212
Bardot, Brigitte 14, 32, 52, 60-61, 65, 94-95, 101-106, 109, 111, 114-115, 119, 129, 197, 203, 209-212
Barrault, Jean-Louis 107
Barry, John 94, 112-113
Barry, Kate 94, 112, 114, 123, 126, 188, 196, 200
Barthélémy, Serge 45
Bashung, Alain 167, 211-212
Béart, Guy 39, 46, 62
Beatles, The 35, 91, 113,

117-118, 130, 140, 145, 152, 155, 159
Berger, Michel 83
Berri, Claude 63, 124, 127, 151, 165, 192
Berry, Chuck 42, 58, 183-184, 186
Betti, Laura 64
Bijou 148-149, 151, 161, 179, 210-211
Birkin, Andrew 92-93, 123-124, 127, 140, 201
Birkin, David 92
Birkin, Jane 14, 92-94, 105, 108-109, 111-113, 127, 131, 137-138, 140-141, 144, 147, 160, 169-170, 182, 188, 197, 199-200, 203-204, 209, 211-212
Black Grape 199
Blackwell, Chris 154, 173
Blier, Bertrand 176, 181
Bourgeois, Denis 42, 75, 106
Brassens, Georges 16, 25
Brel, Jacques 6, 16, 32, 40, 44, 49, 52, 59-60, 62, 66-67, 84, 86, 96, 99, 122, 150, 158, 160, 168-169, 173, 184, 186, 188
Bronski Beat 186
Brooks, Mel 138
Brunet, Alain 14

Brynner, Yul 14, 124
Burridge, Christine 17, 112, 115, 126

Campbell, Judy 92
Canetti, Jacques 41-42
Carne, Marcel 59
Cayatte, André 124
Chamfort, Alain 147, 167, 211-212
Charles, Ray 50, 72, 189
Chevalier, Maurice 25, 43, 60, 119
Clark, Petula 60-61, 64, 85, 99, 105, 173, 201, 210, 212
Claude, Francis 31, 36, 38, 64
Clay, Phillipe 40, 68, 74, 77, 210
Clerc, Julien 161, 166, 211-212
Colombier, Michel 211
Columbo, Pia 47

Dalessandro, Joe 141, 170
Dali, Salvador 27, 32, 77, 106, 116, 121
Dalida 32, 44, 57, 60, 68, 77, 130, 150, 177, 182, 187, 198
Dejacques, Claude 69
Delon, Alain 62, 111, 114,

151
Deneuve, Catherine 14, 52, 75, 107, 165, 190, 211-212
Depardieu, Gérard 165
Devos, Raymond 62, 120
Distel, Sacha 32, 61, 85, 130, 161, 210-211
Doillon, Jacques 164, 194, 201
Drucker, Michel 183
Dufilho, Jacques 39
Dufresne, Diane 166
Dunbar, Sly 153
Dury, Ian 150, 157
Dutronc, Jacques 91, 96, 133, 137, 147, 166, 211-212
Dylan, Bob 88, 91, 97, 149, 153, 181, 186, 190, 196

Faithfull, Marianne 80, 99, 111-112, 193, 210
Fame, Georgie 104, 153
Fast, Larry 175
Ferré, Leo 29
Fonda, Jane 94
Fontana, Wayne 189
François, Claude 65, 74, 77, 96, 118, 130, 150, 181, 198, 210
Frehel 22
Frères Jacques 39
Fulbert 192

Gall, France 75-76, 80, 83, 99-100, 116, 133, 197, 210-212
Gall, Robert 75
Gaudry, Michel 30, 69
Georgett, Gary 178
Gibbons, Steve 153
Ginzburg, Béatrice (second wife) 73, 78-79, 81, 95, 100-101, 105, 144, 164-165, 204

Ginzburg, Charlotte (daughter) 14, 126, 134, 144, 150, 164, 176-177, 182, 188, 194, 196, 200, 204, 209, 211-212
Ginzburg, Lucien (son) 145, 181, 197, 203-204
Ginzburg, Natacha (daughter) 74, 95, 165, 204
Ginzburg, Jacqueline (sister) 203
Ginzburg, Joseph (father) 19-23, 25, 27, 30, 36, 76, 109, 123, 125, 203-204
Ginzburg, Liliane (sister) 21, 123, 203
Ginzburg, Olia (mother) 19-21, 24-25, 76, 100, 125, 145, 177, 203-204
Ginzburg, Vania (son) 100, 165, 204
Goraguer, Alain 42, 45, 53, 68, 75, 78, 81, 87, 103
Gréco, Juliette 32, 35, 50, 59, 62, 68, 109, 125, 158, 173, 203, 210-211
Greenslade, Arthur 78, 86, 110
Grimblat, Pierre 111

Haley, Bill 56, 58, 186
Hallyday, Johnny 57, 62, 65, 77, 84-85, 97, 150, 167, 173, 190
Hardy, Françoise 74, 96, 107, 116, 133, 137, 145, 152, 160, 211-212
Harvey, Mick 200
Hawkshaw, Alan 139, 146-147, 153, 170, 182
Houston, Whitney 13, 182-183

Jaeckin, Just 129, 147
Jeanmaire, Zizi 60, 87,

111, 125, 145, 211-212

Karina, Anna 80, 209
King, Jonathan 88, 150
Koralnik, Pierre 80, 122
Kurant, Willy 81

La Fôret, Marie 52, 97
Lagrange, Valérie 77-78, 210
Laibe, Louis 34
Lalanne, Claude 146
Leger, Fernand 27, 33
Legrand, Michel 42, 75, 96
Lennon, John 91, 117, 159, 183, 199
Levitsky, Elisabeth 27-29, 45, 49, 73, 203, 211
Lhote, André 27
Louki, Pierre 145, 211

Marley, Bob 145, 154
Mathieu, Marielle 84-86, 212
McLaren, Malcolm 71, 156, 173, 199-200
Mistinguett 25, 34
Mitchell, Eddy 58-59, 77, 81, 209
Mitterrand, François 39, 196, 198
Momus 191, 199-200
Montand, Yves 40, 46, 125
Moreno, Dario 84
Moreau, Jeanne 52, 107
Morisse, Lucien 32, 57
Mouskouri, Nana 60, 145, 210-211

Nabokov, Vladimir 21, 25, 153
Nicholas, Paul 122
Nico 68
Noah, Yannick 161

Paradis, Vanessa 195, 212

Parker, Alan 139, 153
Piaf, Edith 22, 62, 92
Plastic Bertrand 149
Poitrenaud, Jacques 51, 68
Presley, Elvis 50, 52, 57, 60, 96, 102, 150, 174
Pretty Things, The 126
Prévert, Jacques 59
Proby, PJ 158, 182, 189

Ramdane, Babeth Si 69, 144, 168, 193
Régine 77, 107-108, 137, 145, 210-211
Resnais, Alain 124
Rivette, Jacques 141
Rolin, Olivier 108, 201
Rolling Stones, The 85, 106, 113, 160
Robinson, Harry 68, 78, 86
Rubettes 130-131
Rush, Billy 174, 179, 185

Sachs, Gunther 95, 101, 106
St Etienne 199
Sarcell, Lucky 34
Sauvage, Catherine 60, 210
Sex Pistols, The 96, 131, 149, 156-159, 183
Shakespeare, Robbie 153
Sheila 64-65, 74, 79, 84, 97
Simenon, Georges 170
Sinatra, Frank 117, 130, 167
Singing Nun, The 74, 150
Slade 55, 140
Smith, Tony "Thunder" 178
Somerville, Jimmy 186, 199-200
Stanley, Bob 17, 199
Stereolab 15
Suede 199

Taylor, Vince 67, 113, 119

Tosh, Peter 154
Trenet, Charles 23, 36
Turner, Joe 68
Twinkle 5, 17, 76, 85, 193, 212

Ursull, Joelle 195, 212

Vadim, Roger 94, 107, 111, 129
Vannier, Jean-Claude 122, 132-133, 212
Vartan, Sylvie 58, 65, 74, 85
Vian, Boris 41, 46
Vincent, Gene 58, 67, 113

Walter, Domenique 211-212
Warhol, Andy 141, 143
Winwood, Steve 154, 173

Zaguri, Robert 102
Zappa, Frank 107, 135, 167